# Evidence-Based Multichannel

Legal deposit: D/2016/13.935/1
ISBN 9789090298405
NUR 802

Book design by Mirror Mirror (MirrorMirror.be)
and Peter Carmen (across.health)
Photography by Tim De Backer (timdebacker.be)
Project coordination by Edward Atkinson-Clark (across.health)



Printed in Belgium by Graphius Group (www.graphius.com)
First Printing, 2016
Second Printing, 2017
Third Printing, 2018

www.across.health
@acrosshealth

# Evidence-Based Multichannel

## Delighting Pharma Customers In The Omnichannel Age

Ruud Kooi

Fonny Schenck

Beverly Smet

# Introduction

Welcome to the third edition of our Multichannel Cookbook! Updated with new insights, thoughts and evidence, we believe that this is truly an indispensable aid to all those who are active in omnichannel customer engagement in life sciences!

You are holding well over 60 years of cumulative multichannel experience and passion in your hands. With this book, we want to address some of the pressing educational needs in life sciences around omnichannel customer engagement.

Some eye-opening facts from the Across Health Maturometer 2018: Only 14% believe their staff are well-trained in digital. Only 15% consider themselves digital experts. "Not enough internal knowledge" is the third most important hurdle for digital success (regulatory / legal / compliance issues is no.1). "Upskilling the organization" is a top-5 priority. And across the board, only 18% think digital transformation is moving 'fast' in their organisation.

The twelve words in the title have probably taken more of our discussion time than any chapter in the book. In the end, we settled on...

- "evidence-based", because that's what we feel is needed for digital to grow to its proper scale in life sciences;
- "multichannel", because it is not about digital, but how all channels work together seamlessly;
- "delighting customers", because the customer perspective is key – rather than marketing at a target group;
- "pharma", as this book blends best practices from other industries into powerful opportunities for life sciences;
- "in the omnichannel age": the newer buzzword, but in pharma speak very similar to "multichannel" – we want to make sure we appear at the top in your Google searches, whichever word you type in ;-)
- "the missing manual", as there is no book on the market (not in 2016, and not even now, in 2018) that brings all these new trends together in an attractive, easily digestible and up-to-date way.

Our missing manual aims to tell you everything you've always wanted to know (and maybe were afraid to ask) about customer engagement in the digital age. We all know that we read less than we should, so it has become a cookbook, with one key ingredient per chapter, spiced up with a wide variety of bite-sized and fact-based snippets and "healthy snacks" that you can consume as you see fit.

Everything changes fast, and certainly in the digital space. You may know of key trends that are not yet included or that have changed drastically since this book went to press. We would love to hear your comments about the book as well as any tips about how to make it better & more complete. We live in a world of constant beta, where the network always wins!

Gent, May 2018

Ruud Kooi
ruud.kooi@a-cross.com

Fonny Schenck
fonny.schenck@a-cross.com

Beverly Smet
beverly.smet@a-cross.com

# Thank you

First and foremost, we would not have been able to pull the second edition of our "missing manual" – with loads of new insights, fresh 2017-2018 data and 3 completely new chapters - together without the unconditional support of our partners and children. So thank you Emile, Lisa, Danielle, Stéphanie, Henri, Emile, Mariken, Quinten and Olivier.

Special thanks go to Philippe Gosseye, whose book The Extraverted Nerd – The B2B Marketing Cookbook was an important catalyst for us back in 2016 to get cracking on our first edition of the "missing manual". Philippe was kind enough to give us access to his treasure trove of content and let us openly repurpose the relevant parts for life sciences.

We would also like to extend our thanks to Peter Carmen and Edward Atkinson-Clark, who coordinated many different people and agendas with endless patience – it surely must have felt like herding cats sometimes!

Furthermore, this book would not have been possible without the inspiration and encouragement of many innovative customers and inspiring thought leaders we've met and worked with over the years.

Last but not least, our heartfelt thanks go to the many enthusiastic experts at Across Health who contributed to this 2018 panoramic picture of the fast-evolving space of evidence-based omnichannel customer engagement in life sciences.

We hope you enjoy the fruit of our efforts!

# About the authors

**Ruud Kooi** is Managing Partner at Across Health. Ruud specializes in defining and implementing worldwide omnichannel strategies for marketing, sales and medical, turning global brand plans into global blueprints and highly measurable local campaign implementations.

**Fonny Schenck** is CEO and Managing Partner at Across Health. Fonny likes to work at the intersection of technology, commercial and medical effectiveness, business strategy and innovation. He helps international clients to 'fix the mix' and boost digital transformation.

**Beverly Smet** is Managing Partner at Across Health. He has a wide experience in large-scale execution of omnichannel programmes both aimed at HCPs and patients. Furthermore he is a professional trainer in omnichannel strategy and a regular speaker at international events.

# About Across Health

Across Health is a trusted advisor to senior leaders of innovative multinational healthcare organizations. With a focus on customer engagement in the digital age, they partner with clients to design, develop, execute and measure digital-second strategies and companywide digital readiness programs – for the short, medium and long term

www.across.health

‘To digitize or not to digitize, that is… no longer the question.’

# 1 From Multichannel Ecosystem to Digital Strategy

# The omnichannel change journey

**Everything has become digital.** With the adoption of wearable smart devices and the advent of the 'Internet of Things', more and more experiences are being digitized. We are 'always on'–anywhere, anytime–and this has drastically changed the marketing profession. But digitization extends well beyond marketing and impacts every part of every business, often disruptively. Digitization spreads across the entire organization and forces departments to **break down silos and start collaborating**. That is what is needed for the digital journey to be successful.

Healthcare in general and pharmaceutical companies specifically have been **lagging in the digital space**, which has already disrupted several industries (just consider the media, travel, electronics, shopping or finance industries). Healthcare is special: it is a very conservative, complex, highly regulated industry. This results in a myriad of challenges and roadblocks for change–even for experts. Within pharma too, digitization and omnichannel customer engagement are still in the early days. Capgemini, for instance, squarely puts pharma in the 'beginner' box (see 'digital transformation' further on).

Leading innovators within pharma are gradually showing the way, but their programmes have largely been restricted to **'pockets of excellence'**: rarely institutionalized or rolled out to other geographic or therapeutic markets. So far, 'bottom-up' and 'let a 1,000 flowers bloom' have been the main (and unsuccessful) strategies. Combine this with 1) limited pressure from customers, competitors or the bottom-line and 2) the high (partly perceived) regulatory hurdles, and **the 'burning platform' for change has proven to be quite limited.**

Nevertheless, **customers are getting tired of waiting** for true omnichannel experiences. Luckily, several companies have responded by adopting massive company-wide programmes. According to Accenture, the size of the prize is quite big: digitization will be fuelling almost 33% of the growth and an estimated 40% of the profitability in pharma by 2020...

The era of acceleration is just around the corner!

> ‘The future is already here. It's just not very evenly distributed.’
>
> **William Gibson**
> **Writer and coiner of "cyberspace"**

## The metrics of omnichannel engagement

**2017**

This was the year when CMOs began spending more on IT than their CIO colleagues. This trend isn't likely to reverse any time soon. (Source: Gartner)

**4,891**

The number of marketing technology vendors on ChiefMartec's 2017 infographic. This is 40% more than the number in 2016 (3,874). (Source: Chiefmartec)

**80+%**

... of marketers say that company silos obscure a seamless view of campaigns and customers. (Source: Forbes)

**87%**

... of marketers consider data the most underused asset in marketing organizations. (Source: Forbes)

**32.7%**

... of healthcare professionals are satisfied with pharma's digital offerings. (Source: Across Health Navigator)

**12%**

... of European pharma professionals are satisfied with their own digital activities. (Source: Across Health Maturometer)

**+35%**

Pharma digital allrounders are expected to grow revenues 35% more compared to laggards. (Source: Accenture)

**+61%**

Pharma digirati can improve profitability by 61%. (Source: Accenture)

> ‘Marketing has become a technology-powered discipline. Marketing organizations must therefore infuse technical capabilities into their DNA.’

**Scott Brinker**
**Blogger at Chief Marketing Technologist**

# The multichannel ecosystem...your customers ARE digital

When pharmaceutical companies launch new products, they spend a lot of money trying to understand the product needs and mindsets of the physicians and other stakeholders. By contrast, when they launch new channels, the same companies mostly rely on their brand managers' **perceptions**, running the risk that decisions are founded on **myths** and **misconceptions**.

But multichannel is not 'something new'. Pharma companies have engaged in multichannel for a long time too, well before the advent of digital. However, these channels tended to be marginal and not really integrated with **the dominant channel,** the **field force**.

The key promise of multichannel is **more impact**: Tannenbaum's table ( 1967) illustrates the true promise of integrated multichannel in pharma.

| Variation of **channel** | NO — Variation of **message** | YES — Variation of **message** |
|---|---|---|
| NO | Lowest effect | Intermediate effect |
| YES | Intermediate effect | Highest effect |

The number of channels has increased dramatically due to the Internet, and one of the main challenges for pharma is to **select the right set of channels** (and content) per segment or, even, at the individual level. Some of these new channels are more personal (e.g. remote detailing, tablet detailing), but most can be considered as non-personal.

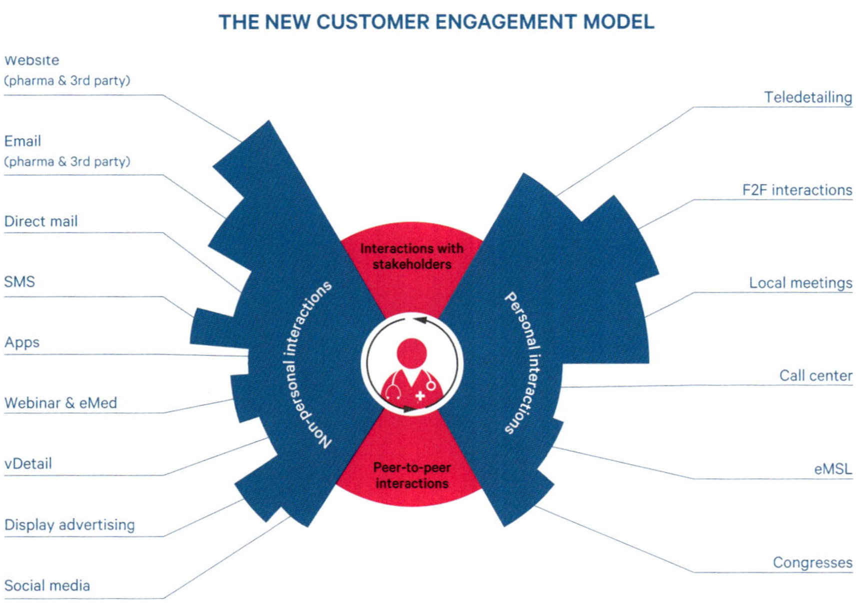

# The channel mix spend

The Across Health Navigator research shows that European physicians now spend about **37 hours/month*** online for professional purposes. In 2009, they spent on average only 16 hours. At the same time, HCPs spend only around 1 hour/month with reps, while the industry still spends over **65% of its budget on the fieldforce** and only about **4% on digital**.** Clearly, **the pharma channel mix is ripe for some serious disruption**!

When we look at the Across Health Navigator data, we get a clear view on **the shift of preferred channels** in the US market. During the period 2011-2017, the reach and impact of the pharma website increased significantly, while the rep's reach dropped sharply - but impact increased ("less is more"?).

**CHANNEL PERFORMANCE MAP: ONCOLOGY US (2011 VS 2017)**

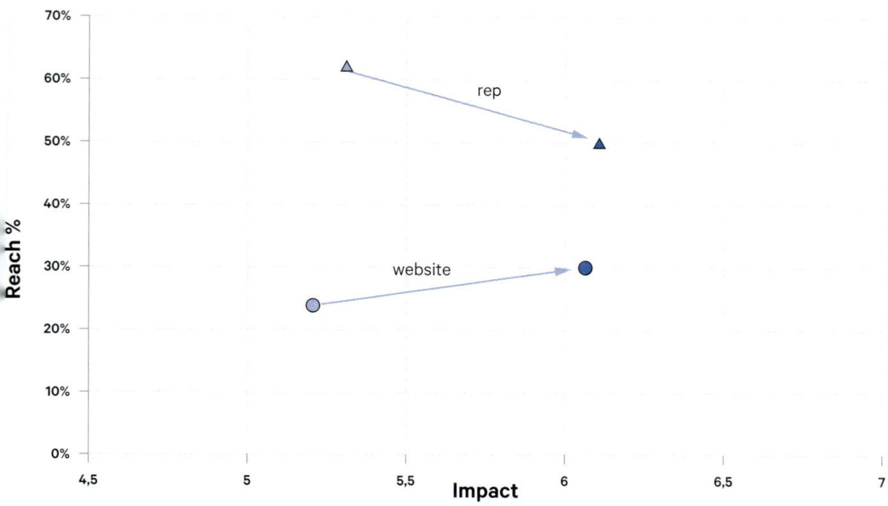


Source: Across Health Navigator 2011-2017, US oncologists (n = 54 (2011) and 75 (2017)).

It should also be borne in mind that, since 2014, **digital native physicians outnumber 'digital immigrants'** (i.e. physicians who studied medicine when the internet was not yet around). These digital natives have different expectations of communication from pharma.

**NORMALIZED CHANNEL REACH BY AGE GROUP**

| | WEBSITE | E-NEWSLETTER | TELEDETAILING | ONLINE MD NETWORK | WEBCAST |
|---|---|---|---|---|---|
| Digital native HCP Age <35 | -- | -- | ++ | ++ | ++ |
| Digital immigrant HCP Age 35-50 | + | - | - | + | - |
| Digital immigrant HCP Age >50 | + | ++ | -- | -- | -- |

Source: The Across Health Navigator

* Source: Navigator 2017, EU5, N=3185

** Source: IQVIA 2017

## Tip

### Digital natives

The term **digital native** was coined by education consultant Marc Prensky in his 2001 article 'Digital Natives, Digital Immigrants'. Prensky posited that "the arrival and rapid dissemination of digital technology in the last decade of the 20th century" had changed the way students think and process information. But the outdated teaching methods haven't followed suit, making it difficult for digital native students to excel academically. What is needed instead, is **a media-rich learning environment** which is better suited to hold their attention.

# The Across Health Navigator

Channels come in many shapes and forms: push-pull, online-offline, social, mobile, ... Forrester created an insightful framework, where channels are attributed to the owned, paid, or earned category:

| MEDIA TYPE | DEFINITION | EXAMPLES | ROLE | BENEFITS | CHALLENGES |
|---|---|---|---|---|---|
| **OWNED MEDIA** | Those media channels that are fully controlled by the brand / the company. | • Website<br>• Mobile site<br>• Blog<br>• Twitter account | To build longer-term relationships.<br>Establish a continuous presence. | • Full control<br>• Cost efficiency<br>• Longevity<br>• Versatility<br>• Targeted audience variation | • Brand / company communication often lacks trust amongst HCPs<br>• Limited guarantees for success<br>• Scaling up reach takes time |
| **PAID MEDIA** | Presence on these channels is bought by the brand / company. | • Display advertising<br>• SEA<br>• Sponsorships | To create and direct traffic to the owned media.<br>Be where your audiences are. | • Immediacy<br>• Control (over costs)<br>• Scale | • Declining response rates<br>• Banner blindness |
| **EARNED MEDIA** | Customers become the channel. | • Word-of-mouth (WoM)<br>• Buzz and viral marketing<br>• Retweets and likes | To establish stronger credibility.<br>Engage in a dialogue. | • Highest level of credibility<br>• Transparent | • No control<br>• Can also be negative<br>• Scaling up is difficult<br>• Hard to measure |

Source: Forrester Research, Inc.

The Across Health Navigator leverages the Forrester owned-paid-earned framework, translates it to the pharma context and adds key offline channels to the digital set, making this a second-to-none omnichannel research in life sciences. From 2013 to mid 2018, over 20,000 HCPs had been surveyed. The 50+ channels include:

| | OWNED PROMOTIONAL | OWNED MEDICAL SERVICE | PAID | EARNED |
|---|---|---|---|---|
| **OFFLINE CHANNELS** | • Promo call<br>• Direct mail<br>• Fax<br>• Newsletter<br>• Rep visit<br>• Rep tablet<br>• Sample<br>• Promotional SMS | • International scientific meeting<br>• Local scientific meeting<br>• MSL<br>• MedEd<br>• Phase IV<br>• Educational call<br>• Service center<br>• Patient adherence | • Advertisement<br>• Congress booth<br>• TV ad<br>• Medical journal<br>• International congress<br>• CME | • KOL<br>• Colleague<br>• Professional association<br>• Patient<br>• Patient association<br>• Caregiver<br>• Nurse<br>• Pharmacist<br>• Hospital<br>• Health insurer<br>• Government<br>• Scientific treatment guidelines |
| **ONLINE CHANNELS** | • eDetail<br>• Newsletter<br>• Teledetailing<br>• Twitter<br>• Website<br>• Rep triggered eMail | • eMedEd<br>• eMSL<br>• Webcast<br>• Smartphone app | • eCME<br>• Online conference<br>• Banners<br>• Scientific website<br>• Scientific eNewsletter<br>• ePrescribing | • Wikipedia<br>• Online medical network<br>• Online medical journal<br>• KOL webinar<br>• Website patient association<br>• Website professional association<br>• Website health authority |

The Navigator data covers both **reach**–the extent to which channels are commonly encountered by HCPs–and **impact**–the extent to which channels influence clinical decision-making. On these unique, data-rich channel findings, a series of analyses are performed. The primary aim is to **support and facilitate fact-based channel mix decision-making**.

In addition, the research also provides insight into **frequency, preferred content & formats, extensive benchmarking (by channel),** as well as **preferred 3d party media** for most specialties (oncology, cardiology, neurology, GPs, ...) in Europe, US and other markets (Navigator 3.0).

You can find an EU5-wide Navigator map for specialists on the following pages (data from 2017), as well as the MCQ map. For the latter, the impact axis has been recalibrated according to the level of impact of the rep. This is what we call **the 'multichannel equivalent' (MCQ)**, which enables comparison between the relative impact of various channels to the rep. In a medical setting, we use the medical meeting or MSL as the standard.

A key benefit of the MCQ is that it allows you to give a relative weight to each channel. After all, **not all touchpoints and channels are equal.**

# Navigating the HCP channel mix: Navigator Performance Map

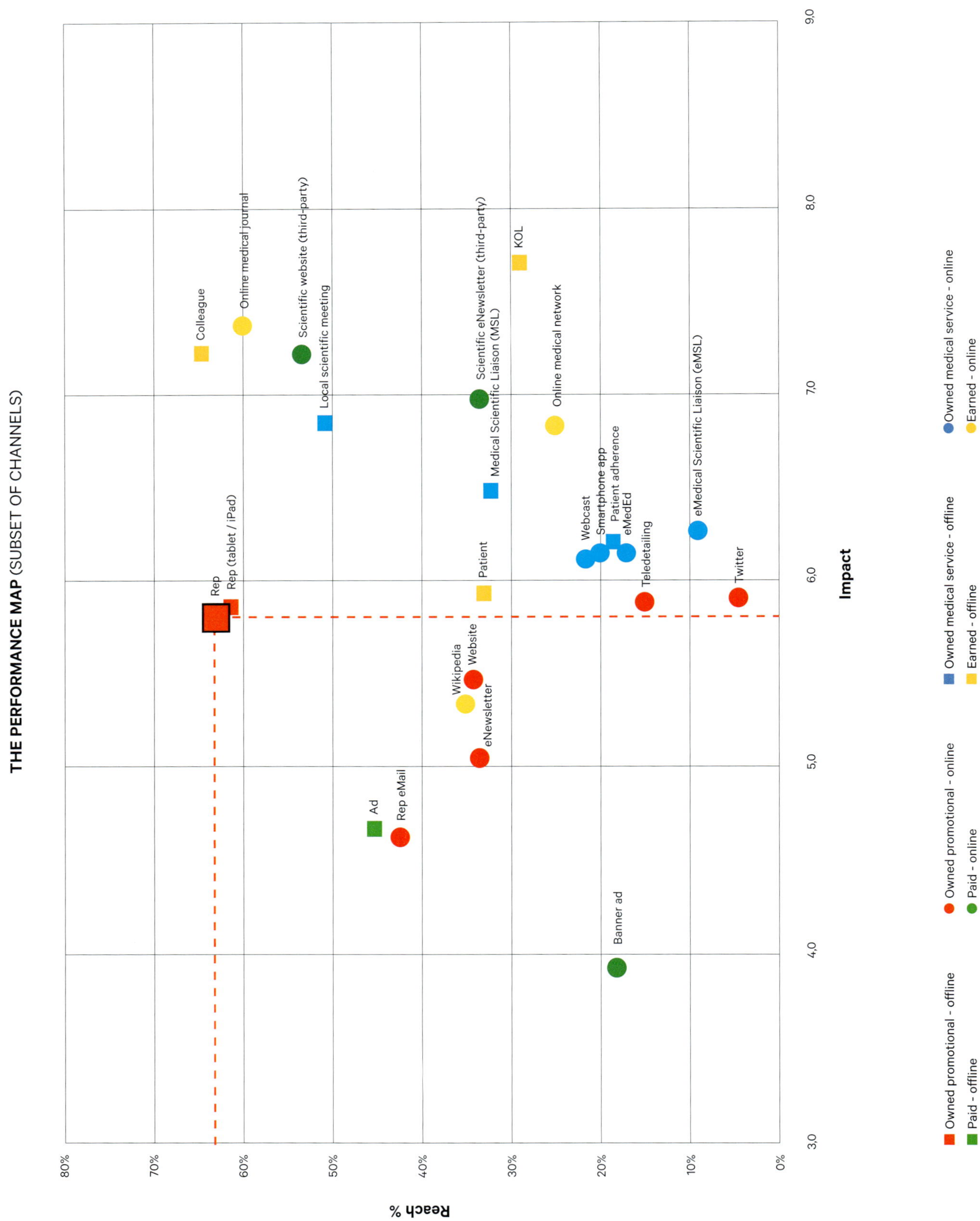


Source: The Across Health Navigator 2018 | N =3,185 | EU5 scope (DE, ES, FR, IT, UK) | Specialists

## Navigating the HCP channel mix: Multichannel Equivalence Map

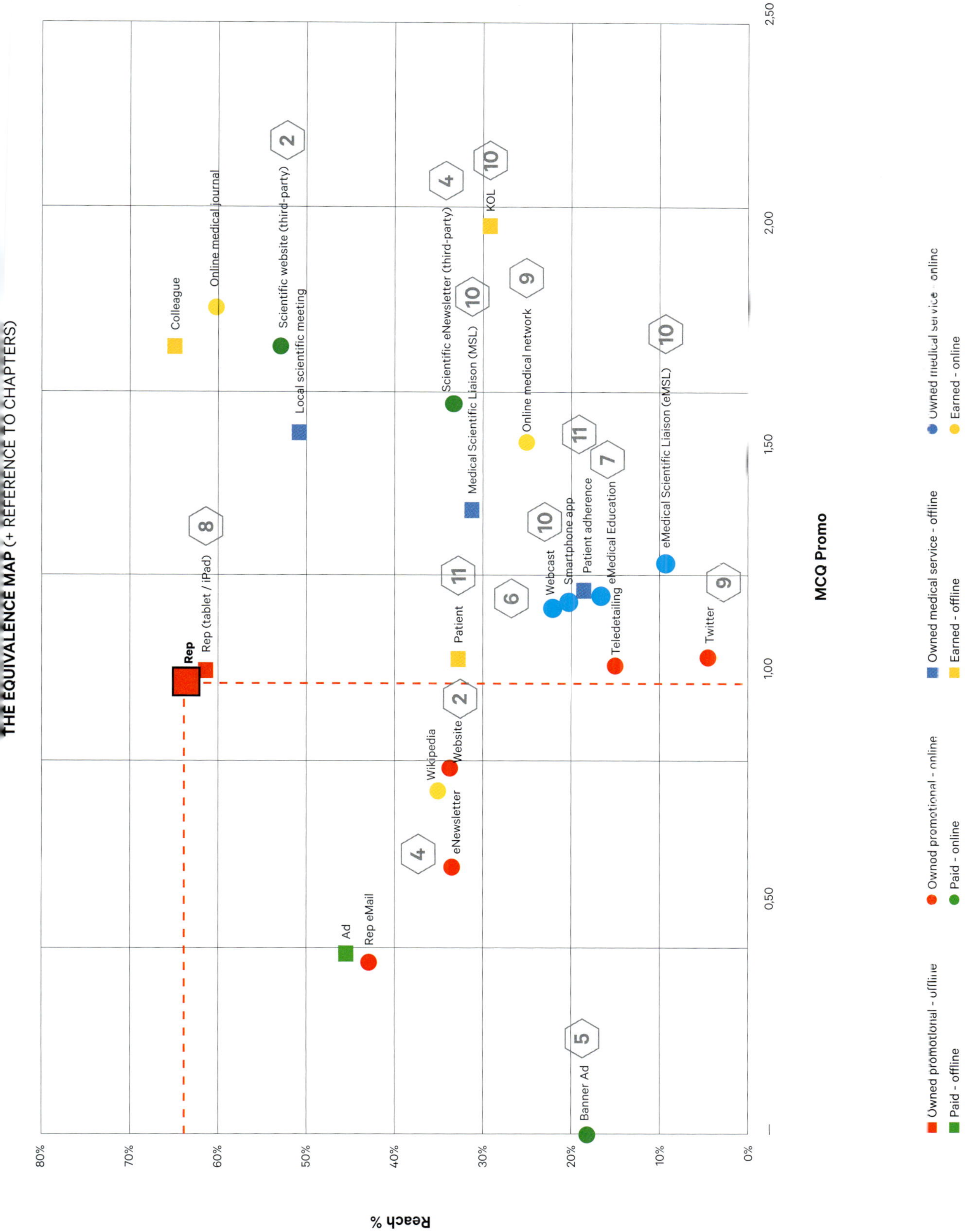


Source: The Across Health Navigator 2018 | N = 3,185 | EU5 scope (DE, ES, FR, IT, UK) | Specialists

# The multistakeholder world of pharma

Pharma is moving towards a **multistakeholder world**: a world in which **stakeholders beyond the prescriber** are gaining importance. Overall budgets, however, have remained flat, making it challenging to reach these additional stakeholders using traditional methods.

Digital must play a key role in reaching these relatively new audiences. As traditional HCP marketing shifts towards a **multichannel** approach, budget can be freed up and redirected to these new audiences. This budget shift is just getting started now, but the impact is expected to be significant and can generate a competitive advantage for **early movers**.

**Payers**
- ✓ Government healthcare spending pressure
- ✓ More proactive management of formularies
- ✓ Legislative support for lower cost generics

**Specialists & GPs**
- ✓ Prescription monopoly under erosion
- ✓ Access increasingly crowded
- ✓ Interest decreasing
- ✓ Purchasing consortia taking on negotiation role

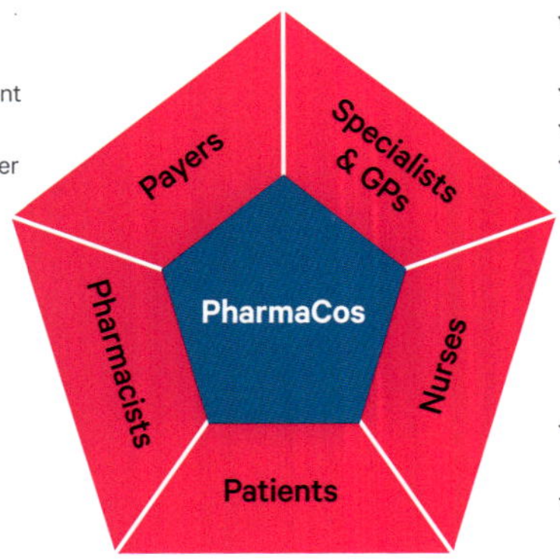


**Pharmacists**
- ✓ Expanded generic substitution power
- ✓ Consultative role

**Nurses**
- ✓ From passive to active influencing role
- ✓ Extended prescription formulary

**Patients**
- ✓ No longer rely on guidance from physician alone

Focus is shifting from HCPs only to multiple stakeholders in pharma marketing. A 2017 analysis by the consultancy **EY** further illustrates the importance of a multistakeholder approach, predicting the following **power shifts**:

Source: EY, Progressions Life Sciences 4.0

# Digital transformation in pharma

Digitization extends well beyond marketing. The combination of 1) **the creative and human side** of digitization with 2) **the analytical and automated side** of it, are equally relevant in departments such as sales, medical affairs, customer service, and others. **Cross-divisional collaboration** has become essential for success. Without it, crucial insights and knowledge about customers and their contact points with the company will leak out of the organization. Companies, therefore, must **break down the silos within the organization**. Research has already shown that digitally mature companies **generate more revenue** and are **more profitable** compared to less digitally savvy competitors. This gap is expected to grow wider as the value chain is becoming ever more digitized.

## Tip

### The MCQ equation

It's not easy to compare **different channels**. For instance, how does a website visit compare to a rep visit? That is what the multichannel equivalent (MCQ) concept enables you to do: you can now **weigh different channels in terms of impact**. For example, if the impact of a rep is 6 and that of a pharma website is 5.4, then it is weighed as 0.9 MCQ's (90%) of a rep visit, as a rep visit is considered one 'unit' of equivalent. Using these figures, you can create multi-channel campaigns which **generate a pre-defined level of impact, directly comparable to a traditional field-force.**

> The challenge within organizations these days is envisioning new omnichannel programmes while breaking down silos.

**Matt Mobley**
**Chief Marketing Technology Officer at Merkle**

**Digital maturity matters!** In 2013, Capgemini ran a cross-industry assessment of digital maturity based on 2 parameters 1) digital intensity and 2) transformation intensity.

❶ **Digital intensity** is defined as the level of investment in digital technologies (social media, customer experience, mobile, analytics, process digitization, internal collaboration, data integration)

❷ **Transformation management intensity** is defined as the ability to drive transformation in the organization, especially by...

- Creating a **vision** that appeals to people
- Establishing **governance policies** to ensure that the company's efforts evolve in the right direction
- Creating **engagement** amongst all employees
- Improving **the IT-business relationship**

Companies can be plotted on these two axes, which creates 4 quadrants and 4 distinct types of companies:

❶ **Beginners** score low on both digital and transformation intensity.

❷ **Fashionistas** have adopted a lot of digital tools, but there is no synergy between the digital assets.

❸ **Conservatives** are late in adopting new digital trends. They are, however, stronger on transformation intensity.

❹ **Digirati** score highly on both digital and transformation intensity. These companies have a clear head start over their competitors. Digirati companies are on average 26% more profitable than their industry peers.

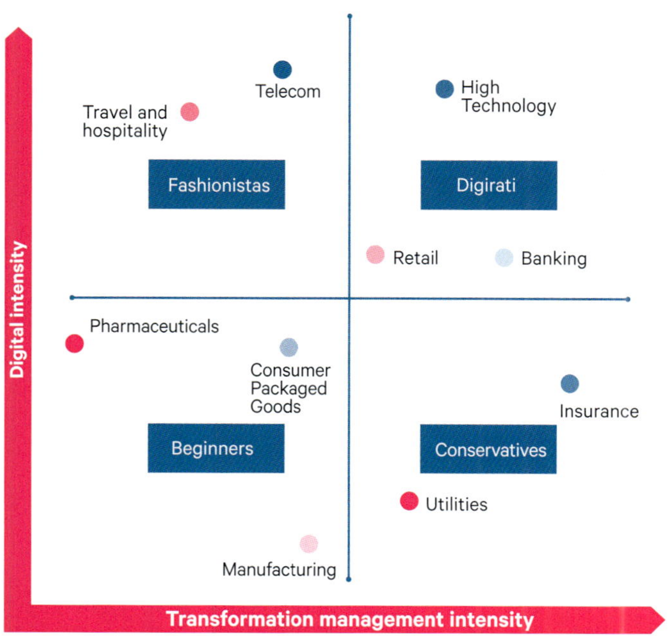


Source: Capgemini Consulting & the MIT Center for Digital Business, 'The Digital Advantage'

Generally speaking, **pharmaceuticals are behind on both axes**. Particularly in terms of transformation intensity, they have been slow to move to **an integrated customer-centric company footprint**. Too often, companies continue to operate more in a silo mode, even within one and the same department.

## Tip

### Digitize everything

Digitization redefines the boundaries of marketing and **the role of the marketer.** Hence digirati companies are digital savvy not just within marketing, but across the entire organization and value chain. Digitization of business processes is crucial to **create synergy** between all domains. Without internal collaboration, the customer experience will fall short in **today's 'always on' reality.** Transformation processes must focus on **breaking down silos** and **redefining roles.**

# The maturity level of digital in pharma

Since 2008, Across Health has run a pharma-specific maturity assessment called the Maturometer.

The Maturometer study confirms **the beginner status of pharma in digital**. It also shows that the top 10% pharma companies in Europe are already clearly ahead of the average on most of the key dimensions (e.g. organization, process, channel mix, measurement). Top performers also spend significantly more on digital, and they tend to have much better staffing levels at both local and international levels.

Interestingly, these leaders 1) feel equally uncertain when **channel mix decisions** are concerned and 2) they are only slightly ahead in terms of **marketing automation**.

| | | KPI | |
|---|---|---|---|
| | | All | Top 10% |
| ORGANISATION | Strong digital transformation vision & strategy | 75% | 95% |
| | Strong digital / MC team with board support | 63% | 90% |
| | Staff well-trained in digital | 46% | 62% |
| PROCESS | Digital / MC team integreted with business / IT | 67% | 95% |
| | Robust process for channel mix | 39% | 55% |
| | MC campaign automation | 27% | 25% |
| MIX | Integrated customer DB across channels | 51% | 81% |
| | Good view of HCP channel acceptance | 37% | 55% |
| | Reps equipped with digital tools beyond e-detail | 70% | 90% |
| MEASUREMENT | Measure results of all channels | 63% | 100% |
| | Measure HCP engagement | 56% | 81% |
| | Good mix qualitative & quantitative KPIs | 53% | 76% |

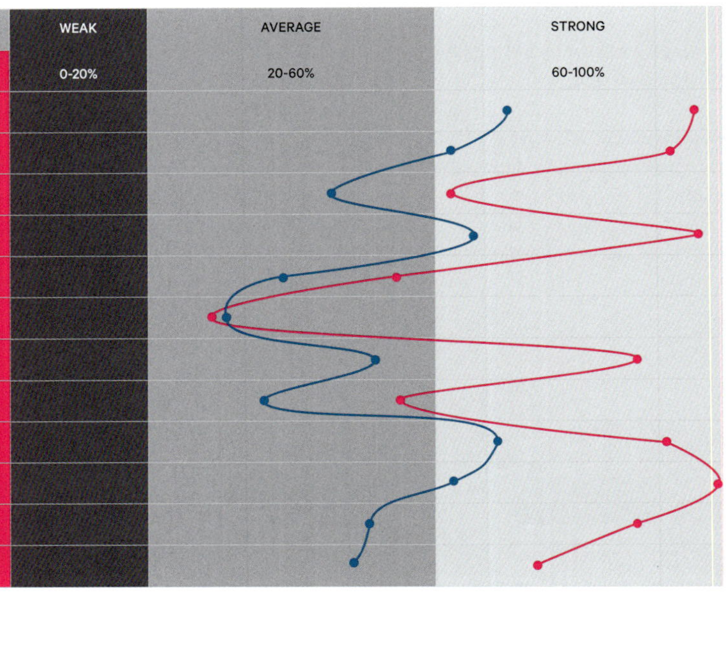

## The eight habits for successful digitization

McKinsey & Company identified a series of habits that make **digital part of a company's DNA**:

1. **Internal journey.** Take your current marketing team on the digital journey. Prophesize digitization throughout the organization via internal communication. Embed digital in the minds of every marketer.

2. **Set aspirational digital goals.** Set digital goals that seem unreasonably high. Lowering the digitization bar increases the chances of failed digitization.

3. **Attract digital talent.** Building digital talent solely from within your own company risks creating delays. Hire external talent and look outside your own industry for digital talent. Talent has no borders.

4. **Cultivate and protect digital talent.** Integrating the new-found digital talent in your regular business risks to quickly stifle digital innovation and slow down ongoing digitization. Create a separate digital hub and consider giving it its own profit and loss account.

5. **Leave nothing unchallenged.** Digitization impacts every aspect of the business. Companies should 1) challenge the way things are done now and 2) investigate how every part of their value chain can be digitized.

6. **Data makes the world go round faster and faster.** Gone are the days of long development cycles and decision-making based on 'hunches'. Data analytics drive 1) the business and 2) digitization. The globalized business reality requires every business unit to be agile in responding to market needs and changes.

7. **Invest where the money is.** Adopt digitization 1) to create new revenue streams and 2) to optimize the current cost structure. Focus simultaneously on these 2 areas.

8. **Obsess over the customer.** Digitization's only purpose is to improve the customer experience. It's a means to an end: the ultimate customer experience.

Successful digital businesses focus on all areas. But before excellence can be achieved, an organization must change and digitize its mindset.

## Digital strategy

There are **2 types of digital strategy**: **companywide** (digital transformation) and **brand/ therapeutic area** (omnichannel brand/TA strategy). Until recently, the latter was the more popular one, as budgets tended to sit within the brand team and brand leaders tended to focus only on their brand(s). Historically, there has been much less interest in, and budget for, the companywide approach. As a result, companywide efforts have been limited, leading to **the digital 'beginner' status** of pharma compared to many other industries.

This is now changing, as senior management becomes more aware of the opportunities of digital as well as of the risks of being left behind. The relatively new trend of **'health tech'** is also helping to create momentum for the company-wide digital transformation strategy.

> 'Tactics without strategy is the noise before defeat.'
>
> **Sun-tzu**

**Two perspectives on digital strategy:**

| **COMPANYWIDE** DIGITAL TRANSFORMATION **STRATEGY** | MULTICHANNEL **BRAND/TA STRATEGY** |
|---|---|
| ← Develop **enablers** for digital transformation → | ← **Integrate** digital/multichannel into the mix → |
| "Transform the organization" | "Fix the mix" |

> "Digital business strategy is the answer to the question: how will our business survive and thrive in an increasingly digital world?"
>
> **Gartner**

**A possible approach for a companywide digital transformation strategy could look like this:**

← DEVELOP ENABLERS FOR DIGITAL TRANSFORMATION →

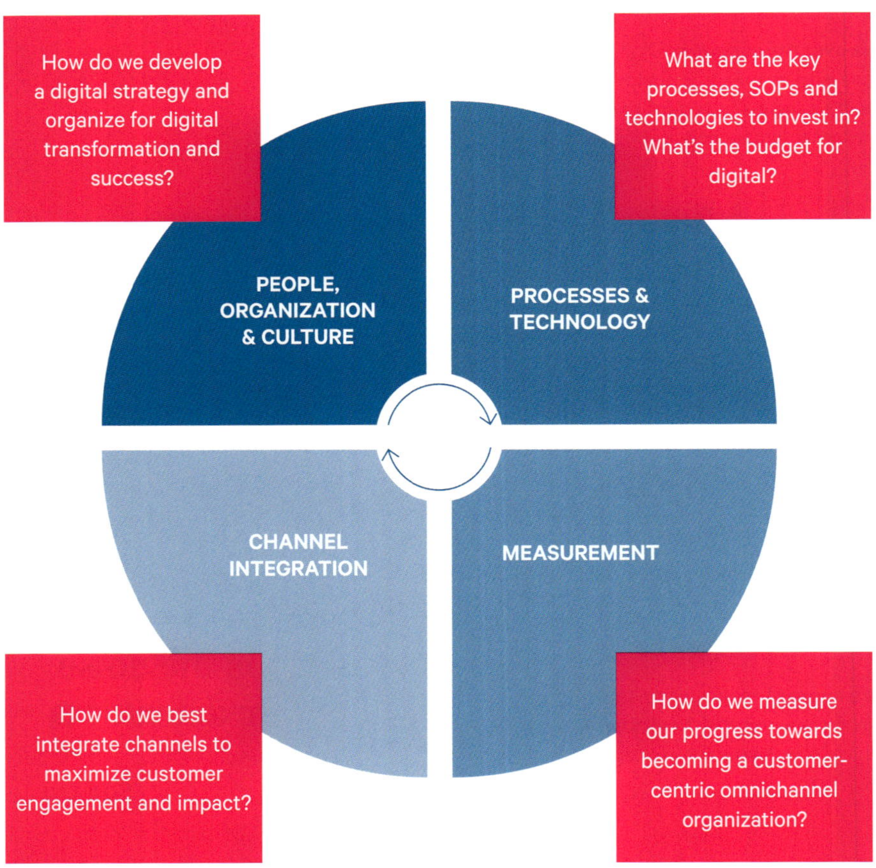

# The multichannel brand/TA strategy

In this section, we focus on **the multichannel brand/therapeutic area (TA) strategy**. The following process is a good starting point:

| 1 STRATEGIC IMPERATIVES | 2 STRATEGIC PROXIES | 3 CONVERSION POINTS | 4 TACTICS | 5 PRIORITIZATION AND PLANNING | 6 MEASUREMENT |
|---|---|---|---|---|---|
| **Brand strategy**<br>• Brand objectives<br>• Positioning<br>• Business opportunities<br>• Key stakeholders | **Translate the strategy into something actionable**<br>• Leverage points<br>• Behavioural objectives<br>• Messages | **What content or services will drive the action/change that we want?** | **What are the ideal channels to achieve this?** | **What is feasible? What is the impact of these tactics?**<br>• Prioritize and plan over time | **How can we measure the interactions and engagement?** |

Notice that the first 3 steps are related to the brand strategy and only as of step 4 do we move to the channel selection.

❶ **Step 1 - strategic imperatives**. In this step, the brand plan is key. What are the brand objectives? What is its positioning vs. competitors? Where do the biggest opportunities lie? Which customer group(s) are key? Have customers been segmented and were different strategies developed for each? Have other stakeholders been taken into account (nurses, pharmacists, patients, payers...)?

❷ **Step 2 - strategic proxies**. In this step, the strategy becomes more tangible. What are the leverage points? What are the behavioural objectives? Which messages are associated with these? What is the contact frequency you need to generate impact? How many multichannel equivalents (MCQs) do you need to generate?

❸ **Step 3 - content & services**. Before you move towards the channels, you need to define how you will achieve conversion, i.e. which content items and services are needed to achieve the behavioural objectives and messages. Some content/services may already exist and will need to be repurposed for digital, while others may have to be created.

❹ **Step 4 - tactics**. It's only as of this step that relevant channels are identified, based on reach, impact, cost and estimated frequency - all of this fully aligned with the customer journey. This typically takes place in the form of a brainstorming session, supported by channel mix data (for instance the Navigator).

❺ **Step 5 - prioritization and planning**. During this step, certain channels will be deprioritized based on the internal maturity of your organization. When an organization is unable to activate a channel at speed, it should be left out for now. Hurdles usually include technology platforms, resources and skills, regulatory concerns, ...

❻ **Step 6 - measurement**. For each multichannel programme, the KPIs need to be defined prior to launch (at the campaign, customer and channel level), in order to assess performance vs. expectations during the execution phase.

This process is repeated for each customer segment or type of stakeholder. At the end of the process, a template can be completed, which can serve as a future reference when the programme is being executed.

| | | | | | |
|---|---|---|---|---|---|
| Brand name | | | | | |
| Leverage point | | | | | |
| Target audience (segments) | | | | | |
| Behavioural objective(s) | | | | | |
| Channel selection | 1 | 2 | 3 | 4 | 5 |
| Channel type | | | | | |
| Expected MCQ | | | | | |
| Impact measurement | Channel related communication effects | | Brand or TA related communication effects | | |
| | Channel related behavioural effects | | Brand or TA related behavioural effects | | |
| Cost per MCQ | | | | | |
| Total MCQ | | | Average cost / MCQ | | |
| Project resources | Internal | | External | | |

Learning about new channels and how to activate them is only one step on the journey to **multichannel excellence**. Most importantly, companies must also tailor the channel mix to customer segments and patient journeys.

> ‘ Companies that perform best on journeys have a more distinct competitive advantage than those that excel at touchpoints. ’
>
> **McKinsey 2016**

> ‘ Only 10% of companies match channels and content to a well-mapped customer journey. ’
>
> **Econsultancy 2015**

## Common multichannel pitfalls

Beware of some of the typical multichannel pitfalls:

- Multichannel is not per se about **adding digital channels to the mix**. Some offline channels continue to do well and should be considered too.
- Many still tend to see **digital as a playground**, or simply a way to spend the remainder of the Q4 budget. A failure to see digital as a strategic investment will lead to overall failure.
- Digital is often **associated with innovation**: "when we do something digital, we do something innovative". This is, however, typical of someone who still lives in The Old Normal! In **The New Normal, digital is a commodity**, and factors like reach, engagement and cost precede innovation.
- Very often, **digital** is seen **as a channel in isolation**, while **the strongest impact is achieved when all channels are activated** along the customer journey in a **well-orchestrated way**. This also includes the integration of key offline channels, such as the field force, medical events, publications, and MSLs.
- Digital is often seen as **a way for reps to enhance engagement with target groups**. But such a stance is too limiting. While digital can definitely help to improve the rep – HCP relationship, at the same time, the internet offers a transformational opportunity to engage with new stakeholders, like patients, caregivers, nurses and pharmacists. Audiences that previously were not reached through the traditional (and costly) pharma channels, but have an increasing impact on the number of diagnoses, prescriptions and adherence, can now be reached cost-effectively as well.
- Digital is seen as **a substitute for face-to-face**. This is not the case. It is a very cost-effective way to amplify the offline activities of the fieldforce, meetings, MSLs, and more.

## Healthy snack

### The use case for multichannel

**The situation:** a top-10 pharma company in Germany calculated that it had made 70,000 rep calls during the previous period to several lower-value HCP segments for 2 mature brands. The calls took up a substantial part of the sales and marketing budget.

**The challenge:** replace the 70,000 calls with a more diverse and optimal channel mix; and to achieve the same share-of-voice using multichannel.

**The approach:** based on the Navigator data, Across Health developed a 12-month multichannel campaign plan. A series of channels and campaign waves were set up. The impact was measured using the multichannel equivalent (MCQ) algorithm. The focus of the campaign was on brand awareness and preference. All materials and content were created to match these brand priorities. Throughout the campaign period, progress was measured both at the channel and the customer level.

**The result:** the campaign achieved its MCQ target, equivalent to 70,000 rep calls. **The sales evolution for both brands was superior** in the segments exposed to the multichannel campaign vs. the target group that received rep visits. Costs were also 80% lower versus the previous (rep-only) situation.

# The omnichannel checklist

To increase your chances of success and improve omnichannel customer engagement, consider the following questions:

1. How well do you understand **the channels your customers are using**? How aware are you about the reach, impact and cost of each channel? How well do you understand the competitive landscape? Which 3rd-party destinations do they go to?
2. Have you looked **beyond your traditional customer groups**? Did you explore 'transformational' opportunities (e.g. nurses, patients, pharmacists ...)?
3. Did you take **a deeper dive into customer segments** and have you developed a segmented (or even individualized) approach? Or do you still focus on 'mass outreach'?
4. Have you put **strategy first** and **channels second**?
5. Have you put **content before channels**? Remember: content is king, channels are princesses.
6. Have you looked at the **cost per engagement** for new channels vs. traditional ones?
7. **How well integrated is your customer-facing organization** (sales, marketing, medical, digital) when it comes to distilling insights and providing a seamless experience for customers?
8. How much did you invest in **promoting your channels**?
9. Is your organization **digitally mature** enough (in terms of skills, resources, technology, MLR, etc.) to launch all these channels today, or do you need to prioritize?
10. Did you develop **a business case** and do you measure the impact of each channel throughout your programme vs. the initial business case?

By observing these 10 items, the holy grail of 'right customer, right channel, right message, right time' is in your grasp.

## Tip

### Central resources and local discretion

**Centralization versus de-centralization** is a never-ending struggle for companies. Organizations that operate on a multinational basis, should look at how to balance digital resources **centrally** with local entities deploying those digital assets at their own **discretion** and adding **local market preferences**. In the meantime, centralization does not have to be 'physical' anymore. Virtual teams dispersed across the globe often have a central support role:

- Through central resources, the company, as a whole, achieves **efficiency gains** and **best practices** get shared
- The local entity 1) **learns more quickly** while 2) localized adaptations **meet local customer needs** better

# Challenges of omnichannel marketing

| Challenges ☹ | Solutions ☺ |
|---|---|
| **How to shift focus from off- to online? From traditional to digital?** | • Analyze your company's **digital strengths and weaknesses.**<br>• **Benchmark against competitors** in your industry. Analyze your digital footprint.<br>• Make **silo thinking** within the company visible and demonstrate how it hurts the business.<br>• Start to break down silo thinking: create **interdisciplinary groups** focused on digitizing your customer engagement strategy.<br>• Start building digital expertise: identify **internal and external resources** for digital marketing.<br>• Add **digital KPIs** to every employee's objectives. |
| **How to become a digirati company?** | • **Assess** your company's digital maturity. Assess your capabilities on digital and transformative intensity.<br>• Create a **transformative digital vision** for the future and provide strong executive support for it.<br>• Identify the areas in which your company should **excel**.<br>• Make someone responsible for digitization. Consider assigning a **chief digital officer.**<br>• Create clear **governance** policies that drive transformation forward.<br>• Adopt a **change management approach** to move the organization towards digirati status: communicate, empower people, create short-term wins, build on the change. |

## To conclude

Digitization has been a disruptive force in many industries and it will continue to disrupt many more. It disrupts not just the marketing profession but the complete value chain. Maximizing the digital potential is the big, inescapable challenge for every organization.

In the pharmaceutical industry, multichannel can no longer be a niche project driven by a small team. Instead, it must form the foundation for a next-generation customer engagement model. It is crucial to understand how the decision-making journey for early adopters plays out: how do these physicians /patients/ payers make decisions, what sources of information do they consult, and so on. Integrating customer insights from all parts of the company—including reps, call centers and marketing, medical, ...—is critical: people must work together across the organization to uncover and meet (and over-deliver on) customer needs.

The New Normal means we are moving away from a static view of marketing to a dynamic one. Rather than having an annual planning cycle, we now receive feedback on an ongoing basis. Plans must be adapted within days or weeks. At the same time, we are moving away from a product-centric view to a customer-centric one. Rather than focusing on the brand and pushing undifferentiated messages regardless of the customer needs and expectations, we are moving to a customer-first approach. Focus must now be on the customer journey, and channel affinity and orchestration have become key in ensuring customer engagement and competitive advantage.

Last but not least, in a true omnichannel organization, we are moving away from trying to measure the impact of individual channels. It is the sequencing of different channels along the customer journey and the frequent encounter across different touch points that will define the ultimate impact. An email in isolation will not have a big impact, but if it triggers a doctor to visit a pharma portal and ask for a rep visit, it becomes highly impactful!

Omnichannel is very much like a relay race: in the end, it is the combination of runners that leads to the final result – not just the last runner.

Rome wasn't built in a day, and the ultimate pharma multichannel organization isn't any different. Companies have to know where they are today, define a roadmap for the next few years and regularly review their progress along the way.

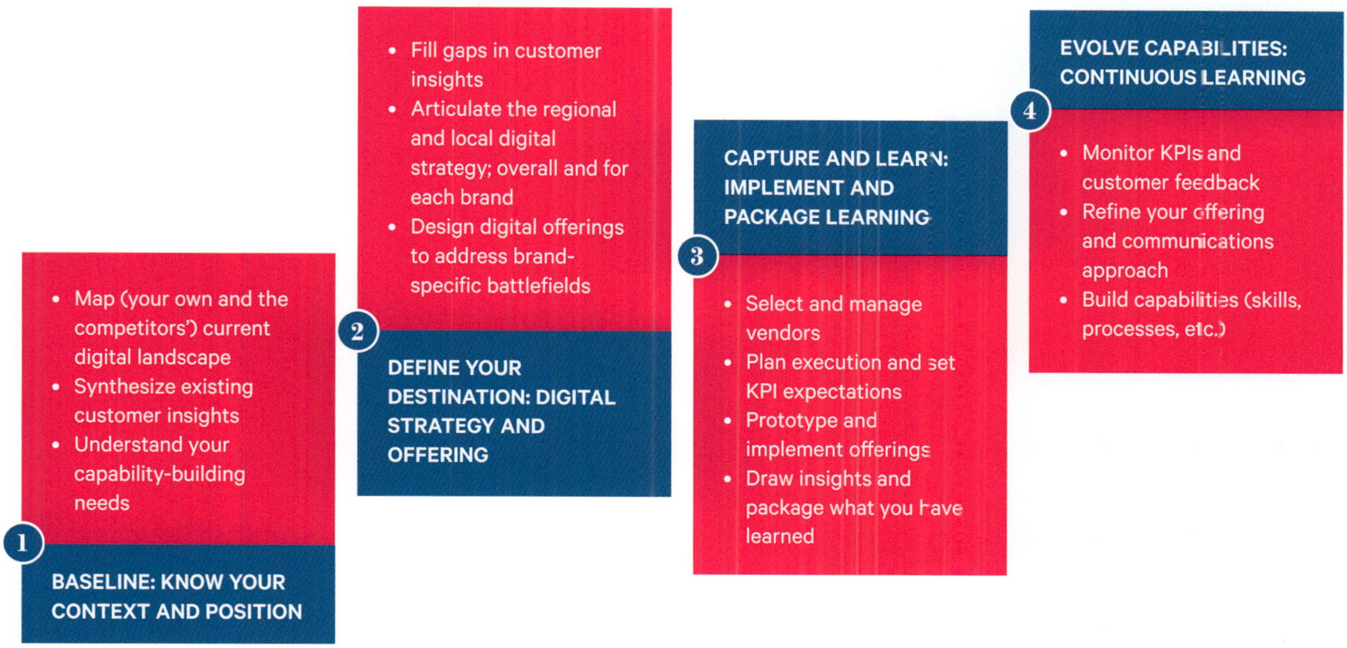


*The digital transformation journey as summarized by Mckinsey and Company (2013).*

# 2 Website Engagement

‘… building and maintaining customer relationships through website activities.’

## The foundation of digital

For many companies, the (mobile) website is the heart of their digital strategy, the hub to which all other marketing activities are directed. For example, inbound marketing best practice states that 60% of all leads generated should come from inbound traffic, and that traffic needs a home.

But the pharma industry is somewhat different: different regions have different regulation over which type of information can be made available to patients and HCPs. Besides the legal constraints, many pharma companies also have further additional internal policies about what can and cannot be communicated. Pharma marketers must continuously balance these different constraints.

In the context of the pharmaceutical industry, the website can fulfill many different roles:

- **disease websites** inform patients about a condition, the possible treatment options and the implications of (not) starting a treatment.
- **product websites** inform HCPs (and, in the US, patients) on specific products, usually containing all the relevant product and prescribing information.
- the **HCP self-service portal**: product sites are gradually giving way to more comprehensive, cross-product, full-service portals, often with 360° personalized features.
- the **corporate website** contains mostly general company information, as well as investor and employee information. It often has only limited relevance to both patients and HCPs.

In the early days of the internet, a website was a simple online business presentation. Since their inception, however, they have evolved from a one-way promotion channel to an integrated, two-way service and education platform.

> ‘ All the competitors in the world are but a mouse click away. ’
>
> **Jakob Nielsen**
> **Usability expert**

## The metrics of website engagement

**over 1.3 billion**

There are over 1.3 billion websites, and counting. On September 16th, 2014, the threshold of 1 billion websites was reached for the first time,  but due to the monthly fluctuations in the count of inactive websites, the number declined again. In 2016, it crossed the 1 billion threshold again. (Source: Internetlivestats)

**64%**

... of website traffic comes via search engines. (Source: Conductor)

**49%**

The average bounce rate of a website. Bounce rate = a visitor leaving your website without navigating to another web page beyond the landing page. (source: Gorocketfuel)

### Tip

#### First impressions and design count

Make **the first impression** count! A visitor decides in a split second whether to stay on your website or to go to that of a competitor. Make sure every page exudes 1) credibility, 2) trustworthiness and 3) professionalism. The **‘tone of voice’** of your website should resonate consistently across every web page.

**Good design matters.** No matter how valuable your content is, know that, in many cases, your visual design will determine the first impression of visitors. Fail on this criterion, and web users will abandon your site and look elsewhere for content.

# Main tactics

The **most important page** of your website is ... every page. Through search engines and social media referrals, visitors can enter your website through any web page. On average, **less than 20%** of visitors ever get to the home page.

The main tactics used within website marketing:

1 **Call to action (CTA):** a web page without a call to action is a lost opportunity. Include a clear CTA **on every page**!

2 **Measure, measure, measure:** monitor your website results and adjust where needed. Define the funnels, identify the weak spots ("at which stage do visitors leave?") and adjust accordingly.

3 **A/B testing**: try out different designs, wording and flows. Changing the wording in a button can have a huge impact on conversion ratios. Never stop testing!

4 **Customize pages:** adjust content to match visitors' needs. Develop multiple landing pages depending on the nature of the visit.

5 **Responsive design:** your website should scale according to the device and screen being used. Make sure that every visitor, whether browsing on a smartphone, tablet or laptop, has a great user experience.

6 **Campaign websites**: separate websites for specific (i.e. temporary) commercial campaigns are becoming less popular. The best option is to ensure your main website **is flexible enough** to also cover temporary campaigns.

7 **Usability testing:** ensure that you do not get 'lost in design'.
The 'how to' of usability testing:

- Testing can be done by any web user.
- Observe visitors' surfing behaviour.
- Ask the user to 'think aloud' about what (s)he's going to do next.
- Provide some crucial tasks the user needs to complete.

## Tip

### Don't re-invent the wheel

**Stick to what people expect** from a website: the company logo can be found top left, the search box top right.
**Copy from industry peers.** Imitate the best and most successful examples.

Some key questions to ask during testing (but beware of 'leading' answers):

- What is, according to you, the purpose of this page?
- Can you find your way around the site?
- Can you (intuitively) perform specific tasks?
- How do you experience the pages?
- Is this what you would expect to find on this page?

When you have made adjustments, retest the updated design. New issues may surface which were not there / invisible before.

## Healthy snack: HCP web portals

**A global pharma company wanted to use a self-service portal as an anchor item for a multichannel and CLM campaign.**

**Step 1: iPad**
After a face-to-face call, the rep selected a relevant contact item on the iPad, that they wanted to share with the HCP.

**Step 2: Rep email**
An email was automatically triggered to the HCP, which contained a deep link to the content item that the rep selected.

**Step 3: Deeplink access**
Physicians clicked on the deeplink in the email they had received, and accessed a web page. This was personalised based on the ID of the HCP, which had been retrieved from the company's CRM system.

**Step 4: Personalised content**
Segmented content was provided at the top of the page, based on the physician's ID. This content was driven by marketing. Tailored content was offered at the bottom of the page, based on historical rep interactions. This content was driven by the field force.

# Website engagement in action

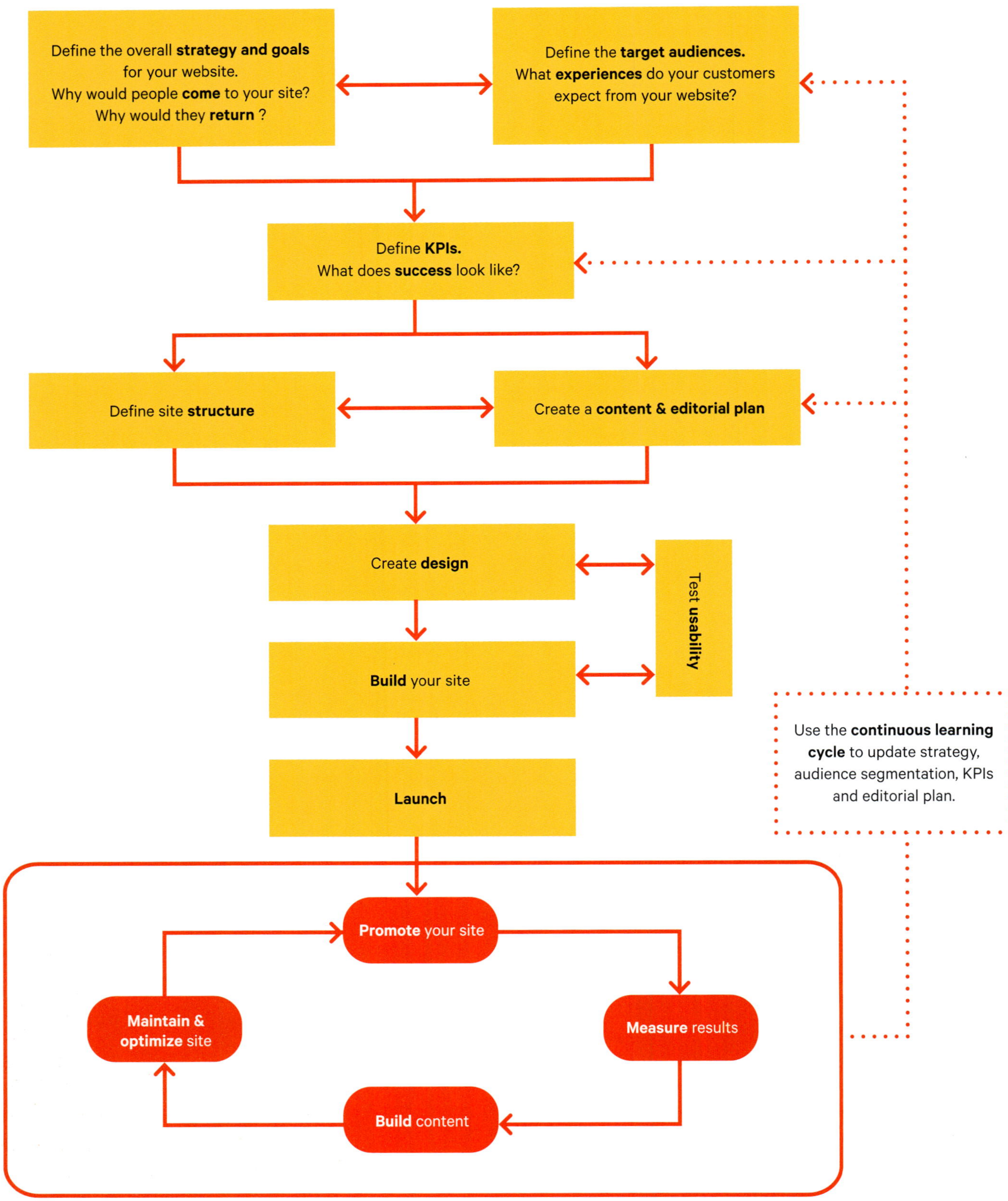

# Challenges of website engagement

| Challenges ☹ | Solutions ☺ |
| --- | --- |
| **How to integrate multiple site goals from different stakeholders?** | • Create a **cross-divisional workgroup** to capture the different opinions and needs from within the organization.<br>• Go through the **website strategy template** to get things right.<br>• Revisit the overall **business goals** to make sure the website's goals are in line with it. |
| **How to stay within time and budget?** | • Avoid **scope creep** (additional functionalities being added to the wish list which were not foreseen in the initial project definition). Thoroughly do your homework before starting website development.<br>• Set up **agile working processes**. Keep business and development stakeholders closely involved and aligned throughout the complete development process. Develop in short sprints according to clearly defined timelines. |
| **How to update the website regularly?** | • Create pre- and post-launch **website content plans** with clearly assigned roles, responsibilities and timelines.<br>• **Integrate** your website content plan into your overall **content marketing plan.**<br>• Create **multiple types of content**, don't use only text. Also include images, video, interactive tools ...<br>• Include **customization and personalization** options. |

> “Design is not just what it looks like and feels like. Design is how it works.”
>
> **Steve Jobs**

## Optimizing landing pages

Prospects and customers can enter your website on any page. But if that page does not offer something meaningful straight away, the visitor will quickly leave. Landing pages—**optimized pages based on the context of the visitor**—help to avoid people leaving your site immediately.

There are several ways to optimize your landing pages:

• **Display ad** landing pages: make sure there is a clear **visual and content continuity** between the display ad and the landing page.

• **SEA** landing pages: make sure the **keywords** related to your search engine ad are clearly included on the landing page.

• **Email** landing pages: **personalize** the page based on the **information** known from the visitor clicking on the link in your email.

• **IP optimized** landing pages: using this more advanced tactic, your website can keep track of the IP addresses of your key customers or prospects. When a visitor enters the website coming from a specific known IP address, the system adapts the web page. It could show, for instance, specific calls to action or reshuffling the content based on what is believed to be more relevant to that company and visitor.

Landing pages are often **'toned down'** versions of regular website pages. Some elements, like the navigation bar, can be removed to avoid visitors getting distracted from the primary goal: completing a campaign-related **call to action.**

Besides optimized landing pages, you can also harness the power of **deep links**. When directing visitors to your website, avoid sending them to the general homepage, but instead, link to pages 'deeper' in the website that contain more specific and in depth information.

> "The main goal of most web projects should be to make it easy for customers to perform useful tasks."
>
> **Jakob Nielsen**
> **Usability expert**

## The maturity level of website engagement

Websites are a **must-have in many industries**, and the pharma industry is no exception. For 7 out of 10 marketers, the pharma-owned website (the company, product, or disease website) is a standard practice. **HCP self-service portals are gaining ground** as well, with 34% of pharma marketers stating it is standard practice and another 39% stating a pilot is planned or ongoing.

The pharma-owned website, which has held the number 1 spot for years, is currently the **2nd most commonly used tactic**, just behind tablet e-detailing. The HCP self-service portal holds the ninth position out of the 25 tactics surveyed.

**The adoption of website tactics by pharma**

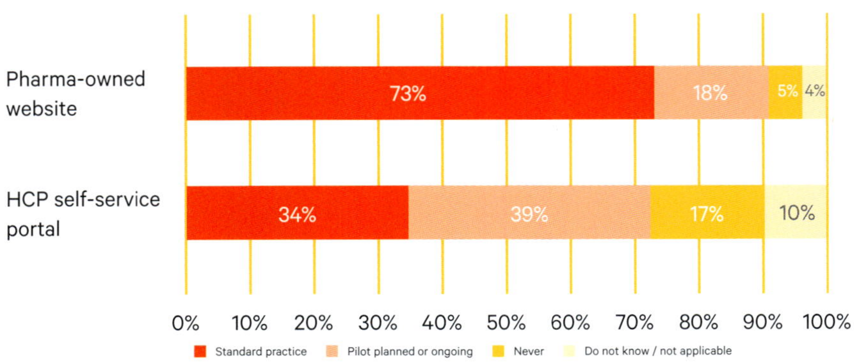


Source: The Across Health Multichannel Maturometer 2017 | N = 221 | EU scope

### Tip

**The F-rule**

Always follow the F-rule when **writing and designing** for the web. Eye-tracking studies show that people read web pages in an F-Pattern. So make sure ...

• the most important information is in **the first two paragraphs,**

• subheads, paragraphs, and bullet points start with **information-carrying words** that entice users.

# Tips for novices

Don't underestimate continued **website management.** Not just from a technical point of view, but also from a content point of view. Only commit to what is reasonably manageable within your organization.

**Consider different options** before embarking on a website adventure. Maybe an existing site already meets your needs? What about third-party sites?

**Combine content and services.** Don't just offer content. By combining content with additional services (e.g. eCME) that are relevant to specific profiles, you can build stronger customer relationships.

Your website is **an extension of who you are** as a company. So get this right before you start designing for the web.

## Tip

### Come again

Two key questions to answer for any website project:
1) Why should people **come** to your website?
2) Why should people **return** to your website?

> The success of a page should be measured by one criterion: do visitors do what you want them to do?
>
> Aaron Wall
> SEObook.com

## Segment and personalize

Pharma websites often face fierce competition from a variety of other websites, and many of these are **perceived as more neutral**. Although this perception is often hard to overcome, some elements can help foster a more positive view and build stronger ties:

• **Optimize segmentation.** Filter the available content, services and functionalities based on different profiles and their interests and goals. By offering different combinations of content to specialists, other HCPs and patients, each profile will find the information most relevant to them faster.

• **Include personalization.** While face-to-face meetings between pharma reps and HCPs remain an important element in the marketing mix, capturing personal interests during the conversation and using this to provide optimized landing pages, can increase relevancy and visits to your website can be stimulated.

• **Create a one-stop shop experience.** By bringing all knowledge sources, support and other services together in one place, you can make it easier for HCPs and other customers to quickly find what they are looking for.

## The analogy of the diamond

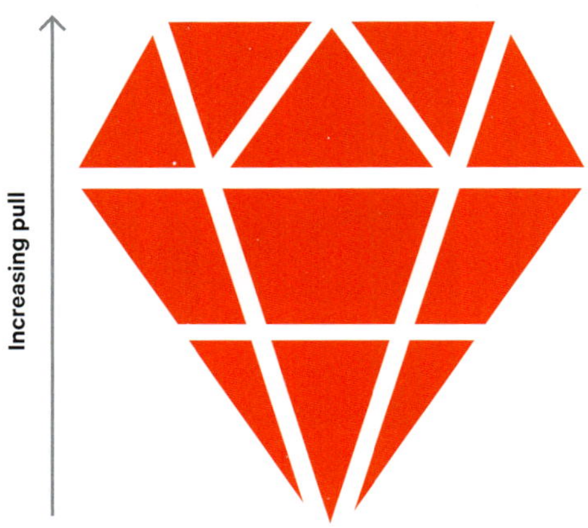


**Community**
Add a community aspect to your website. Don't make this too complicated by immediately thinking about discussion forums. Keep it simple: let your visitors rate content and present the most-liked or most-read articles.

**Self-service**
Websites are available 24/7 and can increase your reach and frequency. Add forms (requests, order materials, event signup...), call-me-back functionalities, CRM and ERP integration, etc. to enhance the service aspect of your website.

**Content**
Content is the foundation. Keep it short and sweet. Provide frequent content updates in a bite-sized format. If content production is a challenge, you may use content packs from third-party providers. Chances are that they have a lot of the content you need available off-the-shelf. Don't aspire to be a publisher... stay close to your company's services and brands.

## Are you an HCP?

Various kinds of HCP-oriented information cannot be made publicly available. But different countries have different regulations around this. In the UK, for instance, **confirming HCP status** by simply clicking an 'I am an HCP' button is enough. However, in many European countries a more formal check of HCP status is necessary.

This can happen in different ways. By including a third-party validation tool you outsource the trouble of confirming a person's HCP status. The disadvantage of this is that you can miss out on relevant data when the HCP visits your site, as third-party implementation is usually **anonymous.**

It therefore may be worthwhile to handle the HCP confirmation process yourself. Although this takes up resources, you can gain a great deal by capturing highly relevant visitor data. It becomes easier to build **a 360° view of your customers** when you know what they're doing on your HCP portal.

It's therefore also recommendable to **limit the use of product sites** (which also require a HCP confirmation in many countries) and, rather, go for one comprehensive self-service HCP portal. These can contain various kinds of product information and services, often presented in a personalized manner and integrated with backend systems (CRM, ERP ...).

## Tip

### the GDPR

After years of preparation, the EU Parliament approved a systematic reform of the EU data protection rules on 14 April 2016, the so-called GDPR (General Data Protection Regulation). Stronger rules on data protection mean people have more control over their personal data and businesses benefit from a level playing field. The enforcement date was 25 May 2018, after which non-compliant organizations may face heavy fines. For life science companies, this has important implications for their customer database (optin, anonymization, etc) - as well as for their business partners processing such customer data.

*ec.europa.eu*

## Website engagement: reach & impact in Europe 2017

| Website | | Rep |
|---|---|---|
| 34% | ... reach versus... | 63% |
| 5.4 | ... impact versus... | 5.8 |
| 0.81 | ... MCQ versus... | 1.00 |

The Across Health Navigator studies the impact and reach of 57 off- and online channels amongst HCPs. From this, the multichannel equivalent (MCQ) is derived: a measurement of relative impact, which makes comparing between channels possible. Find out more about the Navigator data in chapter 1.

Source: The Across Health Navigator 2017 | N = 3,185 | EU5 scope (DE, ES, FR, IT, UK) | Specialists

## The role of the third-party website

HCPs prefer independent medical websites to those provided by the pharma industry. Knowing this, and the difficulties with setting up an HCP site, such as password protection, governance and compliance processes, adverse event monitoring and traffic building, pharma companies can save both time and money by **partnering with a third-party website**.

The benefits of partnering with third-party websites:

- **They are considered more trustworthy.** HCPs have a natural skepticism towards pharma resources, and about continued medical education (CME). By partnering with third-party websites and enabling them to incorporate your information as they see fit, pharma companies can add an additional layer of trustworthiness to their content.
- **Increase reach and engagement.** Instead of trying to attract HCPs to your (password protected) site, meet them where they already are: third-party websites. This can also be a great means to (potentially) reach out to a wider audience (your indirect target groups).
- **Limit the number of review processes.** Although you give up some control over your content, this comes with the advantage of potentially reducing the number of internal medical, legal or regulatory reviews.

In summary, third-party sites ensure high reach and trust. Ideally they can be integrated with a pharma-owned property, where conversion can occur and 360° relationships can be developed.

## The site taking centre stage

Campaigns use and combine many different tactics, but these need to revert back to a central hub. In many cases, this is the website.

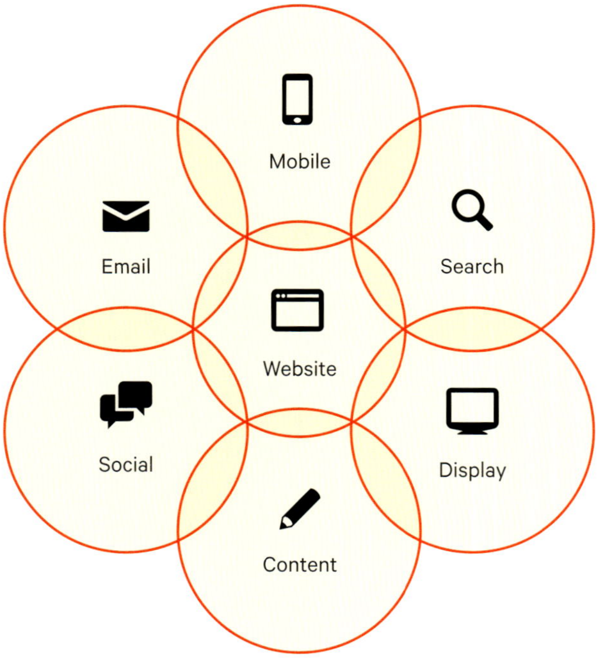

# The rise of the self-service portal

The HCP self-service portal is gaining ground as the central location for all multichannel interactions. Best-practice examples take into consideration 3 key elements:
1. The **brand** journey tailors promotional information to the HCP's fields of interest.
2. The **knowledge** journey provides segmented medical information.
3. The **customer relationship** journey facilitates getting in contact.

Through **segmentation**, content is tailored and filtered according to the segments and behavioural objectives as defined in the brand plan and the customer journey.

Via **personalization**, the presented content is directly related to the most recent client interactions, both face-to-face and online.

**Campaign triggers** can link directly to new content, activity suggestions or online interactions.

Lastly, to make sure everyone is fully involved, clear **ownership roles** need to be defined.

This way of working helps to gain commitment from the sales force. The personalized experience ensures that each visit becomes more **impactful.**

| HCP self-service portal | | |
|---|---|---|
| **1) Promotional information**<br><br>→ The brand journey<br><br>E.g. webcast suggestions and product information according to treatment preferences. | **2) Medical information**<br><br>→ The knowledge journey<br><br>E.g. congress suggestions and medical courses according to knowledge preferences. | **3) Personal information**<br><br>→ The customer relationship journey<br><br>E.g. shared files, contact info, personalized agenda and services. |

# What to measure

Websites have the great advantage that you can track almost everything. Some relevant KPIs and metrics to consider:

| EXPOSURE | ENGAGEMENT | CONVERSION |
|---|---|---|
| • # of website visitors<br>• # of unique website visitors<br>• # of pages visited | • # of pieces of content accessed (e.g. downloadable videos)<br>• # of segment-specific activities completed | • # of connections / user<br>• # of returning users<br>• # of completed call-to-actions<br>• Duration of video viewing<br>• Net Promotor Score for therapeutic area, brand or company |

## To conclude

**Company-owned websites are like a Swiss army knife, offering a range of interesting features, brand building, lead and sales generation through to (self-) service and fostering customer loyalty. Very often, it's the hub to which all communications refer. A strong website is therefore crucial in realizing your overall objectives and optimizing 360° customer engagement. Combining it selectively with 3d-party website activities will yield even higher reach, frequency and engagement.**

> ...the promotion of websites and content pages through search engines.

# 3 Search Engine Marketing

## To be found or not to be found

No one types out URLs anymore. They remain important to structure the web, but web users, patients and healthcare professionals alike, use search engines for virtually everything. With search engine marketing, you make sure you can be found. Because if you can't be found, you may just as well not exist.

**Search engine marketing** (SEM) covers **2 key tactics: search engine optimization** (SEO) and **search engine advertising** (SEA). SEO—also referred to as 'organic results'—is mainly achieved by optimizing the content of websites with the aim getting a higher 'organic' ranking in search engines and hence higher visibility. SEA—also known as 'sponsored results'—shows specific search-related text ads.

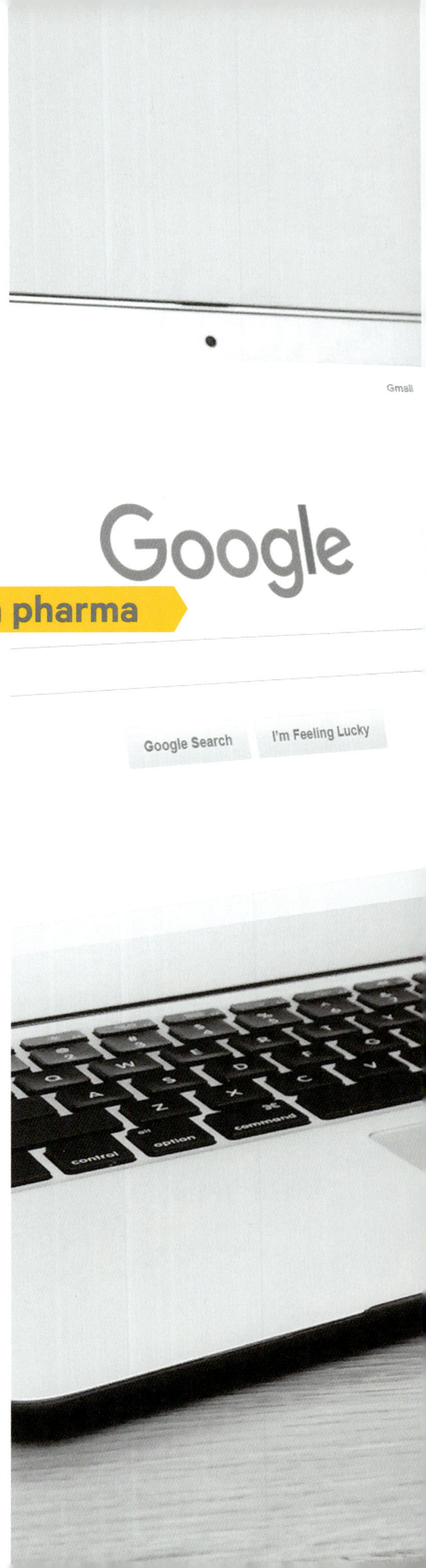


## The metrics of search engine marketing in pharma

**160 million**

The average number of health-related searches on Google every day (1 out of 20 searches on Google is health related!). (Source: Google Ignite)

**60%**

... of patients regularly use search engines for health-related decision making. It's their most frequently used channel. (Source: Google Ignite)

**44%**

The first link in the search engine results page receives on average 44% of all search engine traffic (Source: SEOprofiler)

**92%**

The links on the first page receive 92% of all search engine clicks. The second page receives only 4.8% of them. (Source: Impact BND)

**72% vs. 28%**

Organic search results typically capture 72% of the potential clicks from a search engine results page. Sponsored results capture the remaining 28%. (Source: Isobar)

## SEM versus display advertising

**Search engine marketing** (SEM) and display advertising (e.g. bannering) are distinct, but receive similar budgets. According to Dentsu Aegis (2017), across industries budgets for paid search are slightly higher (15.9%) than display (12.7%). While **SEM** is a **pull tactic** (pulling in people), **display advertising** is more of **a push tactic** (pushing ads towards people). The latter is more frequently used at the early stages of the customer journey, when, for example, patients or physicians are not actively looking for a solution to a problem. Search, on the other hand, is more frequently used in the later stages of the customer journey, closer to treatment and product decision and drug adherence.

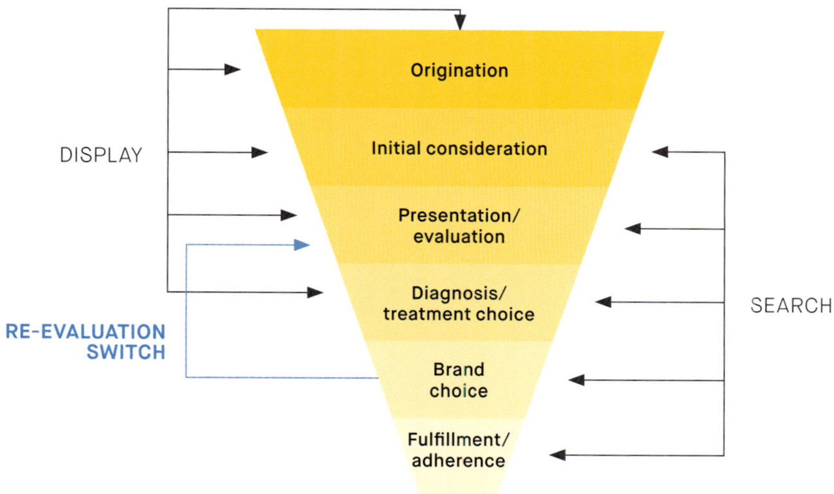


## Tip

### Choose your keywords wisely

To help you select the right keywords, Google has developed a 'keyword planner' tool. A list of relevant keywords for a therapeutic area or product can be generated as well as the monthly search volume and estimated cost-per-click for them. The tool helps you select the right keywords for both search engine optimization (SEO) as well as search engine advertising (SEA).

adwords.google.com/KeywordPlanner*

* *Google account and active Google AdWords campaign needed to utilize this tool and its full set of features.*

## SEM along the customer journey

Understanding how patients and healthcare professionals search throughout the customer journey is crucial. Actionable insights into search behaviour allow you to align the content of your website and your SEM strategy. As a result, your content will be perceived as more relevant and is more likely to appear more prominently on the results pages of search engines.

For patients, search peaks can be expected when experiencing first symptoms and right after being diagnosed.

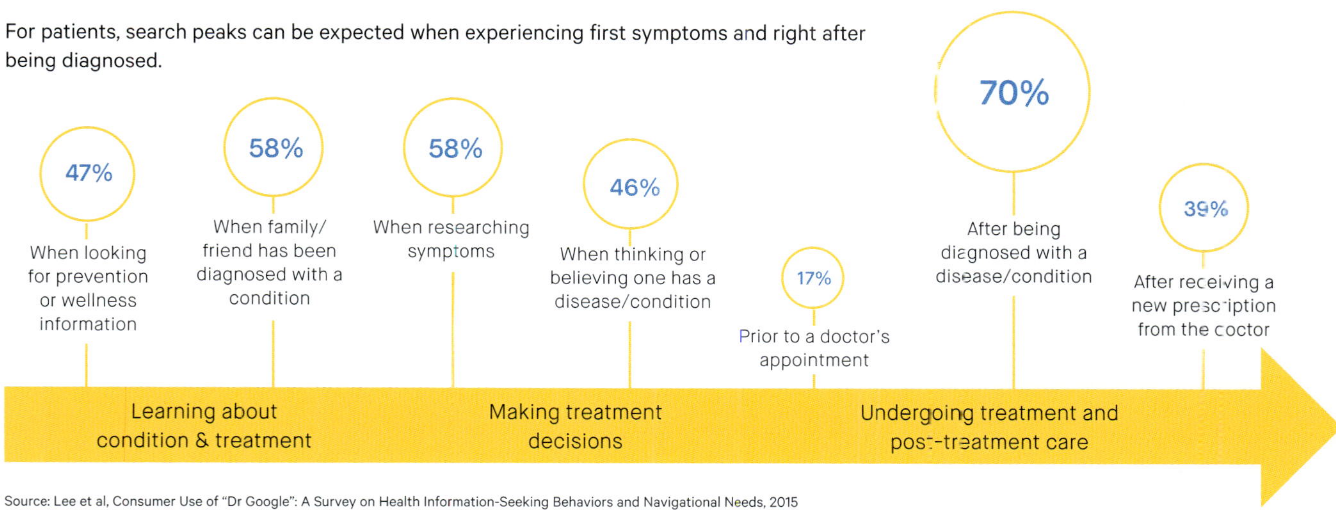


Source: Lee et al, Consumer Use of "Dr Google": A Survey on Health Information-Seeking Behaviors and Navigational Needs, 2015

# The success of SEO

With SEO, you optimise **your website and other digital channels (Youtube, blogs, ...)** for search engines. With over 1 billion websites available on the web, finding what you're looking for without the help of search engines has become impossible. Search engines are, for many web users, **the starting-point for everything.** Despite the fact that a significant portion of internet traffic comes from search engines, only 36% of pharma companies are actively optimizing their websites to improve search engine visibility. Ensuring that your content can be found by search engines is vital for every company.

The success of SEO is based on ...

- **Value:** in a sense, SEO is 'free' advertising. As a company, you don't pay to be shown in search engine result pages. But this does not mean that there's no cost! Continuously optimizing your website and related channels for search engines does take time and effort.

- **Content:** SEO is content driven. You optimize your content for search engines by incorporating relevant keywords. The more relevant and recent your content is, the higher the chances of being shown in search engine results pages. The higher your content appears in the result lists, the greater the likelihood of people visiting your content.

- **Technology:** SEO is also technology-driven. Make sure your website is easily accessible for search engines. Optimize the site structure to facilitate both surfing and crawling. Tag all the visual elements on your site, such as images, video, PDF... Search engines only interpret text and content tagging (text descriptions) enables them to interpret and index these visual elements. Optimize your website also for mobile. Next to providing a better user experience for the ever growing number of website visitors from mobile devices, having a mobile-friendly website might also improve your positioning in search engines.

- **Credibility:** the more credible your website is, the higher it will rank in search engines. A way to improve the credibility of your website is by having other websites link to your site. This technique is called "linkbaiting". The more important and relevant to your content other websites are that link to your site, the more favourable this will be for your position in search engines. Also enable social sharing: the additional links to your website might also improve your ranking over time.

## Tip

### How search engines work

A web crawler - also referred to as a web spider - is **an automated software application** that systematically browses the World Wide Web. Web crawlers copy all the pages they visit and store these in a **'web index'.** Thanks to the index, a search engine can generate result pages in **a split second.**

The index is like a massive book of the internet. When we perform a search, the search engine flips through this huge book. It 1) locates all the relevant pages and 2) selects the pages it thinks are the best to show first. The 'selection logic' is defined by the 'algorithm'.

## Tip

### The black box of SEO

Search engines create their result pages based on **a series of algorithms.** These algorithms determine whether your page gets a high ranking or not. The inner workings of the algorithms are as mysterious as Coca-Cola's formula.

Search engines regularly update and change their algorithm. This can have a big impact on the positioning of your pages. **Monitoring the positioning** of your web pages in search engines on business-critial keywords is crucial. With a significant portion of traffic coming via search engines, a drop in position can have a big impact on on your traffic and hence on your business results.

# Pharma challenges of SEO

Due to its regulated nature, the healthcare industry faces some SEO challenges unknown to most other industries:

- **Content challenges:** due to copy approval and compliance reasons, it is difficult to compete with big third-party websites in keeping content fresh and up-to-date. SEO therefore needs to be considered as soon as content development starts. It is often very time-consuming to implement or adjust at a later stage due to Medical-Legal-Regulatory (MLR) timelines. A detailed mid- to long-term content plan is also recommended to circumvent this crucial challenge.

- **Keyword challenges:** while potentially very powerful for organic search the use of your own (Rx) product names on publicly available websites is highly restricted. You cannot make any promotional claims nor mention anything beyond (a link to) the summary of product characteristics (SmPC).

- **Password challenges:** most websites for healthcare professionals are password-protected. But search engines cannot index password-protected content. As a result, only the landing page(s) of your HCP sites will be indexed and shown in the search results. Due to limited access to your content, these sites will likely not show up high in search results. It's therefore very important to include as much descriptive content as possible on the landing page of every password-protected site, or add a section that can be publicly accessed from your landing page, for example, for patients.

- **Tagging challenges:** meta tags (page titles and descriptions which appear publicly in the search engine result pages) have to go through the same approval process as site content, as search engines will display title and description tags in the search results. This can lengthen approval times while simultaneously restricting your freedom in making your search engine result listing as attractive and relevant as possible.

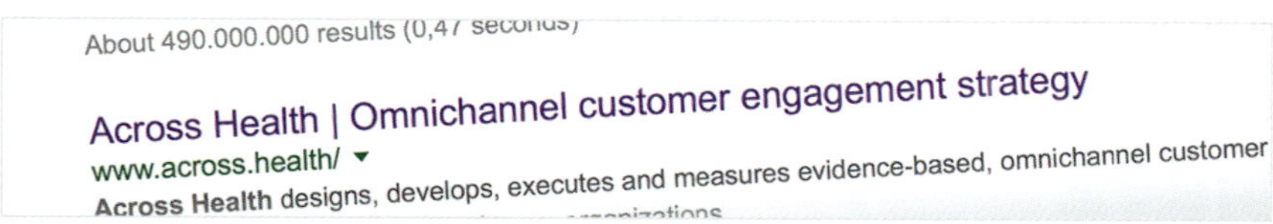


## Tip

### Combine channels

**Blog sites** sometimes outperform websites in organic search engine results. This is because blog sites are, by nature, 1) fully optimized for search engines and 2) they usually contain very specialized, highly relevant and fresh content.
Consider combining different website formats (corporate website + blog site) to optimize your ranking. **Extend your online media mix** to comprise multiple sources that refer to one another. Companies that blog tend to be seen as respectable authorities in their field and typically attract more website visitors from search engines and beyond.

# The maturity level of search engine marketing

The maturity level of SEM among pharma companies still has **room for growth**. 37% and 32% of pharma marketers use SEO and SEA, respectively, as standard practice.
For now, these tactics are ranked 9th and 11th among the top 25 digital marketing tactics, respectively. This is surprisingly low, knowing that a significant part of online journeys start with a search engine.

## The adoption of SEO and SEA by pharma

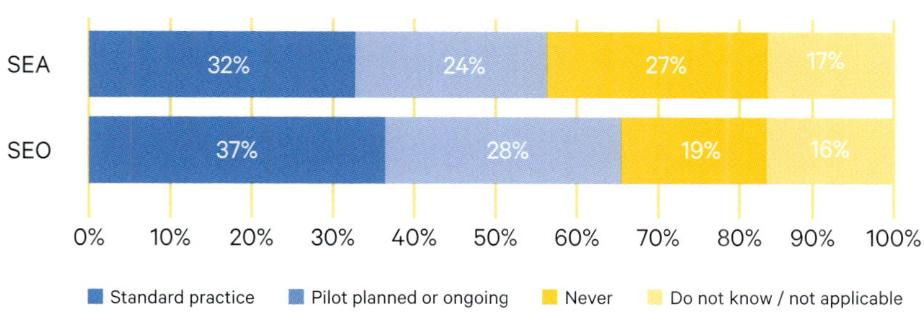


Source: The Across Health Multichannel Maturometer 2017 | N = 221 | EU scope

## SEO – how to...

Some important rules when optimizing for search engines:

Create **quality content**! Sites with with unique and interesting content will typically have a better search engine ranking:

- Write **easy-to-read** text and update the content frequently.
- Use **heading tags** (i.c. titles and subtitles on the web page)
- Write strong **anchor text**. The anchor text (link label, link text, or link title) is the visible, clickable text in a hyperlink.
- **Optimize** the use of **images**: add an 'alt' attribute description for every image. This will increase the likelihood of your images showing e.g. in Google images.

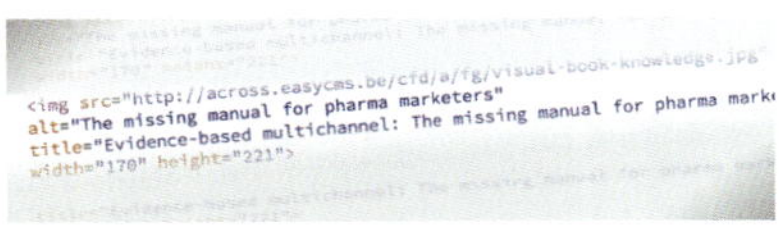


Create unique **title tags** for each page and use brief, descriptive titles:

- Provide a **meta tag** description (= a concise explanation of a webpage's content, added to the page's code).
- Include **relevant keywords** in titles and tags. Avoid internal speak and use keywords that web users use to search for your type of content in your industry. Regularly perform keyword analyses.
- Create **URLs** that are easy to understand for both users and search engines. Use understandable words in URLs and avoid 'code speak'.

Create a simple **directory structure**. Provide only one version of a URL per content item:

- **Create** two **sitemaps**: one for users (in HTML), and one for search engines (in XML)
- Create a **mobile sitemap** if you have a mobile website

**Optimize linking** to and from other sites. Look for 'quality' links: links from websites with relevant content and high traffic are more beneficial to your site ranking. As most pharma companies have many websites, a quick win is to interlink between these sites as much as possible to increase credibility.

**Promote your website**: Due to the specific challenges for SEO in pharma you should not rely solely on this channel for web traffic generation. Invest in other promotion techniques (including SEA and display advertising) to build traffic. In the long term, websites with more relevant traffic are deemed more relevant and can get a better positioning.

**Monitor** your search engine positioning **continuously**. When search engine algorithms change or competitors become more active, your position may quickly fall!

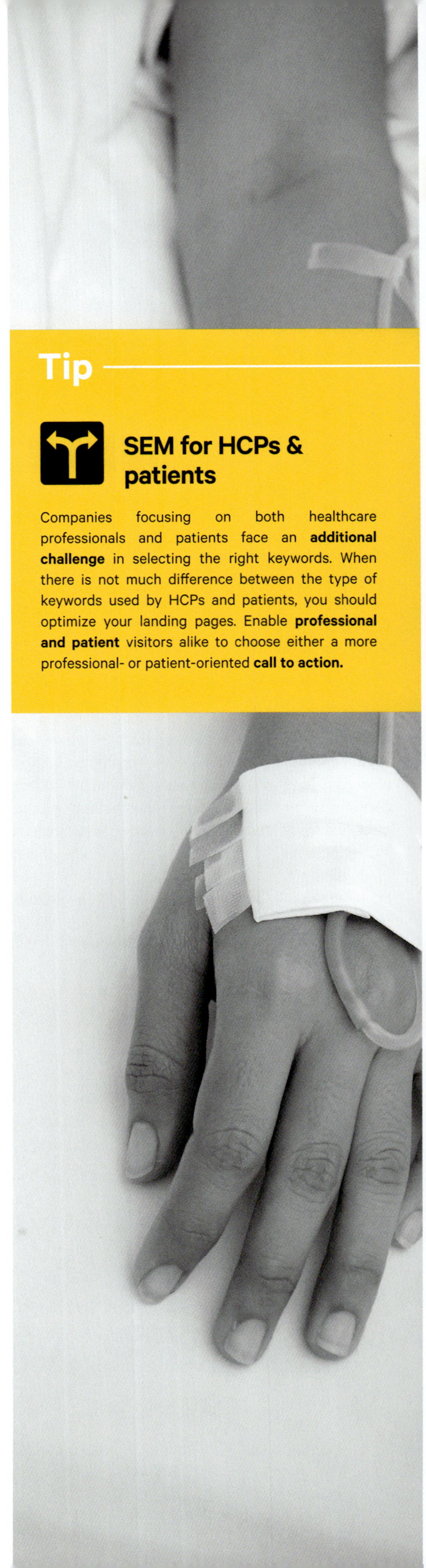

### Tip

#### SEM for HCPs & patients

Companies focusing on both healthcare professionals and patients face an **additional challenge** in selecting the right keywords. When there is not much difference between the type of keywords used by HCPs and patients, you should optimize your landing pages. Enable **professional and patient** visitors alike to choose either a more professional- or patient-oriented **call to action.**

# The success of SEA

Many pharma companies struggle to attain a good position in the organic search results due to industry-specific challenges and the competition of big 3rd-party websites. In such cases, search engine advertising or paid search can be a cost-efficient channel to leverage.

With **search engine advertising,** companies submit **text ads** to search engines combined with a series of **keywords**. Web users searching the web receive search result pages which include both 'organic' and 'sponsored' results. Sponsored results are marked as being 'ads'. When a user clicks on an ad, the company is charged a certain amount.

Currently, only 32% of pharma companies invest in search engine advertising.
**The success of SEA is based on ...**

- **Value:** advertisers pay for actions (= clicks), not for views. SEA is a form of results-driven advertising.

- **Relevancy:** SEA is relevant advertising. The ads shown are related to the keyword search by a user. Compared to traditional advertising such as TV or radio, there is very limited waste with search engine marketing. SEA enables you to show different ad texts depending on the keywords used. As such, ad copy can be tailored to meet specific search needs, and visitors can be directed immediately to the most relevant page on your website.

- **Low-cost clicks:** many keywords and especially 'targeted keyword combinations' are sold for as little as 0.10 € per click. For very popular keywords, the cost per click (CPC) can vary from a few cents to a few euros. It's therefore worthwhile to also buy less popular keywords, even including misspellings, to optimize SEA expenditure.

- **Control of costs:** companies fully control their SEA budget in real time. With the 'daily budget cap', advertisements are stopped as soon as the daily budget is reached.

- **Auctioning:** keywords are auctioned in real time. The supply and demand equation is transparent to the advertisers. Consequently, campaigns must be monitored daily, as competition on a keyword changes over time, which affects the click price.

- **Real-time monitoring:** Google Analytics enables real-time monitoring of SEA campaigns.

- **Insights:** keyword analysis helps advertisers create campaigns based on frequently used keywords. This further increases relevancy and minimizes advertising waste.

- **Reach:** Google is not only the most visited website worldwide, its search engine advertising also extends well beyond its own website. Through AdSense, Google's text ads are shown on third-party websites, based on the same keyword relevancy logic. Besides contextual text ads, video ads in YouTube and in-app advertising on mobile apps are also options to be considered.

- **Localization:** different campaigns in different languages can be deployed for different geographic areas. Advertisers can determine a range (e.g. miles) around a company location to add relevancy.

- **Text advertising:** text ads are perceived as less intrusive compared to traditional banner advertising, adding to its success. This translates into higher click-through-rates. Text ads on search engines on average have a CTR of 2% or more while banners typically achieve less then 0,3%.

- **Control of timing:** campaigns can be turned on or off with the flick of a switch depending on advertiser's needs. Or you automate your ad rotation by e.g. only showing your advertisements on certain times of day or days of the week.

## Tip

### AD Building your ad

Search engine ads force you to communicate your message in as **few characters as possible**. Make sure to include your most important keywords and provide a clear URL and call-to-action. Different variations of your ad copy (e.g. 2 – 3 per ad group) can be run in order to see what works best. It is preferable to include variations from the inception of the campaign, to avoid having to go through the approval process many times.

**Search engine ads have very strict limitations:**

| | |
|---|---|
| [headline] | two headline fields (up to 30 characters each) |
| [URL] | a display URL that uses your final URL's domain + two optional 'Path' fields, used in the ad's display URL (up to 15 characters each) |
| [description] | a single, expanded description field (up to 80 characters) |

**For example:**

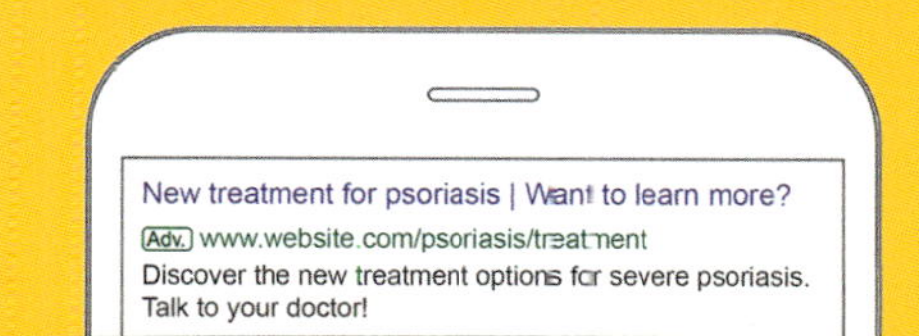


To make your ad stand out more, you can also include **Google AdWords extensions.** This allows you to add your most important call-to-actions on top of your regular ad copy, without additional costs.

## Tip

### How to target HCPs through SEA?

As ads are visible to everyone, it is not easy to explicitly target healthcare professionals. One approach is to buy keywords that are rarely used by the general public. These keywords can contain specific scientific terms, names of key opinion leaders (with their permission) or names of scientific events.

## Pharma challenges of SEA

• **Keyword selection:** legal and regulatory restrictions make it difficult to buy certain popular search terms such as your own product names. More specific or niche medical terms—comorbidity, side effects, related conditions, symptoms—are often searched so infrequently that Google AdWords may mark these highly specific keywords for having a (too) 'low search volume'. This may lead Google or other search engines to show these ads irregularly or not at all. Best practice suggests that you should focus on keywords which have at least 100 searches a month (according to the Google keyword planner) in your targeted region, although this can be altered depending on the desired outcome of the campaign.

• **Creative ad text:** the ad text must include the required language or keywords, while still fitting within the limits and guidelines of the search engines. Ad texts must also be submitted for approval as they can appear to the general public in the search engine results.

• **Getting the right audience on board:** as search engine advertisements can be seen by everybody, it is not easy to use SEA explicitly for targeting healthcare professionals. Especially as you cannot buy Rx brand names or molecule name keywords in most countries and regions (outside of the US).

## SEA versus SEO

| Search engine advertising (SEA) | Search engine optimization (SEO) |
|---|---|
| **LEVEL OF CONTROL** | |
| Guaranteed visibility | No guaranteed visibility |
| Control over budget (monthly spend cap) | Less clear allocation of budgets |
| Full control over text that appears in listings | Limited control over text that appears in listings |
| **EFFORTS** | |
| 24x7 management to efficiently run campaigns | First months are the most work-intensive |
| Costs may increase over time (due to competition) | Costs typically decrease over time |
| Limited website changes may be needed for optimal campaign results | Significant websites changes and optimizations are typically required |
| Once solid landing pages are in place no need for major content updates | Regular and relevant content updates are key |
| **REACH & VISIBILITY** | |
| 1/3rd of potential clicks | 2/3rd of the potential clicks & higher credibility |
| Virtually unlimited number of keywords including those with high search interest and competition | Number of keywords is typically more focused on smaller set of relevant yet specific niche terms |
| Instant visibility (possible short-term solution) | Will take time (longer-term solution) |

### Tip

#### How to measure success of SEA?

Many marketers use number of clicks and cost per click (CPC) as metrics to measure the success of a campaign. But the fact that someone clicks on your ad and visits your website, tells you nothing about the quality of that visitor. Always consider the goals of your campaigns. What do you want visitors to do, once they land on your web page? In other words: how should visitors 'convert'? Examples of conversion are 'downloading a factsheet', 'subscribing to a newsletter', 'registering for an event', etc.

By tracking these conversions, you can calculate the cost per conversion and compare different channels. With Google Analytics, you can monitor in real time how well your paid ads are performing.

> 'You can spend every penny you have on a website, but it will all be for nothing if nobody knows your site is there.'
>
> Marc Ostrofsky
> Author of 'Get Rich Click: The Ultimate Guide to Making Money Online'

## Lost in abbreviation

A glossary for digital campaigns:

**CPC** = cost per click. A system where advertisements are shown, but the advertiser only pays for actual clicks on them and not for the number of views. Sometimes referred to as pay per click (PPC).

**CPM** = cost per mille. An advertiser pays per thousand views of an advertisement. Mostly used in display advertising.

**CPL** = cost per lead. An advertiser pays per actual lead generated through advertising. CPL is often combined with CPC or CPM.

**CTA** = call to action. Website visitors are invited to complete an action, for example completing a form, finding more information, taking an online test, ...

**CTR** = click-through rate. The number of times an ad is clicked as a percentage of the total number of times it is viewed (CTR = # of clicks / # of views). For example: 50 clicks out of a total of 1,000 views = 5% CTR.

**PPC** = see CPC.

**URL** = Universal Resource Locator; a synonym of a website address.

> "There's nothing that cannot be found through some search engine or on the Internet somewhere."
>
> **Eric Schmidt**
> **Executive chairman of Google**

## The long tail of search

There's a lot of value to be gained from **the long tail of search engine marketing**. Getting a top position on popular keywords can be 1) **challenging** in organic search result lists and 2) **expensive** for search engine advertising. Becoming **more niche** and **specialized** in keyword selection can help you gain a top position for **more targeted audiences**.

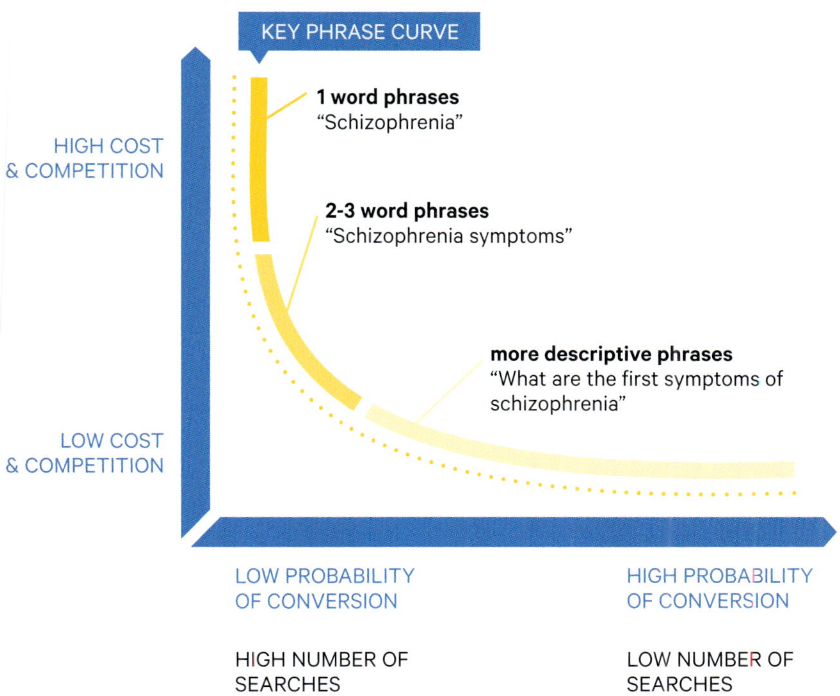

## Search engine marketing in action

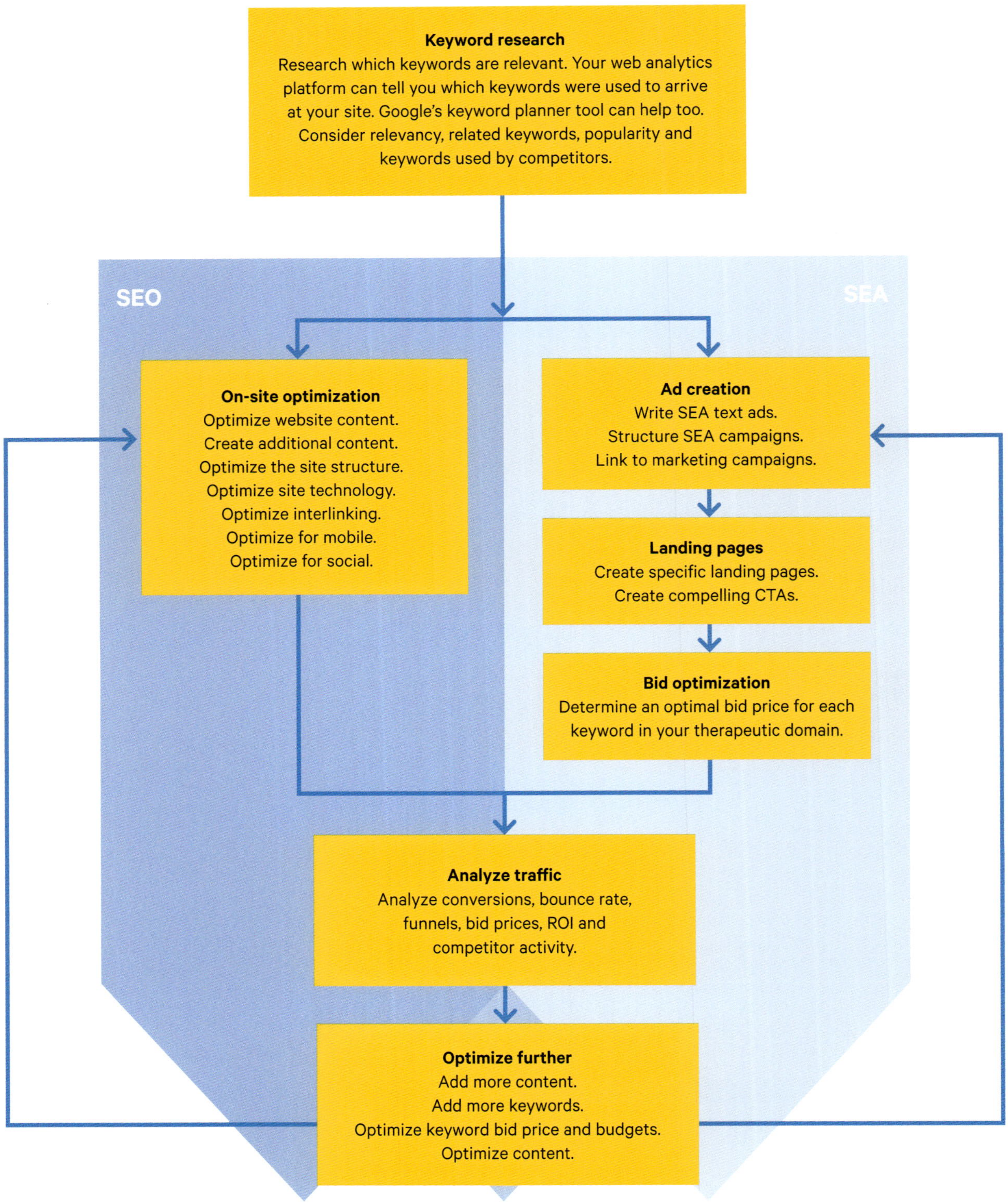

## To conclude

In comparison with other industries, the adoption of SEM in pharma is still very low. This is remarkable, as search engines are the starting point of the online journey for most patients and healthcare professionals.

If you can't be found online, you might as well not exist. Make sure your online content is fully optimized, whether on your own website or through other channels. When adding search engine advertising to the media mix, optimize these SEA campaigns continuously. Search engine marketing demands ongoing monitoring and optimization efforts to stay ahead of the competition.

> Our goal is to organize the world's information and to make it universally accessible and useful.
>
> Larry Page
> Co-founder of Google

‘… building long-term customer relationships through email.’

# 4 Email Engagement

## You've got mail

Through email marketing, different types of emails are sent to different target groups to build and maintain customer relationships. Messages change throughout the customer journey to reinforce lead generation, lead nurturing, conversion and loyalty building.

## The metrics of email engagement

**2,600,000** — On average nearly 2.6 million emails are sent every second. (Source: Radicati)

**225+ billion** — The average number of business (120 billion) and personal (105 billion) emails sent every day. (Source: Radicati)

**22.53%** — The average open rate of an email campaign in EU5 (Source: Across Health Illuminator)

**21.44%** — The average CTR of an email campaign in EU5 (Source: Across Health Illuminator)

**51%** — ... of emails are opened on a mobile device. (Source: Litmus)

**77%** — 77% of emails are optimized for mobile. (Source: Litmus)

**0.22%** — The average unsubscribe rate for emails sent by pharma companies. (Source: Mailchimp)

> ‘Email has an ability many channels don't have: creating valuable, personal touches – at scale.’
>
> **David Newman**
> **Marketing expert**

## The success of email engagement

Email has drastically changed the way we work and communicate. It's hard to imagine a workday without email or a business contact without an email address. Although social media has gained a lot of ground, email is still standing strong as a lead generator and loyalty management channel. Email marketing remains a crucial marketing tactic thanks to its...

1. wide **reach**
2. **diversity** in use (from lead generation to conversion to loyalty building)
3. **measurability**
4. **automation possibilities**
5. **customizability**
6. **low cost**

## Main tactics

We distinguish 3 main types of email: 1) **marketing**, 2) **notification** and 3) **transactional** emails.

1. **Marketing** emails are commercial in nature. E.g.: newsletters, sales and promotional announcements.

2. **Notification** emails are more informative. E.g.: registration confirmation emails, status update changes (e.g. update from a free to a premium account), subscription abandonment email, notifications on recently browsed products or feedback request emails ...

3. **Transactional** emails are expected by the recipient and confirm the customer relationship. E.g.: welcome message / account opening, shipment tracking and order status updates, account termination emails, order confirmation messages or invoices.

Companies can manage these many different email messages by...

- Creating a **flow matrix** which indicates which message is sent when and how often, in order to avoid 'over-sending'.

- Creating **different scenarios** for different types of customers or buyer personas.

- Making sure every email message is **tailored to a specific purpose**.

Emails are useful in building trust with your customers but don't violate this trust by being overly commercial.

### Tip

#### Click-through rates

Email click-through rates (CTR) represent the percentage of clicks that an email generates. This number is often used to **measure the success of an email campaign**. The ideal click-through rate varies depending on the nature of the email.

CTR is impacted by:
- The **frequency** of emails sent,
- The **quality** of the list of recipients,
- The **relevancy** of the content to the audience,
- The **industry,**
- The **time** of day,
- The **day** of the week,
- The **visibility** of the CTA button/link

> 'What you prefer or what your designer prefers doesn't matter if it's not getting you conversions.'
>
> **Jen Gordon**
> **Web designer and marketer**

# Email marketing in action

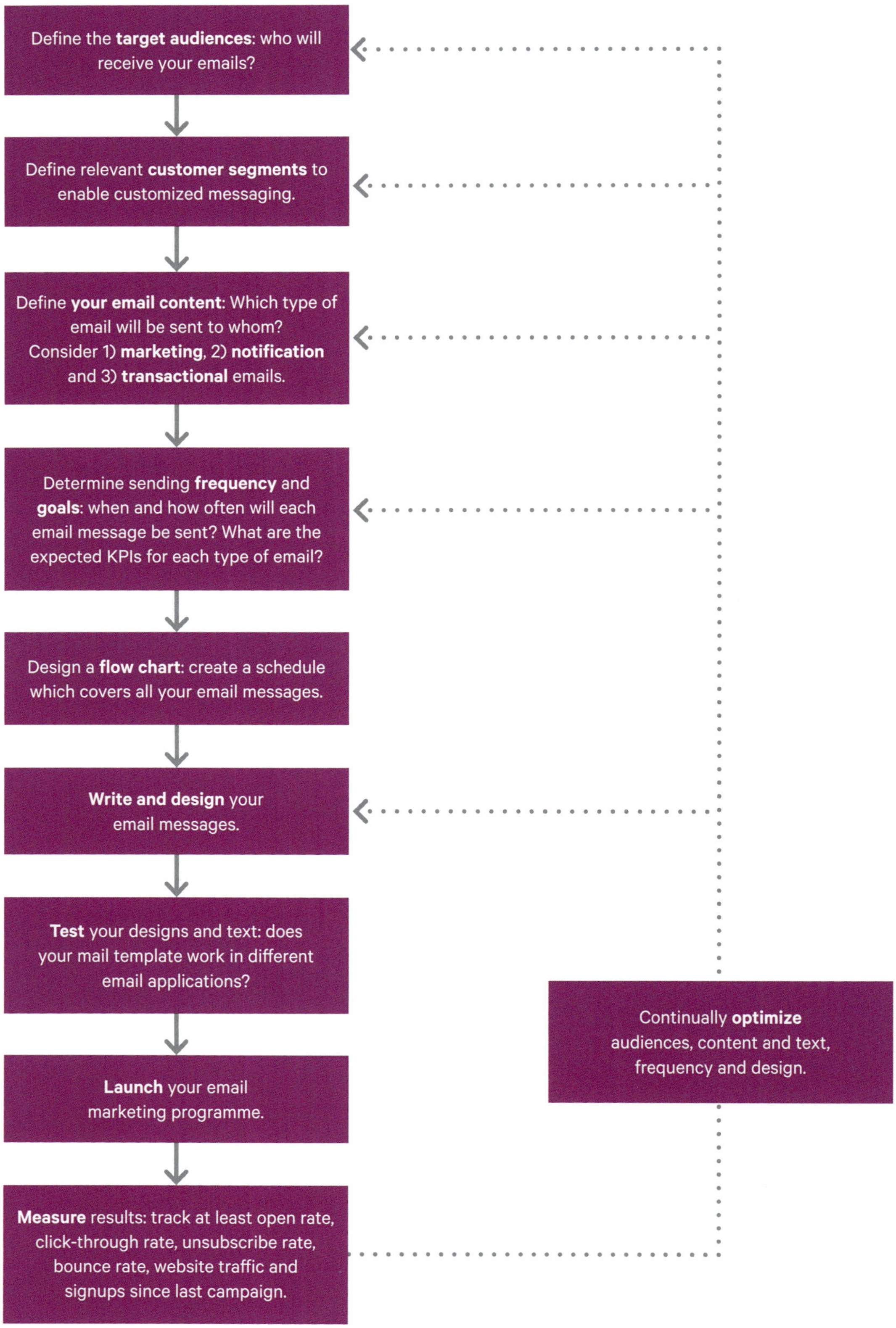

## Building email lists

The foundation of good email marketing is a **high-quality email** list. That's no different compared to the old days of printed direct mail. Some tips on how you can build and continuously extend your email list:

1 Your **current customer database**: start with what you've already got. Your CRM system is filled with relevant target customers who you can connect with through various email formats. DO make sure you have their formal (and documented) opt-in (by channel & content type(s)! Also look at how you can **re-activate older contacts**.

2 **Create eye-catching (email) content**: great content will be shared and forwarded and this can trigger new people to sign up. Enable people to sign up for niche content instead of general content. This increases relevancy for both the recipient and your company.

3 **Facilitate subscription**: make it easy for people to subscribe. Limit the number of fields to be filled in, enable 'auto-fill' on your forms, add a QR code on your offline material, collect subscriptions at offline events, promote your email services through other (social) channels, ...

4 Check whether your database is **GDPR-compliant** (and if you obtained the information from a third-party, that they are GDPR compliant)

It's best to **build your email list the 'smart way'.** You can't buy your way into the hearts of new customers. You have to earn that. Consequently, the old practice of **buying lists** never led to huge traction - and from May 2018, **is actually prohibited** within the EU. Many companies will update their regulations to reflect this worldwide - so be sure to check with your local compliance teams to find what is legally permissible in your jurisdiction.

## Collecting email addresses from HCPs

No one likes spam or unsolicited email, and that's not different for HCPs. When it comes to collecting email addresses from HCPs, there are a few specific approaches possible.

- Via your **website:** enable different ways for HCPs to get in touch with you or to 'stay up to date', for example by simply filling in an email address, combined with an opt-in permission box.
- Via the **sales rep:** your reps are in direct contact with your target audiences, and should be trained to pro-actively capture opt-in email addresses. This can be done through collecting (paper) cards or with iPad detailing during sales visits.
- Via **(medical) events:** ask for opt-in email addresses from HCPs at the events they attend.
- Via a **call centre:** you can set up specific call campaigns to collect email addresses from HCPs, for example to inform them on a new product or service.
- Via a **third party:** you can also work via others to attain additional email addresses. But beware of rented or bought email lists, as these can be **of lower quality than those you develop yourself.** Always check whether third parties are **GDPR-compliant**.

## Tip

### Personalizing messages

Know **when** and **how** to personalize your emails (and when and how not to). With more and more people worrying about cybersecurity, personalization has to be **used with caution**. Like in real life: you build a relationship of trust over **time**. Insincere familiarity can put readers off.

Consider not just **classic personalization** (e.g.: 'Dear [first_name] [last_name]'), but also include **personalized content**. Use **customer journey and information preferences** of a person to suggest the content, products or services, without including the classic personalization. Giving people more of what they want helps forge closer ties.

## Timing is everything

The right day and time to send out emails differs from industry to industry - and from target group to target group, from campaign to campaign ... and from individual to individual. It's best to **A/B test different moments of the day and different days** to see what works best for your recipients.

• When sending out regular newsletters, keeping **a fixed timing** may be helpful to recipients: they get accustomed to receiving your email at the same time and – if you manage to provide relevant content – they may even look forward to it.

• When you're active in an international setting, bear in mind how **different time zones** may impact your emails.

• In our **'always-on' reality**, the importance of timing has become a bit more fuzzy. With 51% of business email being read on a mobile device, it's clear that the time people consume their emails is shifting as well. Keep testing to establish the best moment to generate the highest possible returns.

• **Resend emails** to people who did not open the first email. This can yield an additional 5-15% to your open rate. Beware: do NOT resend emails to everyone!

While there are no set rules for days and times, there are some rules of thumb which can be used to start your testing:

• **Midweek** generates the best results: Tuesday, Wednesday or Thursday.
• **Monday**: the 'blues' at the start of a new workweek reduces the chances of open and click rates.
• **Friday**: people are preparing for the weekend or they are finishing some last-minute job. It may be worthwhile to have a more 'fun'-oriented newsletter on Fridays to boost open rates.
• **Weekends** can have surprisingly high opening rates in a B2B setting, but also a very low CTR.
• Send out emails between **10 am and 12 pm** and **3 pm and 5 pm.**
• Before **10 am**, customers are either commuting or handling email from the night before.
• After **5 pm**: they are getting ready to go back home.

But the only essential rule is... **never stop testing** to see what time works best for what type of email communication to which target group.

> ‘It takes little knowledge or depth of relationship to place someone's name in your greeting. It shows far greater care to send personalized email that is specific to a recipient's needs and history.’
>
> **Kevan Lee**
> **Content crafter**

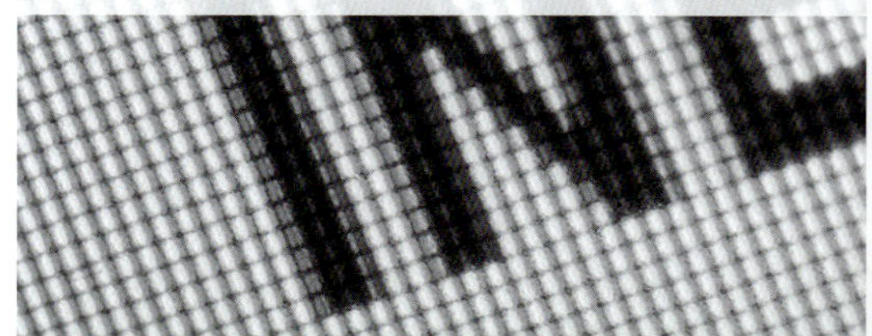

## Tip

### Who's sending?

The sender has a big impact on **open rates.** Usually, e-newsletters are linked to a campaign or a brand and the receiver expects this to be sent on behalf of **the campaign or brand name.**

But, as soon as you have a more personalized message—for example for invitations to events or webinars or follow-up mails after a face-to-face contact—it's better to send the email from a rep's address. **An email sent under a rep's name is twice to three times more likely to be opened** than one sent from your general company or campaign email address.

## What to measure

Some relevant KPIs and metrics to consider for email engagement:

| EXPOSURE | INTERACTION | ENGAGEMENT |
|---|---|---|
| • # of **optins** collected<br>• # of emails **sent**<br>• # of **permissions** (cumulative, over time) | • # of emails **opened**<br>• # of emails **bounced** | • # of emails **clicked** (CTR)<br>• # of **call-to-actions** (CTA)<br>• # of **opt-outs**<br>• # of **forwards** |

## The importance of subject lines

Your recipient's **first impression** of your email communication is through the subject line. Based on this, a recipient determines whether to **open your email or not**. Considering the number of emails we all receive, the subject line has to be really convincing to generate an action.

- Subject lines of 70+ characters engage readers to **click through** to the content.
- Subject lines of under 49 characters generate the best **open rates**.
- Avoid 60 to 70 character-long subject lines (the 'dead zone of subject length'), as these deliver the least clicks and lowest open rates.

If your aim is to generate **lots of clicks, create long subject lines.** Adding several titles of the topics covered in your email message in the subject line will generate more clicks to your website (e.g.: [title_topic_1], [title_topic_2], [title_topic_3]).

If your main objective is **a high open rate, create short subject lines.**

Whether you go for a short or long subject line, always put information-carrying and **descriptive words first** in the subject line.

Always **avoid generic, meaningless subject lines** (e.g.: 'Newsletter 159 from [company_name]).

Test your subject lines against the 'Four "U" Approach' to email subject writing:

1. **Useful**: in what way is the message of value to the recipient? Follow the 'WIIFR-rule': 'What's-In-It-For-The-Recipient'.

2. **Ultra-specific**: make it immediately clear to the recipient what can be expected from the email.

3. **Unique**: in what way is the message compelling and inviting?

4. **Urgent**: can you create a need to read it now?

> ‘A small list of recipients that wants exactly what you're offering is better than a bigger list that isn't committed.’
>
> **Ramsay Leimenstoll**
> **Marketing consultant**

## Make it easy to (un)subscribe

Any human relationship is built on trust. When people trust you with their email address, it's only logical to treat that trust with care.

Two basic rules to **begin and end** email relationships:

1. Make it **easy to subscribe**: limit the number of fields to fill in. Someone signing up for your newsletter may be willing to give you their email address, but perhaps not their full address details with additional demographic information.

**Always link the required fields** to the purpose of the visitor. It's OK to ask for full address details when a person orders something that needs to be shipped to their home or practice. Not so when the person simply signs up for a newsletter.

2. Make it **easy to unsubscribe**: a 'one-click' un-subscription process is ideal. Enable recipients to unsubscribe **with one click** from within one of your emails.

Optionally, you can **ask why** the person no longer wants to receive your emails. Do this after they've confirmed un-subscription on your website.

When you make it difficult to unsubscribe, people get annoyed and they may even **mark you as spam**, which can be far more harmful than losing 1 recipient as spam filters can be shared within companies or email services.

### Tip

SPAM

#### Spam was invented by ... Monty Python

The infamous **'Spam' sketch** by the legendary comedy series 'Monty Python's Flying Circus' was first aired in 1970. In the scene, a waitress in a café is reciting the Spam-filled menu to a customer, when a group of Vikings start to chant "Spam, Spam, Spam, lovely Spam! Wonderful Spam!", interrupting or 'spamming' the conversation. Spam as mentioned in the sketch is, in fact, a US brand of tinned meat which was imported intensively after World War II, as Britain was rebuilding its agriculture.

The term 'spam' was adopted in email marketing, after the first spam email was sent in 1978 by a marketer at DEC (Digital Equipment Corporation). The email, which promoted an open house to check out DEC's latest product, was sent to 400 of the 2,600 people on ARPAnet—the predecessor of the Internet. Besides a lot of negative remarks, the email also generated some commercial success.

# The maturity level of email engagement

**62% of pharma marketers** state that email marketing is a standard practice for their organisation, clearly demonstrating that it is one of the most mature marketing technologies for pharma companies. Email marketing (#4) is only preceded by direct marketing (#3), the pharma website (#2) and tablet eDetailing (#1) on the list of the 25 most commonly used pharma marketing tactics. Rep email is gaining traction fast as well.

## The adoption of email tactics by pharma

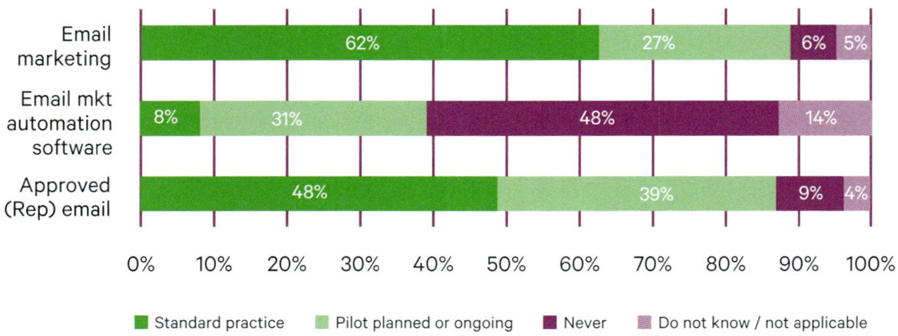


Source: The Across Health Multichannel Maturometer 2017 | N = 221 | EU scope

## Tip

### Drip marketing

Drip marketing is popularly applied as a sales tool, particularly in long customer journeys (high-involvement decisions). Whereas persistent follow-up can become a deterrent and too costly to ensure conversion, drip marketing offers the ability to remain top-of-mind, and even prompt action, without jeopardizing the relationship. Defining customer journeys in advanced marketing automation software can boost the impact with a potential customer of these programs while reducing resource use.

## The case for email engagement

**1 hr**

**The lifespan of an email is very short.** 24% of all opens happen during the first hour after delivery. The chances of your mail being opened after 24 hours is less than 1%!

**x2**

It pays to **invest in your own email database** (first-party), instead of just buying your way into a third-party email. The open rate of owned emails is up to two times higher than third-party emails. Also the click through rate (CTR) can be twice as high for first-party emails.

**GP vs. SP**

There are **differences in email behaviour between GPs and specialists**: the **open rates** are **slightly higher** for specialists (25.8% vs 23.19%), but the **click-through** rate is **much higher** (20.7% vs 12.4%)
(source: Across Health Illuminator database)

**+12%**

**Reminder emails work.** Resending the same mail to people who didn't open the first email pays off. One specific case showed that throughout a campaign with several email blasts, reminder emails added an additional 12% to the open rate (the average is 5%). In this specific case, the CTR for the reminder email was even higher than that of the initial email.

**REP vs. MASS**

**Open rates for rep-triggered email** can be twice as high as those for mass campaigns (50% and higher).

# Tips for novices

**Make it easy for your recipient to click.** But ... 1) balance the links with the content and 2) make sure the links are relevant.

**Email marketing is owned by the business,** not IT.

Make it easy to **share** and forward email content.

**New subscribers are more engaged.** After a while, subscribers' interest may begin to wane and their click through rates can drop off. Look how you can maximize the potential of email marketing through the different customer life cycle stages.

**Never stop testing!** Try out different content, different designs, different CTAs, ... Changing the location or wording of a button can have a significant impact on your ROI!

**Be the recipient!** Add your own email address to your mailing lists and make sure that you regularly receive a copy of all the different emails sent. Receiving your own marketing emails in a real setting can give you additional insights on how to improve them.

**Add calls-to-action** to every email: every email is an opportunity for a subsequent action. Think about how you can generate additional clicks from every email you send out.

**Standardize formats.** Use **standardized email templates** to create a consistent customer experience as well as to ensure the inclusion of standard legal clauses and opt-out possibilities.

## Challenges of email marketing

| Challenges ☹ | Solutions ☺ |
| --- | --- |
| **How to manage and integrate a wide variety of email marketing messages?** | • Construct **a flow chart** with clear timelines and a fixed number of touch points. Consider **different scenarios** of (potential) customers and how often they're contacted by email.<br><br>• Create an email **marketing matrix**: what gets sent to whom, when and how often? Link this to the customer journey and your overall multichannel marketing customer view.<br><br>• Buy a **marketing automation platform** to automate the above.<br><br>• **Measure** the impact of email marketing on the business KPIs. **Track visitor funnels** and optimize weak spots (= places where people leave).<br><br>• **Coalesce data** from different resources centrally: create an overview of all email communication and other channels in a central customer intelligence hub. |
| **How to ensure continued engagement?** | • Make sure your **value proposition** is a nice blend of what the customer and you value, while creating unique content in the marketplace. Test, learn and redefine! |

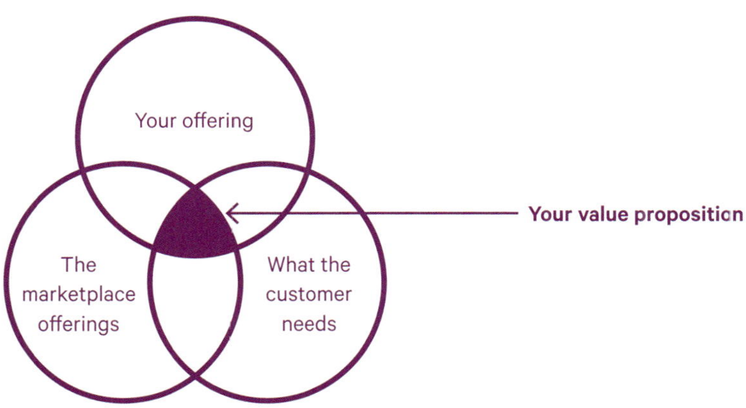

## Collecting first-party email addresses

**First-party email addresses** are extremely valuable for HCP engagement for several reasons:

1. The **cost of acquisition** for your target group is low compared to continued dependence on third-party databases

2. **Open and click rates** are higher

3. You can **measure results at the individual level** and hence truly personalize offerings.

4. You can **ensure GDPR compliance**

For non-core HCPs or for core HCPs whose email address you do not have, you can leverage third-party email databases (but make sure to deduplicate vs. your own database - and ensure your partners are GDPR-compliant!)

## What kind of content is best?

The short and right answer is: it really depends...

1. For **mass newsletters**, the content should be a mix of customer interests, your offering and uniqueness vs. the marketplace. You can ask customers what they are looking for and/or test different formats and topics through A/B testing.

2. For **segmented offerings**, content should be customized for different personas or customer segments. Towards loyal customers, content could, for example, be focused on expanding Rx use in a new group of patients. On the other hand, towards non-prescribers, the focus may be on overcoming the hurdles to prescribe for the first time. You can send different content towards a science-oriented HCP vs. a more relationship-oriented HCP, towards GPs vs. specialists, etc.

3. For **event-triggered email**, content should (of course) be relevant to the event.

Regardless of the type of content, it is recommended to review the key metrics (open rate, CTR, opt-outs) over 60, 90, 180 and 365 days to fully understand and optimize customer engagement.

## Whither marketing automation?

At its broadest, marketing automation allows its users to collect data, automatically segment customers, control content flows, and schedule content without the need for extensive human interaction. At its best, it can make interactions between the customer and a brand or company fluid and responsive, ultimately improving customer engagement.

Examples range from an automated email flow, which would allow a customer to receive ever more specific information about a product or service based on their actions (opens, clicks), to a fully integrated experience with an app, email, and a customized website.
While obviously this can be a very powerful tool to create seamless customer engagement, pharma has been slow to fully embrace it. To an extent, this is endemic in all technical processes within the industry – that to get all parts of a system working, takes longer. However, also questions over the role of the rep in shepherding different streams of this information, and of the overall quality of data and content which pharma owns (and rules for its usage), have slowed its adoption.

That said, companies who move quickly in the space will enjoy significant first mover advantages as they develop the ability to more comprehensively engage with a broader group of HCP customers and other stakeholders.

## Tip

### Manage unsubscribes

Very few physicians will unsubscribe from your email channel, provided that you offer relevant content. Numbers as low as 0.1% per wave are commonplace. When HCPs do unsubscribe, it is important that you try to minimize the number of email lists from which they unsubscribe. They may still be interested in other offerings than the one they unsubscribe for... **so give them the option** to check channels one by one.

It is a best practice to also ask why they unsubscribe. This will give you additional insights, enabling you to further optimize your future email activities.

(Source: Econsultancy)

# GDPR & consent

Pharma has long been aware of the sensitivity of the data it collects and uses – and this is especially the case when dealing with the kind of information essential for effective multichannel campaigns.

However, the introduction of **The General Data Protection Regulation (GDPR)** in mid-2018 creates an extra dimension of regulation, focussed on personal data being owned by users themselves (and not the companies holding the data). This is founded on seven key principles: 1) lawfulness, fairness & transparency, 2) purpose limitation, 3) data minimisation, 4) accuracy of information, 5) storage limitation, 6) integrity & confidentiality (i.e. security), and 6) accountability.

The rules **apply to any company which owns or processes any personal data from any European citizens** so applies to any company working in the EU, but also to companies working outside the EU but processing personal data from EU citizens. Under GDPR, organizations in breach can be fined up to 4% of total company global revenue or €20m (whichever is greater). This is the maximum fine for the most serious infringements (e.g. not having sufficient customer consent to process data), and emphasises how seriously companies should take these regulations.

Broadly, personal data is anything which is identifiable (either directly or indirectly to a natural individual). This can be a person's name, an identification number, location data, an online identifier or one or more factors specific to the physical, physiological, genetic, mental, economic, cultural or social identity of an individual. If we focus on online identifiers, IP addresses, cookies, mobile IPs and even search engines also fall into scope.

From a marketer's perspective, this has a big impact, especially in the way consent will need to be collected. The conditions for consent collection have been strengthened, and companies will no longer be able to use long illegible terms and conditions. This is because the request for consent must be given in an intelligible and easily accessible form, using clear and plain language, stating the purpose the data is being collected and processed related to that consent. Furthermore it must be as easy to withdraw consent as it is to give it.

**The general transition looks like this:**

| Then | | GDPR |
|---|---|---|
| Assumed permission acceptable; use of pre-filled boxes; difficult opt-out procedures | ➡ | Explicit permission mandatory; using clear and plain language; offering opt-out procedures in a transparent way |
| Data can be built up organically over time | ➡ | Precisely defined purpose of data collection (i.e. not transferrable) |
| Companies kept data after customers opted-out of specific contact methods | ➡ | Right to be forgotten entitles companies to erase personal data |

*This is not an exhaustive list of the changes covered in the GDPR*

Each company will interpret the regulations in different ways, and many will have a person in charge of processing data. In all instances, please check with them about the internal company processes you should follow.

**That said, the rules generally to ask are:**

- Do you have a clear privacy policy in place, to say what data you are collecting, on what basis you are collecting it, and what you will do with it?
- Do you have a clear record of all of your opt-ins, including the time, the scope of the opt-in, and the privacy policy which was in place when this consent to be contacted was given?
- Is it clear and easy for customers to opt-out, at any time?

While regulations can be seen as somewhat burdensome, this will lead to higher quality communications.

# The anatomy of a five-star email

0 A preheader (otherwise known as a 'Johnson Box') is the short summary text that follows the subject line when an email is viewed in the inbox. Many mobile, desktop and web email clients provide them to tip you off on what the email contains before you open it.

1 Use an actual person as sender (avoid 'info@your_company.com' as sender)

2 Create a clear, attention-grabbing subject line

3 Include your company branding

4 Personalize salutation

5 Value proposition and context

6 Personalize the offering

7 Clear call-to-action

8 Relevant imagery

9 Secondary call-to-action

10 Social sharing options

11 Link to privacy policy

12 Link to unsubscribe

13 Link to website

14 Have a web version

## eNewsletter: reach and impact in Europe 2017

| eNewsletter | | Rep |
|---|---|---|
| 33% | ... reach versus... | 63% |
| 5 | ... impact versus... | 5.8 |
| 0.60 | ... MCQ versus... | 1.00 |

The Across Health Navigator studies the impact and reach of 57 off- and online channels amongst HCPs. From this, the multichannel equivalent (MCQ) is derived: a measurement of relative impact, which makes comparing between channels possible. Find out more on the Navigator data in chapter 1.

Source: The Across Health Navigator 2017 | N = 3,185 | EU5 scope (DE, ES, FR, IT, UK) | Specialists

## To conclude

**Email is an essential part of every company's communication mix. However, getting the balance right between different types of email communication remains a challenge. And so is continually building and enriching your address lists. But investing time and resources in GDPR-compliant marketing is a 'must-do', despite the advent of newer forms of social media sharing.**

'...activating HCPs and patients through online advertising.'

# 5 Display Advertising

## Advertising we love to hate

Declared dead a number of times, display advertising has always managed to climb back up. Nowadays, using sophisticated targeting methods, it can be of relevance when fully integrated into your overall customer engagement strategy.

## The metrics of display advertising

**1,700** The average person is served more than 1,700 banner ads per month. (Source: Comscore)

**77%** ... of display ads are never seen. (Source: Forbes)

**0.1%** The average click-through rate (CTR) across all display advertising formats. The first-ever banner ad (in 1994, on hotwired.com) had a...44% click-through rate. (Source: Google Display benchmarks tool)

**60%** ... of all clicks on mobile ads are accidental. (Source: MediaPost)

**50%** ... of pharma companies consider display advertising a standard tactic. (Source: Across Health Maturometer)

> ‘Increasingly, mass marketing is turning into a mass of niches.’
>
> **Chris Anderson**
> **Author of ‘The Long Tail’**

> ‘What’s measured, improves.’
>
> **Peter Drucker**
> **Strategy guru**

## The metrics of display advertising

The click-through rate (CTR) of display advertising has **fallen over time**. In the early days of the internet, it was not uncommon to have CTRs of 2 to 5%. Nowadays, a display campaign reaches an average CTR of only 0.1%. This means that for every 1,000 views of a banner campaign, **only 1 click** is generated.

Initially, display ads could only be bought on a CPM basis (cost per thousand views). With the arrival of search engine marketing, pricing models have moved towards **performance-based pricing:** cost per click (CPC), cost per lead (CPL), cost per acquisition (CPA).

Through **performance-based pricing**, the risk shifts from advertiser to publisher. Today, 2/3[rd] of all online advertising is performance-based (CPC, CPL or CPA) compared to 1/3[rd] on a CPM basis.

## The formats of display advertising

Being creative – or **more creative** than your competitors – can attract extra eyeballs and clicks to your ads. But stay away from too intrusive advertising, which causes annoyance.

Some suggested formats:

- **In-banner video**: adding video to your display ad can help generate more views and clicks. Add, for instance, the video footage of one of your webinars to a display ad.
- **Interactive ads**: polls or simple games embedded in ads can create an interaction which, in turn, can help build engagement.
- **Coupons or free offers:** offering something for free (or at a reduced rate) can be inviting for people to click. For example: promote through your display ads relevant content that's downloadable for free.
- **Avoid intrusive ads**: ads that are intrusive will be ignored and may cause negative sentiments about your brand or company.

## Humour sells

Consumers can easily identify when they are being sold to – in particular when marketing messages are in spots traditionally reserved for this, such as TV adverts or website banner ads. However, consumers respond differently to adverts, according to the content of the message. Understanding the key levers to break through perceptions of 'advertising' is therefore paramount. As seen here, in an analysis of television adverts, humour, fantasy, and ads which focus on real people are more emotionally impactful than those based solely on information or science.

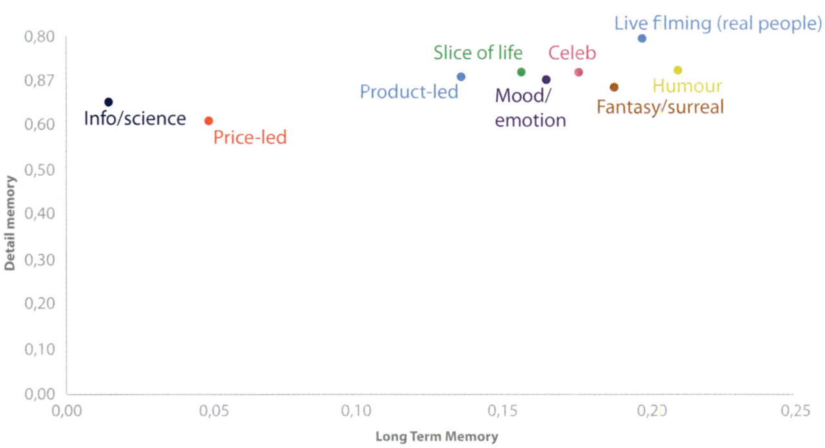


Peaks of response at end branding
Source: Creative Drivers of Effectiveness, 2016, Neuro-Insight/Thinkbox.

## Tip

### Once more: monitor, monitor, monitor... then monitor some more

Don't rest on your laurels. What worked yesterday, may not return the same results today. As the investment for display advertising is often **higher** than other online marketing tactics, you cannot afford to lose sight of the impact of your e-campaigns.

When results for a campaign start to falter, **move it around** (e.g. move the ads to other publishers) or **change** the ad (e.g. try out a different wording or design).

# Main tactics

Tactics to help you optimize your display ROI:

• **IP geographic targeting**: based on the geographic location of the visitor, you can promote the most relevant offering. For instance: suggest the nearest hospital or doctor, list the feedback of nearby patients that use your services, ...

• **Contextual targeting**: place your ads near relevant content. For example: if you want to raise awareness around a programme for diabetes patients, make sure your display ads appear on blogs and other health websites that discuss the topic. Tip: Google offers a network of websites (Google Display Network) that allows you to do contextual advertising. Based on specific keywords, websites that could be appropriate for placing your ad content are suggested automatically. You can also exclude certain websites that are deemed inappropriate or not compliant, from showing your ad. Different ad types (text, image, video) are possible. In 2017, several blue-chip FMCG companies instantly suspended their online advertising efforts, when it became clear that their ads were shown next to dubious third-party content.

• **Social targeting**: while actively engaging with patients or HCPs on social media presents some challenges for the pharma industry, social networks, such as Facebook and LinkedIn, offer some great advertising opportunities. The benefit of placing display ads on social media is that they can be **targeted at specific demographic profiles** (age, gender, income, ...) **or interest categories** (disease, specialty,...). As a result, these ads are much more relevant than a banner on a general website. As a rule of thumb, Facebook is more appropriate for targeting patients, while healthcare professionals are better reached via LinkedIn.

• **Behavioural targeting**: use the person's behaviour to push the most relevant display ads. For example: undiagnosed patients display different online behaviour than diagnosed patients. This should result in different display ads being shown. For the first category, you might want to advertise a symptom checker tool, while for the second category, you may want to promote a condition tracker.

• **Variety in ad design**: when the same ad appears over and over again, it is ignored faster. Even if the suggested offering does not change, do change the ad design. This can help catch the attention of the viewer and it can be a great means to test different designs as well.

• Consider **frequency**: a rule of thumb is a frequency of 4 to 8 times within a 3-month period. But this can differ greatly per offering, therapeutic area and target group (healthcare professionals vs. patients). Abandoning a campaign too soon may be the cause of poor results. This, in turn, can lead to flawed conclusions about campaign effectiveness.

## Tip

### Retargeting? No can do!

Ad retargeting - having your display ads shown to people who have visited your website before - is a common practice in many industries but it is **not possible for pharma companies,** unless it is not directly related to a drug or disease. An example of this is advertising for events. Google, for instance, prohibits all health and medical related remarketing campaigns, such as retargeted advertising for disease awareness information or wellness-based products that are sensitive in nature.

For example, you can advertise a pregnancy test, but you cannot retarget the same pregnancy test ad based on visits or searches a surfer may have done before.

## Healthy snack

### The use case for social ads on LinkedIn to reach HCPs

**The situation**: a leading pharma company launched a medical education platform aimed at European psychiatrists. The medical education website contained a series of educational webcasts that were recorded during international symposia and congresses.

**The challenge**: create awareness around the website and scientific webcasts; generate relevant traffic and subscriptions.

**The approach**: a display advertising campaign on LinkedIn was launched. The ads were targeted at LinkedIn profiles that explicitly mentioned 'psychiatrist' in their job title. Different ads were created to invite physicians to register on the medical education site and watch the webcasts.

**The result**: close to 5 million impressions were generated across the target group; a total of 1,085 relevant individuals signed up at a cost of € 12 per conversion.

| LinkedIn ad impressions | Clicks | CTR | Avg. CPC | # registrations (conversions) | Registration % | Cost per registration |
|---|---|---|---|---|---|---|
| 4,750,000 | 6,980 | 0.15% | € 1.85 | 1,085 | 16% | € 12 |

## Display vs. search

Despite the possibility of measuring everything online, even online advertising suffers from **the attribution problem**—which ad contributed to the buying decision and to what extent? When you examine the impact of display advertising, make sure you **dive deep enough** into the data. Companies that don't go beyond CPC and CPA metrics, may decide to decrease investments, which may have an indirect impact on ROI in general.

Display advertising is often considered diametrically opposed to search engine advertising. A recent study showed that **display ads do have a positive effect** on the number of people who 1) click on search ads and 2) ultimately become customers.

However, this does not necessarily mean that display spending should increase. The study also showed that ...

1. search ads have a **longer-term effect** compared to display ads
2. although display ads do drive prospects to click more on search ads, this process also increases the **overall ad cost.**

Ultimately, this study recommended the company—a major player in the banking industry:

1. to **downscale** (but not stop) their investment in display advertising
2. to **increase** investments in search advertising.

Although different industries may produce different results, this study showed that 1) the **decision about where to invest** in advertising is anything but simple and 2) despite the possibilities to measure everything online, marketers have to **dig deep into the data** to make correct investment decisions, as rudimentary statistics may lead to wrong budget allocations.

> "It no longer makes sense to send an advertising message to the many in hopes of persuading the few."
>
> **M. Lawrence Light**
> **Former Chief Marketing Officer**
> **McDonalds**

## Healthy snack

### The business case for social advertising on Facebook for patient activation

**The situation**: health statistics in Belgium indicated that 'pertussis' (also known as whooping cough or 100-day cough) was on the rise again. To stop this highly contagious bacterial disease from spreading, family cocoon vaccination is recommended.

**The challenge**: get fathers and grandparents to go see a GP and get vaccinated. As pregnant women are already vaccinated in the hospital before giving birth, they were not directly targeted.

**The approach**: different ad groups on Facebook were created that specifically targeted new fathers and grandparents. The ads directed people to a patient activation website, where they could participate in a quiz, download a checklist to facilitate a doctor's appointment, and request the vaccination.

**The result**: during the 9-week campaign period over 14 million impressions were generated across the target groups. The Facebook campaign generated 33% of all visits to the website and 30% of all conversions.

| CTR | Avg. CPC | Conversion % | Cost per registration |
|---|---|---|---|
| 0.03% | € 0,25 | 6% | € 4 |

# The inner workings of display advertising

A **demand side platform** (DSP) is a technology platform that enables marketing agencies and advertisers to buy media across different inventory sources. In combination with real-time bidding, **automated computer programs** buy relevant ad space on a multitude of websites. By combining real-time visitor data and an auctioning system, **the most relevant ad space** can be purchased at the optimal price range.

How it works:

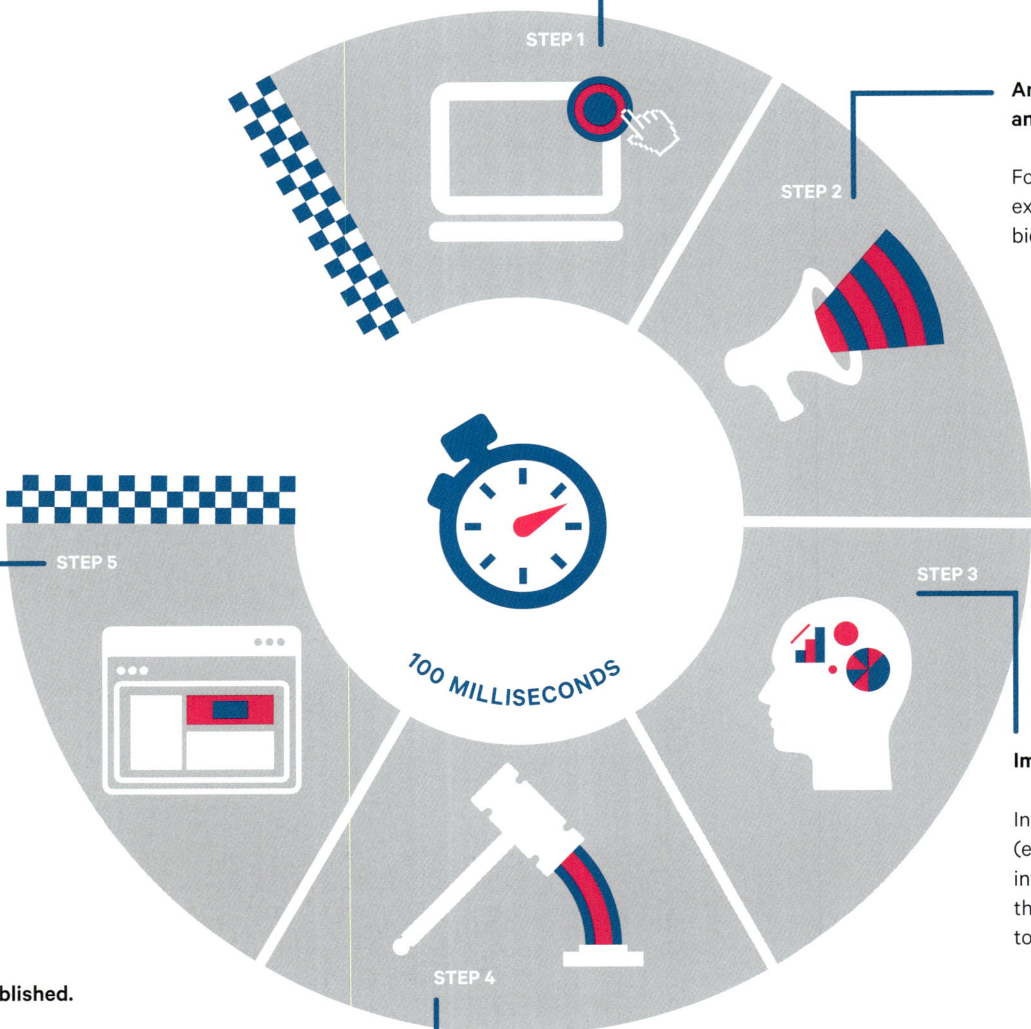


**Person visits a web page.**

**An impression is announced.**

For every impression, the exchange system sends a bid request.

**Impression is evaluated.**

Information about the impression (e.g.: website, web page, user information ...) is provided and the system can decide whether to bid or not.

**The auction.**

Within milliseconds, the system decides to place a bid. The exchange system that runs the auction evaluates all bids and a winner is assigned.

**Ad is published.**

The winning ad is shown on the website. The whole process took less than 100 milliseconds.

***Real-time bidding** works because it is fast, automated and it optimizes investment and inventory for advertisers and publishers.*

Source: Doubleclick, by Google

## Tips for novices

**Be aware of banner blindness.** All too often, people no longer 'see' display ads. Although the ads appear in the periphery of view, people automatically block them out. Eye-tracking research shows that, most of the time, display ads are above all... ignored. An estimated 77% of all display ads are completely ignored.

Avoid **display overload** by producing multiple variations of your ad.

**The online advertising paradox:** although a banner ad contains more visual elements and has more options for interaction with prospects (meaning display advertising seems more appropriate for brand-building), the search ad, in general, generates a better ROI. Less is more, even in online advertising.

**Watch out for web traffic fraud:** in a 2014 article in the Wall Street Journal, the Interactive Advertising Bureau (IAB) estimated that more than a third of all online traffic could be fake or fraudulent! Automated ad buying is believed to contribute to the problem as automation increases, there's a concurrent decrease in transparency and accountability. "About 36 per cent of all Web traffic is considered fake: the product of computers hijacked by viruses and programmed to lure recipients to visit specific sites."

**Not core:** display advertising is hardly ever the backbone of an e-campaign any more. Most often, it's an 'add-on', a means to extend or strengthen another marketing tactic.

# The maturity level of display ads

Although the pharma industry faces many limitations when it comes to display advertising, **half of pharma marketers** (50%) state that they use display advertising as a standard practice. With a 5th place amongst the 25 surveyed tactics, it clearly trumps search engine optimization (9th) and search engine advertising (11th).

## The adoption of display and search tactics by pharma

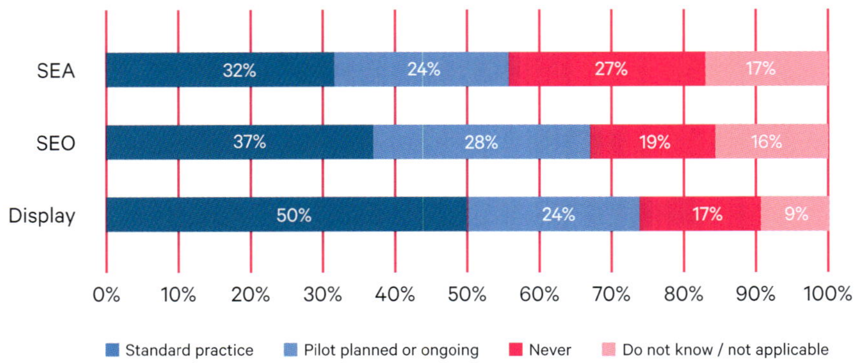


Source: The Across Health Multichannel Maturometer 2017 | N = 221 | EU scope

# Banner: reach and impact in Europe 2017

The Across Health Navigator studies the impact and reach of 57 off- and online channels with HCPs.

Source: The Across Health Navigator 2017 | N = 3,185 | EU5 scope (DE, ES, FR, IT, UK) | Specialists

## Tip

### Once more: test, test, test... then test some more

As with any marketing tactic, display ads must be thoroughly tested and retested.

Consider:

- The **wording**: rephrase your offer to see what generates the best ROI.
- Test different **offerings** to the same target group.
- Change the **call-to-action** (CTA). Even a simple change from 'download e-book' to 'download free e-book' can have a substantial impact.
- Try out different **formats** for different offerings. E.g.: the promotion for your new webinar may work better with a video integrated in your ad.
- Try out different **publishers**: different websites attract different types of audiences.
- Different **periods** can generate different outcomes for your campaigns. Consider time of day, different days during the week, seasons....

Testing never stops. Remember, in e-marketing, **one size fits all = no fit at all.**

## To conclude

Display advertising used to be **'carpet-bombing'** marketing. But it is recovering, as real-time bidding and (re-)targeting give it renewed relevancy. Thanks to technological improvements, this tactic is now helping marketers reach the right audience, at the right time, with the right message. Deployment of display advertising should be considered carefully. Campaign results should be monitored closely and data should be cross-referenced to find the right balance in budget allocation.

Only display advertising which is fully integrated in the overall communication mix and helps create a strong "surround sound", yields results.

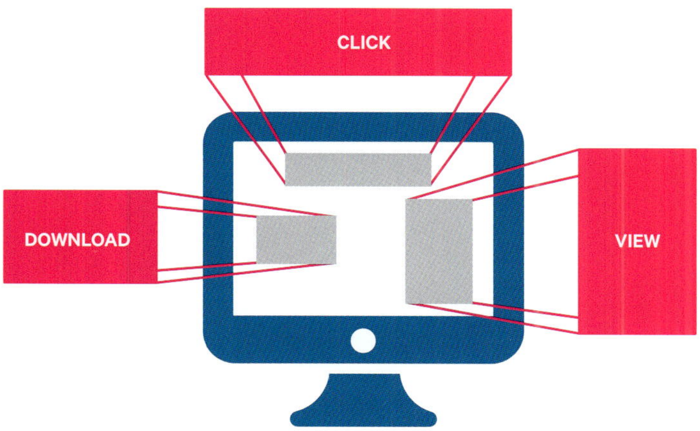

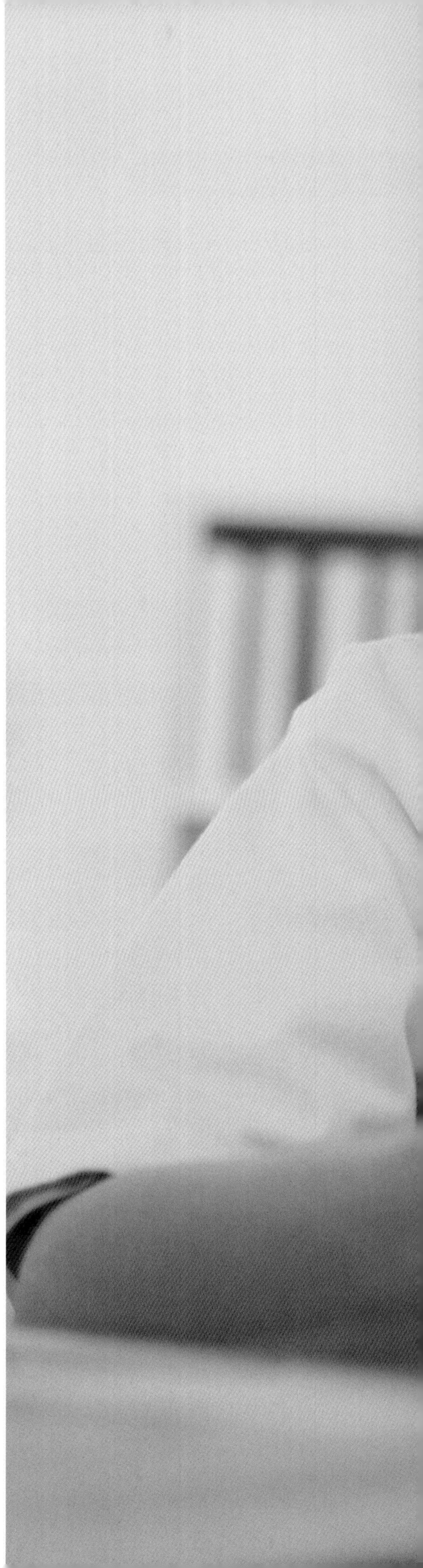

‘… creating seamless, mobile customer experiences.’

# 6 Mobile Engagement

## Experiencing life at your fingertips

Social sharing, searching the web, making payments ... literally **every digital activity has gone mobile**. As one of the most recent disruptions in the digital landscape, mobile has an enormous potential. But getting mobile right is tough. It presents marketers with a very particular challenge. Companies get only one chance to make a first impression, and increasingly, that's via a mobile device. If your website does not scale properly to whatever mobile device your customers are using, you're likely to lose customers. Companies willing to adopt a mobile-first mindset can reap big rewards and build strong competitive advantage.

## The metrics of mobile marketing

| | |
|---|---|
| 65% | ... of all digital minutes are mobile. (Source: statista) |
| 2.3 | There are 2.3 billion smartphone users globally. (Source: statista) |
| 325 K | In 2017, there were about 325,000 healthcare apps (and 84,000 health app publishers). (Source: Research2Guidance) |
| 3.8 bn | Healthcare apps were downloaded 3.7 billion times in 2017. |
| 55% | 55% of all health apps are downloaded less than 500 times and 3% over 1m times. (Source: Forbes) |
| 83% | ... of all EU5 physicians use a mobile phone. 65.5% also use a tablet. (Source: Across Health Navigator 2017) |
| 57% | 57% of internet users say they won't recommend a business with a poorly designed mobile website. (Source: ImpactBND) |
| 20% | By 2019, 20% of brands will abandon their mobile apps. (Source: Gartner) |
| 30% | By 2020, 30% of web browsing sessions will be done without a screen. (Source: Gartner) |

‘In today's modern world, people are either asleep or connected.’

**Janice H. Reinold**
**Rosetta Marketing**

## Tip

### The multi-screen reality

Not long ago a mobile phone was just for calling, now it is used for pretty much everything. Today, many of us simultaneously interact with a computer screen, a smartphone and a tablet. Mobile devices have changed **the way we multitask** and this also has an impact on ... the level of impact that messages have.

Research from Stanford University has shown **that people who multitask are less productive** than those who focus on one task at a time. A constant stream of electronic messages reduces people's ability to pay attention or recall information. Another study from the University of London even showed that **IQ scores drop** for people who are multitasking during a cognitive task.

So next time you need something done that requires lots of brain activity, better turn off those other screens.

## Main tactics

Mobile marketing includes a wide variety of tactics, each with their own characteristics. Matching the right channel to the right activity and target group can sometimes be challenging. However some, like the mobile-optimized site, mobile apps and social sharing have reached a 'must-have' status. The key options include:

**1. Mobile-optimized site:** the responsive website has become the norm. Websites that do not scale properly to whatever mobile device its customers are using, are bound to lose customers. Various online tools enable you to test the level of responsiveness of your website(s).

**2. Mobile optimized landing pages:** while regular landing pages already offer concise and dense content with a minimum of distraction, the mobile optimized landing pages take this one step further. Every word, image and link has to contribute to the objective of the page and the campaign. The central adage is: (much) less is (much) more.

**3. Mobile app:** the mobile app has become an increasingly important sales and business facilitator. Apps come in many different forms: from simply sharing content and building peer-based customer communities to transaction and adherence support.

**4. Mobile search:** with over half of all searches happening on a mobile device, companies must take into account the mobile reality of bandwidth, responsive site experiences and location-based optimizations.

**5. Outbound SMS/MMS:** using text and multimedia messages for marketing purposes. This 'old' channel still works very well.

**6. Mobile advertising:** like almost any type of advertising, mobile ads have a poor reputation. In the early days, when display advertising was simply migrated to a mobile environment, the results were often very poor, with 1 out of every 2 clicks on mobile ads being accidental. As mobile advertising matures, video and native (contextual) ads have taken over and their reputation is improving. Moving forward, more contextualized and personalized mobile ads are expected to create an even more relevant customer experience.

**7. Mobile bar code (QR, SnapTag):** codes that can be scanned by a mobile device that redirect customers directly to a URL.

**8. Short-code SMS reply:** replies to SMS campaigns are facilitated by providing customers with a short code (usually 3 to 7 letters and/or numbers).

**9. Geo-targeting:** the GPS position of a website visitor is used to deliver specific and more relevant content.

**10. Wearables:** mobile devices with sensors that track motion, heart rate, sleep, or other physiological metrics. You can find them on many recent mobile phones or on dedicated devices (wristbands, watches and even shirts).

> The mobile phone acts as a cursor to connect the digital and physical.
>
> **Marissa Mayer**
> **ex-CEO of Yahoo**

## A day in the life of a Mobile User

As the amount of time which consumers spend on their mobile phones grows, fewer and fewer 'apps' take up the majority of the time. This is becoming ever truer, as certain apps, for instance **Facebook**, begin to take on other roles – moving from being a social network, to allowing interaction with customer services, banks, and websites themselves. Never has it been more the case that smartphones are less phones, and more computers with multiple entry points into the digital world. Another example is **Wechat**, in China. What started out as a chat app has become a payments platform, an electronic medical record and many other things besides.

| | Average # Apps Installed on Device* | Average Number of Apps Used Daily | Average Number of Apps accountng for 80%+ of App Usage | Time Spent on Phone (per Day) | Most Commonly Used Apps |
|---|---|---|---|---|---|
| USA | 37 | 12 | 3 | 5 Hours | Facebook, Chrome Youtube |
| Worldwide | 33 | 12 | 3 | 4 Hours | Facebook, WhatsApp, Chrome |

Source: KPCB (Kleiner Perkins Caufield & Byers) Internet Trends 2016.(kpcb.com/internet-trends)

# Mobile-first

Mobile's 'always-on' mantra has dramatically changed the customer journey. It now more closely resembles **a maze with customers popping in and out** as they see fit. And, all too often, a poor mobile experience is a key reason to drop out.

Although a majority of pharma marketers acknowledge the importance of mobile, only 32% of them state that mobile is **a standard practice** in the overall marketing strategy.

The wide variety of devices and operating systems can make embracing a 'mobile-first' mindset a complex process for companies. Partially because of this, many companies are stuck in a 'mobile campaign' mode, and very few are able to reach a mature 'mobile digirati' or **'mobirati' status.** While the digirati framework considers digital intensity and transformation intensity, the mobirati framework separates mobile from the other digital activities and compares 1) the level of **mobile marketing intensity** to overall digital intensity and 2) the **integration** between both.

1. **Beginners** score low on both digital and mobile intensity. There is little to no integration between mobile and other digital activities.

2. **Fashionistas** have adopted a lot of mobile tools, but there is little synergy with other digital activities.

3. **Conservatives** are late in adopting mobile, but they are strong on digital intensity.

4. **Mobirati** score high on both mobile and digital intensity, and both are fully intertwined, often starting from a mobile-first mindset.

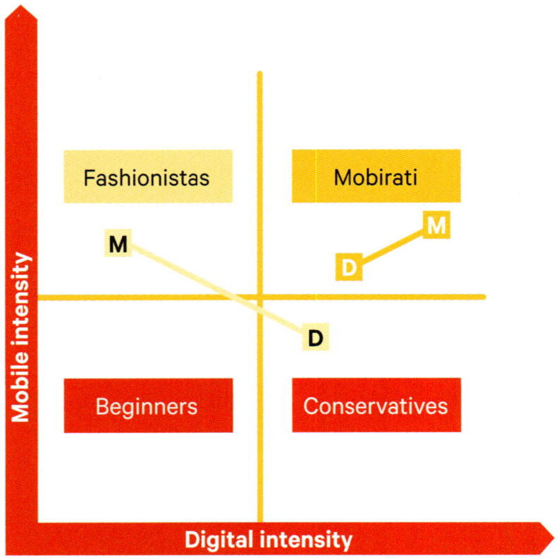


***Mobirati companies** are truly omni-channel, placing mobile at the centre of a great customer experience. This creates a first-mover advantage over competitors. Fashionistas have a large number of mobile activities, but these are largely disparate from their other digital activities.*

Source: the mobirati scheme is an adaptation of and variation to the digirati scheme, as developed in 'The Digital Advantage' report by Capgemini Consulting & the MIT Center for Digital Business.

> "The smartphone is the greatest medical device ever made."
>
> **Dr Ausiello, Healthgrades**

# Mobilizing the funnel

While it is worthwhile to plot your mobile activities across the customer journey to see how well you cover different stages, it's just a small step up from there to **a more holistic approach.** This should include all contact moments, whether mobile, digital or offline. To capture the full scope of the customer experience, your next step is to ensure all touch points are aligned and that the level of intensity is well balanced. It's important to realize that your customer is probably not making a distinction between devices (and experiences) anymore anyway.

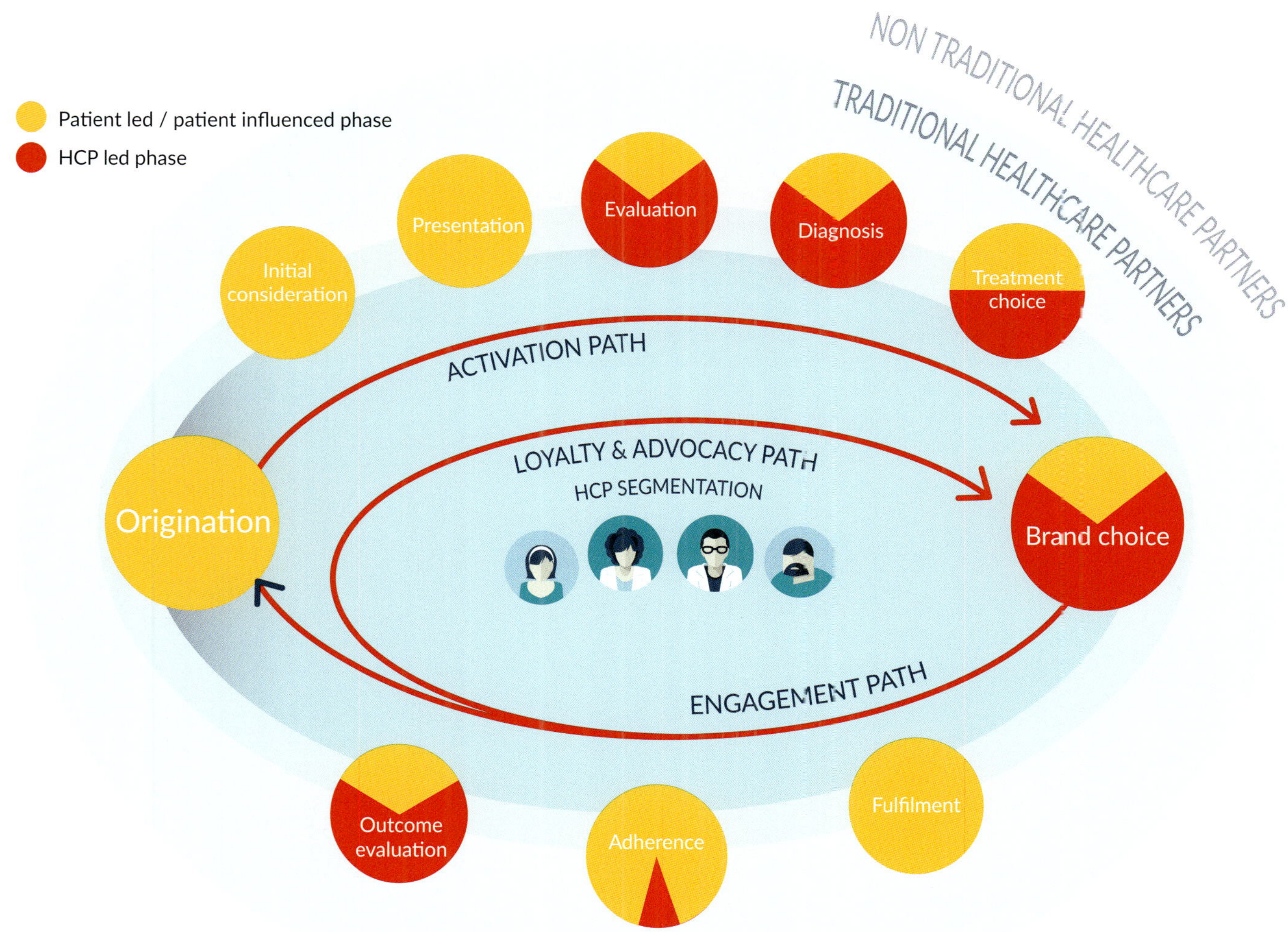


Source: the closed loop model is inspired by McKinsey's Consumer Decision Journey.

# Blurred lines

The lines between our professional and private lives are blurring. In today's **always-on mindset**, people cross over from one to the other throughout the day, and often well into the night too. One research report found that 9 in 10 smartphone users have their mobile device within arm's length 24/7. Many people check their updates and emails before getting out of bed in the morning or before dozing off at night. Another study by MailChimp found that 87% of the market research participants read **work and personal emails** together on their mobile device.

Many healthcare professionals and consumers search and consume content on mobile devices outside of normal business hours and locations, and this should impact how companies design mobile services and content for different user contexts and times.

# Mobile app disruption

After the industrial and digital revolution, we are now in the midst of **the mobile revolution**. In less than a decade, mobile has become a key channel for going online. This is fuelling innovation: a lot of today's innovations are driven by companies that have mobile at their core (e.g. Uber) or that take their business model mobile (e.g. Facebook, Google).

Between June 2013 and July 2014, the major app stores paid software developers more than $15 billion. Mobile has, thus, given ground to a whole new industry, from app developers to data mining and everything in between. But only a limited amount of that money flows back to large companies, as most provide **free apps**. Generating direct revenue from apps is for many companies not the primary objective, and the same applies to pharma.

**50%** ... of US patients used health apps in 2016 (vs. 16% in 2014).
(Source: Accenture)

**21%** ... use wearables for health purposes.
(Source: Accenture)

**45%** ...of UK oncologists own at least one wearable (and 21% intend to buy one)
(Navigator 3.0 2017)

## Tip

### There's an app for that

The (relative) ease of developing apps has led companies to deeper sub-segmentation. With so many apps available and additional customization options within apps, we are gradually moving towards a 'segment-of-one' situation. Got a problem that no-one else has? There's probably an app for that.
But with this comes a new phenomenon: **app burnout.** With so many apps around, which one should a customer choose? The average mobile user has over 30 apps installed and a substantial amount of time is spent on them. But it's the most popular apps (e.g. Facebook, games, ...) that take up most of users' time. In this respect, apps are not that different from other products or services: **we only use and continue to use those apps that deliver real value.**

## Tip

### Don't fall in the app trap

Pharma has created a lot of apps in the past few years, but, very few have found widespread success. The fact that most people use a smartphone does not imply they will be using your apps. Research2Guidance studied the pharma app field in 2017 and found that the only pharma company that had **a good mix of breadth (number of apps) and depth (use)** was **J&J** (but their consumer-facing franchise may explain some of that). Only 3 others had over 500K downloads in 2016 (**GSK, Sanofi** and **Bayer** - again, pharma companies with a strong Consumer business). About half of the majors had over 150 apps, with **Novartis** and **Bayer** close to 350 (Research2Guidance 2017).

When it comes to mobile, creating **mobile-responsive websites** should be your first priority. If you do consider an app, do a landscape analysis first (you may find third-party apps with whom you can partner) and develop a solid business case secondly.

Also look beyond apps! The Internet-of-Things is approaching fast and will offer many unique opportunities for fast movers!

## You can wear this

Wearables are devices that are worn on the body and which continually collect data, such as biofeedback and physiological data. This data is then **uploaded automatically to the cloud** and made available for review by the consumer, or the HCP. This automatic upload has the advantage that it greatly improves the accuracy and consistency of health data. There is, however, still a long way to go before this data is connected and integrated directly into a more holistic healthcare records and analytics systems.

The growth of devices has mainly been fuelled by consumers interested in their own **dietary and fitness habits,** although disease-related wearables are also gaining ground.

Most wearables today are designed to be worn on the wrist and almost all devices (90%) synchronize wirelessly with an app to automatically collect the data. A growing number of wearables are being developed now that connect to a body part which is unobtrusive (e.g. the ear) and that collects real-time sensory information, such as heart rate, blood pressure, respiration rate, oxygen saturation and more. In 2017, the FDA approved the first pill with a sensor (Otsuka, Abilify Mycite).

Wearables fit perfectly within the concept of **the quantified self** or **lifelogging**: people keeping track of their own health records in order to adjust their behaviour and stay healthy.

> ‘Today the majority of wearables solve a problem called December.’
>
> **Robert M. Pearl**
> **CEO of Permanente**

## The maturity level of mobile marketing

With **32% of pharma marketers** stating that mobile marketing is a standard practice the maturity level of mobile in pharma companies is still fairly limited. Considering, however, that another 38% indicate that a pilot is ongoing or underway, this may mean that mobile marketing is ready to make a strong leap forward in the coming years.

The outbound call center, although not directly associated with 'mobile', is also quite popular and has its place in (inbound and) outbound customer outreach programmes. It continues to be very effective and efficient- just like another 'old-timer', SMS. Ignore them at your own peril...

### The adoption of mobile tactics by pharma

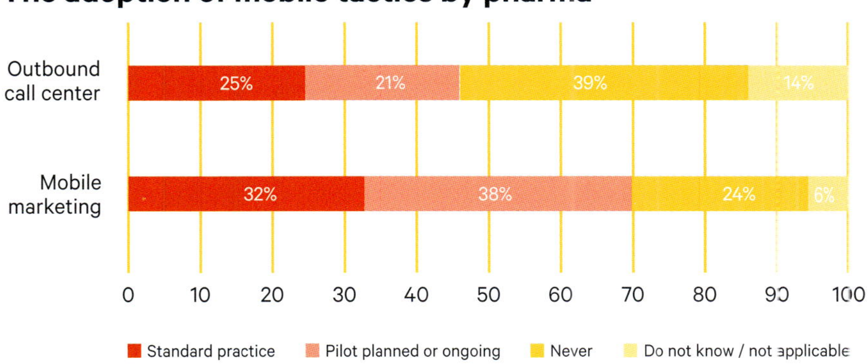


Source: The Across Health Multichannel Maturometer 2017 | N = 221 | EU scope

# Health apps on the rise

The number of mobile health apps has increased drastically in recent years:

- A 2017 Research2Guidance research report took into account a total of **325,000 mHealth apps** across different operating systems.
- Health app downloads increased 16% between 2016 and 2017 to 3.2 billion, with over 60% coming from Android (Research2guidance 2017).

Most mHealth apps are centred around wellness, dietary advice and exercise, but **disease and treatment management apps are on the rise** and already comprise 25% of all mHealth apps. The breadth of functionalities that can be included in such apps makes them very interesting to many stakeholders within the healthcare ecosystem.

mHealth apps are used to...

- **Inform** on a condition or disease in a variety of ways (text, photo, video).
- **Instruct** the patient on how to use a medicine or how to optimally apply a device.
- **Record** data, either manually or automatically.
- **Display** recorded data in a visually interesting way and show progress.
- **Guide** a patient towards next steps or provide specific recommendations.
- **Remind/alert** a patient when to take medication and, thus, improve adherence to a treatment.
- Set up **communication** between patients themselves, and between patients and healthcare professionals.

Although the maturity level of mHealth apps is still limited, **one in three physicians** state that they already **recommend mHealth apps to patients.** In terms of their own professional use, HCPs tend to prefer non-pharma apps (close to 50% do not use any pharma app); in terms of content, they prefer literature apps by a wide margin (Across Health Navigator).

**Number of medical apps used by EU5 oncologists**

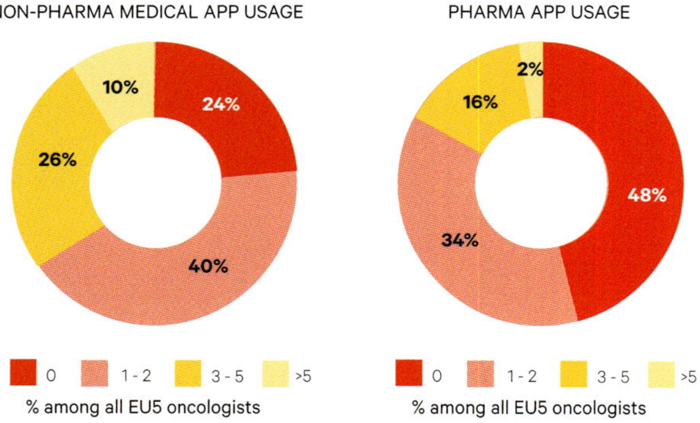


Source: Across Health Navigator 3.0 2017, EU5 oncologists, N=367

**What are your most preferred healthcare-related apps?**

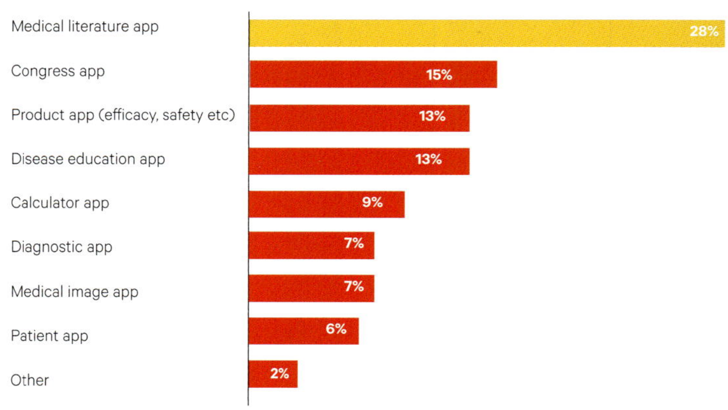


Source: Across Health Navigator 3.0, 2017 EU5 oncologists, N=367

**84%** ...of consumer mHealth apps are available for free.

(Source: IMShealth)

**53%** ...of US millennials agree wih the statement "I want my doctor to use my fitness tracker and/or health app data."

(Source: Apigee)

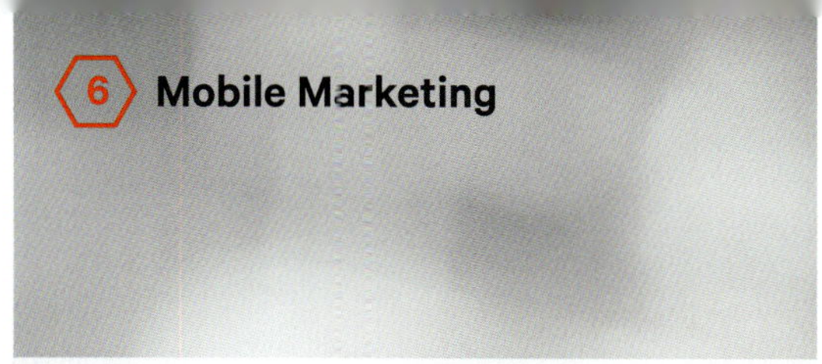

## Challenges of mobile marketing

| Challenges ☹ | Solutions ☺ |
|---|---|
| **How to grow a mobile-first mindset?** | • Analyze your **mobirati status**: how many mobile initiatives do you have? How well integrated are they in your overall marketing strategy?<br>• **Compare** your mobirati status to that of your main competitors. How well do you score in comparison?<br>• Begin by harvesting **some low-hanging fruit** by extending and building on the first crucial mobile tactics: make sure your websites are responsive, and provide - and partner with leading - apps where appropriate.<br>• Begin **your next few marketing campaigns** or activities with a 'mobile-first' mindset: instead of looking at mobile as an add-on at the end of all other activity, start with mobile and grow the campaign from there.<br>• Use lessons learned from the first trials in the field to build your **mobile expertise.**<br>• Be serious about the Internet of Things (IoT) - sensors, wearables, ... |

> "You don't get to decide which device people use to access your content. They do."
>
> **Karen McGrane**
> **Author of Content Strategy for Mobile**

## Mobile Engagement: reach and impact in Europe 2017

| Smartphone app | | Rep |
|---|---|---|
| 20% | ... reach versus... | 63% |
| 6.1 | ... impact versus... | 5.8 |
| 1.18 | ... MCQ versus... | 1.00 |

> "In the medical device segment, the largest market will be wearable devices for chronic diseases."
>
> **Casper De Clercq**
> **mHealth entrepreneur**

The Across Health Navigator studies the impact and reach of 57 off- and online channels amongst HCPs. From this, the multichannel equivalent (MCQ) is derived: a measurement of relative impact, which makes comparing between channels possible. Find out more on the Navigator data in chapter 1.

Source: The Across Health Navigator 2017 | N = 3,185 | EU5 scope (DE, ES, FR, IT, UK) | Specialists

## To conclude

With few companies having adopted a 'mobile-first' strategy, there's still ample opportunity to take advantage of the full mobile spectrum. The potential benefits are enormous as mobile activities continue to evolve. They hold the potential to change almost every part of the pharma industry they touch: from improving the efficiency of internal teams, to guiding patients and physicians through the customer journey, to helping patients adhere to medication, to improving patient-physician connectivity. Almost anything that patients and HCPs did before, may well become possible through mobile. And a whole lot more than that, too.

The Internet of Things (IoT), boosted by a myriad of sensors in mobile devices and beyond, is adding a totally new - and very exciting - dimension to this already strategic field. We can see the next stage of this trend already on the horizon, as wearables are giving way to 'disappearables' (sensors inside the body). Several pharma companies are taking IoT very seriously and are moving at a fast pace. Shouldn't you?

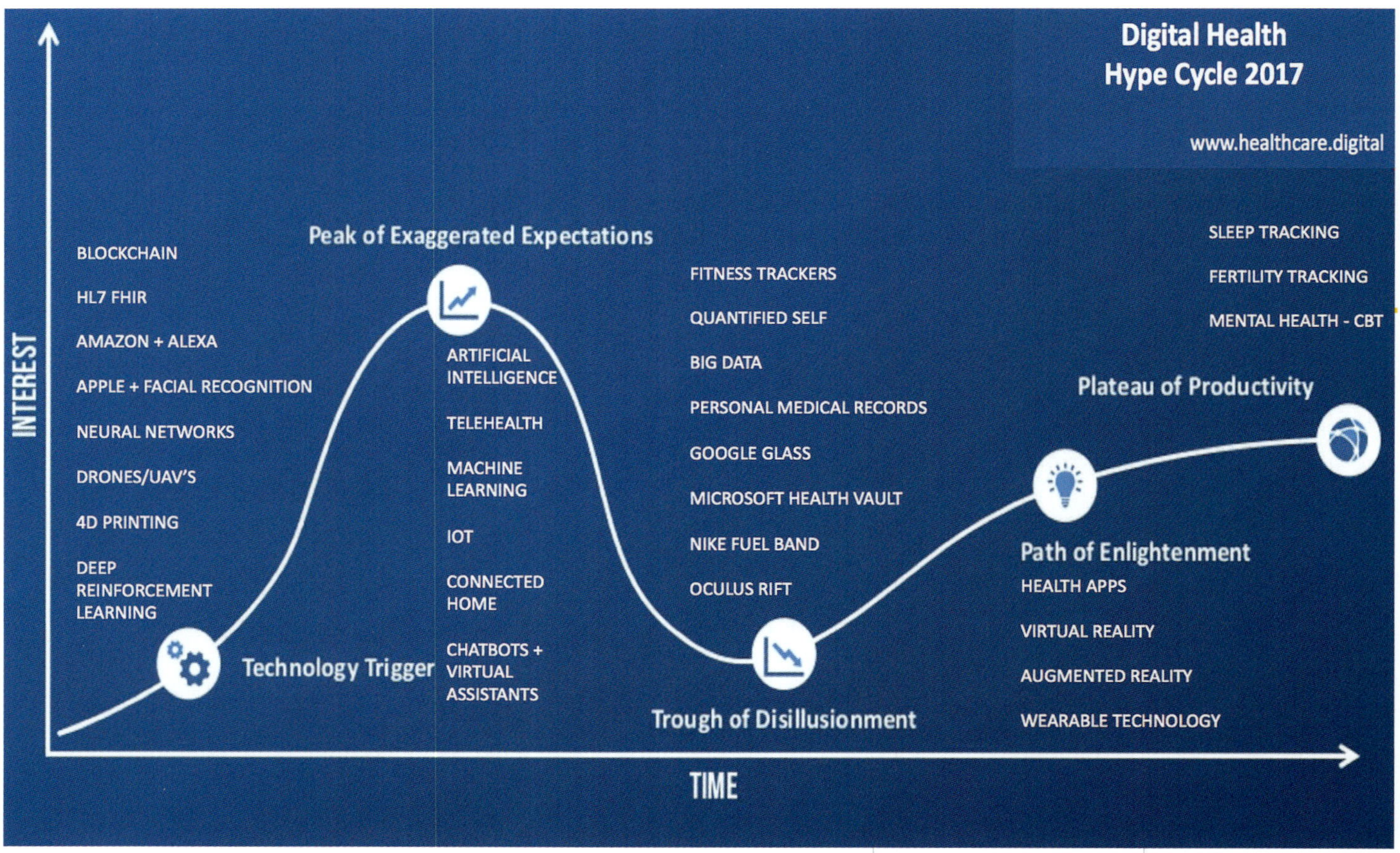


The digital health hype cycle. Source: healthcare.digital

# 7 Teledetailing

## The HCP engagement model of the future?

Teledetailing—also referred to as 'remote detailing' or 'web calls'—boils down to conducting **an interactive, online, real-time meeting** with a healthcare professional (HCP).

The typical process of teledetailing, as it is applied within pharma, begins with an appointment being scheduled with the HCP one or two weeks ahead of time. At the end of each call, an evaluation survey is triggered.

As technologies such as Skype and Facetime have become an integral part of our personal communications, remote professional communications between pharma companies and HCPs are expected to further grow. Teledetailing will increasingly be adopted to complement face-to-face (F2F) visits, especially with digital native HCPs.

This trend will also become more significant as **physician access becomes increasingly difficult.** In some (mainly northern) European markets, sales reps can do as few as 2 calls per day.

Teledetailing is therefore a great way to extend reach or contact frequency and create impact.

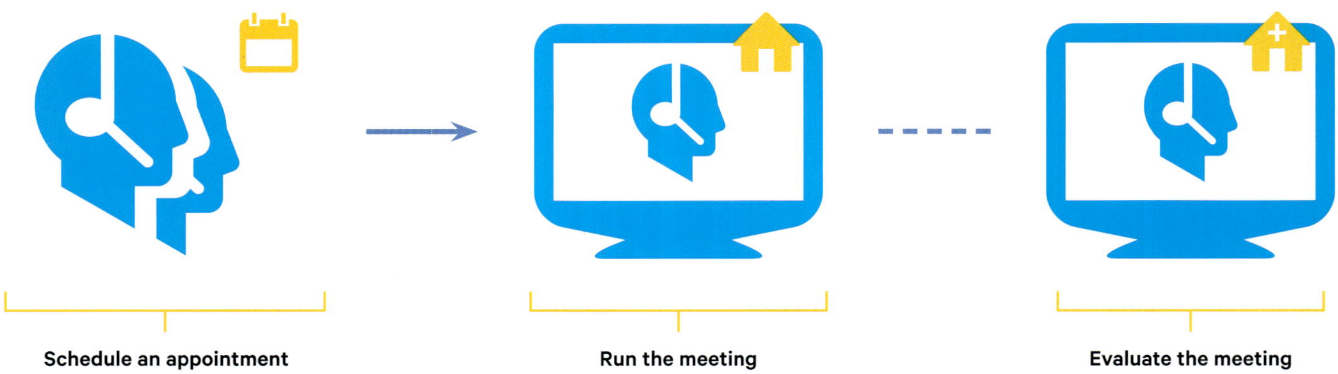


## The metrics of teledetailing

**50%** ... of HCPs find the timing of normal F2F calls inconvenient.

**20%** ... is the average acceptance rate for teledetailing among general practicioners.

**30%** ... is the average acceptance rate for teledetailing among specialists.

**14%** Only 14% of pharma sales reps actively use teledetailing. This shrinks to 12% for medical science liaisons.

**15'** 15 minutes is the average length of a remote call, which is 3 times longer than an average F2F visit.

**90%** ...is the retention rate of teledetailing for those customers that have accepted it the first time. Satisfaction levels are typically very high for HCPs who participate.

Based on aggregated results of Across Health teledetailing projects

# Teledetailing strategies

In general, there are 5 strategies that explain why pharma companies engage with physicians via remote detailing.

1. **Coverage:** teledetailing can be a means to extend the reach towards customer groups that are currently not seen by the field force, as these physicians are difficult to reach or because they are part of a secondary (lower focus) target group.

2. **Frequency:** with teledetailing, the number of calls can be increased compared to F2F meetings. The assumption behind this strategy is that a remote call can, in theory, take place every 30 minutes, which would be very challenging to realise in the field.

3. **Distant or vacant territories:** teledetailing can be an efficient way to cover vacant territories.

4. **On-demand service:** companies can offer physicians the online possibility to request a remote call to address a specific need.

5. **Differentiated messaging:** in a hybrid scenario, where reps alternate between F2F calls and remote calls, the latter can be used to talk about other products or to focus on specific services that aren't discussed during a F2F call.

## Tip

### VoIP or telephone?

Although most remote detailing platforms offer the possibility to deliver voice communication over the internet (VoIP), it is advisable to still use the telephone for audio support. This is less prone to interference and best practices show most HCPs feel more comfortable with this.

# The business models of teledetailing

In general, three business models of teledetailing are applied by pharma today, the main difference being the level of outsourcing and implementation complexity.

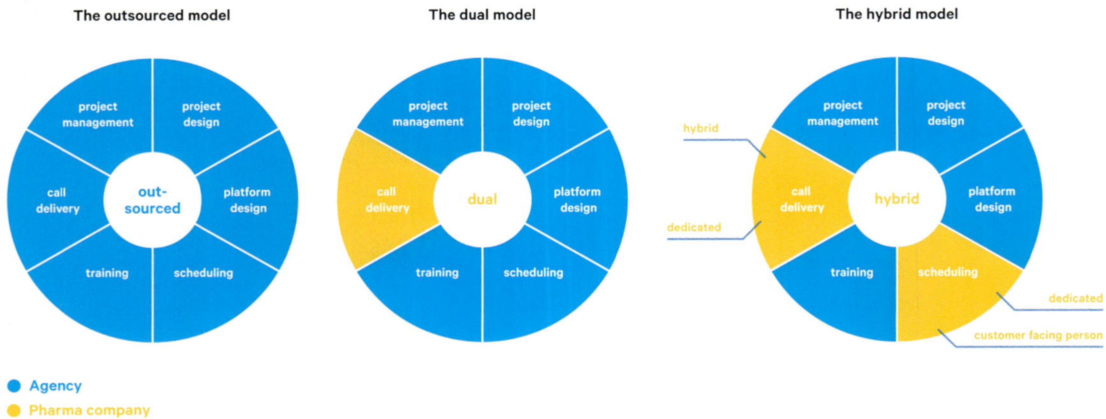


**1. The outsourced model**

In the outsourced model, all components of teledetailing are managed by **an external agency**: ranging from project design and platform configuration to scheduling and executing the calls with customers.
In this model, **external sales reps** are contracted with the sole intent to perform remote calls. As a result, few internal objections can be expected, and there's no change management needed.

The big benefit of the outsourced model is that it can be **set up very quickly**. It also allows you to gain significant coverage or frequency in a short period of time, as external reps are often paid per call.

If your company has **no prior experience** with teledetailing, then the outsourced model is probably the easiest - and fastest - to implement with limited change management issues.

## Tip

### Which technology should I select?

When selecting a teledetailing technology, it is extremely important to choose a platform that doesn't require any plug-in downloads on the side of the HCP. Especially in hospital environments, firewalls will block the download and, as a result, the call cannot be executed. A technology that is frequently used is Zoom, as it only requires a browser and an internet connection.

### 2. The dual model

With the dual model, most activities are still done by an external agency, including the scheduling of calls. The only component managed by the pharma company is **call delivery** itself. This is an activity that corresponds closest to the core competency of the field force.

Especially in the start-up phase of the programme, it can be quite challenging to make customer-facing staff replace time in the field with remote calls. If they are **not properly trained** or the value proposition isn't clearly explained to them, they might be reluctant to schedule remote calls when they can see their contacts face-to-face.

One way to overcome this, is by having the calls scheduled by an external call agent. When calls are scheduled, it is important to take into account that 1 out of 2 calls are postponed or cancelled on the day they are supposed to take place. As a rule, during a normal working day, 16 calls should be scheduled upfront (one every 30 minutes) in order to have at least 8 properly executed calls and, thus, make the model cost-effective compared to a pure F2F setting.

For companies that have little prior experience but still want to use their own field force, the dual model may be the most appropriate one to start with.

**1 in 2**

**1 in 2 scheduled calls is cancelled or postponed on the day it is planned for.**

Source: Across Health campaign results

> "Start with volunteers and then use them as ambassadors to convince the rest of the field force."

### 3. The hybrid model

Pharma companies that already have some teledetailing experience can consider implementing the hybrid model. In this model, only the set-up, training and platform configuration (or parts of these) are done by an agency, while the **call scheduling and execution is done internally** by company employees.

A couple of combinations are possible:

- In the initial phase, it is advisable to have **a dedicated person** within the company or the service centre to schedule the calls. This way, field reps can focus on their core competency: making calls to customers. Resistance to this type of change can be strong at the beginning of the project. By having the calls scheduled by someone else, you ensure that the call volumes are high, which allows the field force to gain experience with the new model.
- Over time, as the field force begins to understand the value of teledetailing for themselves and their customers, call scheduling too could be **transitioned to the field force**. After all, most of them are already scheduling the appointments for their F2F visits.
- Some pharma companies decide to hire **dedicated agents** for the sole purpose of planning and making remote calls. Especially if you want to start quickly, book success in the short term and avoid change management issues, this could be a good approach.

*The hybrid model is preferred by most EU5 oncologists*

TELEDETAILING BY REP - ONCO EU5

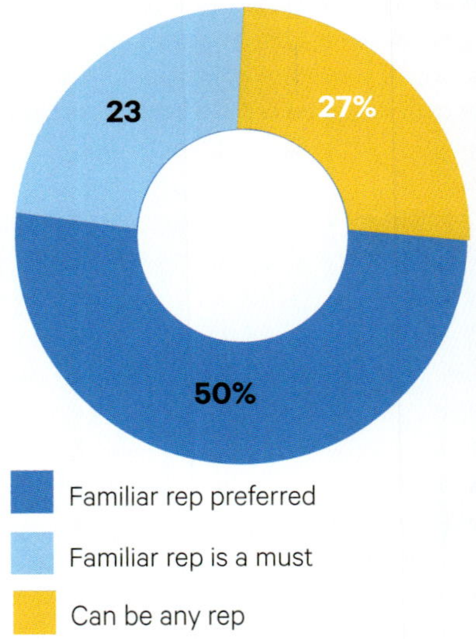


% among all HCPs

Source: Across Health Navigator 3.0 2017, EU5 oncologists, N=367

The hybrid model is the most difficult model to implement as it requires both a large amount of change management and training efforts.  It is certainly not the model to apply if your aim is to create short-term business impact. Given the 'social' nature of the field force, many of them will be **reluctant at first** when asked to be in the office for 1 or 2 days a week (although others may/will see the benefit of not having to be on the road the entire week).

If you want to adopt the hybrid model, it is advisable to **identify volunteers first** before asking everyone to make remote calls. Volunteers are often younger people that are already using technologies such as Skype in their daily lives. They are more comfortable and confident about using the technology and many of them also like the flexibility of the model, allowing them to work from home.

Once these volunteers are generating their first successes with the model, they can act as **ambassadors** to convince the rest of the field force.

## The outsourced vs. the hybrid model

| Outsourced model | Hybrid model |
|---|---|
| Little prior experience with teledetailing is required | Some initial experience is required |
| Preferably used with target customers who are not seen by the reps (to avoid channel conflicts) | Can be used with new as well as existing (and already visited) target customers |
| Works well to cover vacant territories | To differentiate the field force's activities from its competitors |
| Complement internal reps when not enough capacity available to reach all target customers | To optimize field force resources (increase productivity) |
| Works best for early PLC stages: to cover target groups not seen by internal reps | Works at all stages, also in the mature stage (because of established relationship with rep) |
| Short-term (one or a few waves) | Long-term (integrated waves) |

# Healthy snack

## A case study on the implementation of the hybrid model

**The situation:** a top-10 pharma company in Europe, specializing in vaccines, had limited experience with teledetailing but believed it could be a good addition to their communication and marketing mix.

Its primary target audience were specialists who had already been visited face-to-face by the field force. The secondary target audience were GPs who had not been visited before by the reps.

**The challenge:** in the first phase, the dual model was used, with an external call agent scheduling the calls. After this initial experience, the firm switched to the hybrid model, using a dedicated outbound service agent (an employee on the company payroll) to schedule all the calls for the reps. Reps were asked to dedicate 20% of their time (1 day per week) to teledetailing.

After each remote call, physicians were asked to evaluate the web call on three parameters: the quality of the content, the technology and the presenter. They could also indicate their desire to be contacted again via teledetailing and the extent to which they would recommend teledetailing to their peers (Net Promotor Score).

**The approach:** the company worked with a professional call centre to schedule the appointments for the reps. Both GPs and specialists were contacted and asked for their opt-in.

**The result:** the firm was able to greatly extend its reach, while the HCPs were very positive about teledetailing. The overall satisfaction score for teledetailing was 8.1 on a scale of 10 with a positive Net Promotor Score (the extent to which physicians would recommend teledetailing to their peers) of 11%.

71% of all contacted specialists had a preference for a combination of rep visits and teledetailing and 23% even stated that they only wanted to have remote calls in the future. Of the GPs—who were not contacted before—8 in 10 indicated a preference for being contacted through teledetailing in the future.

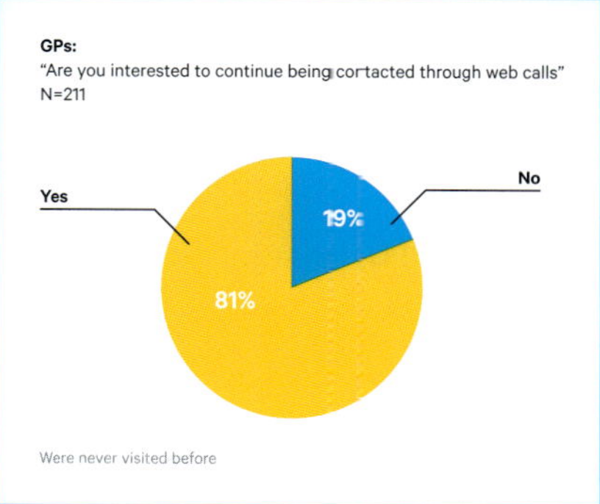


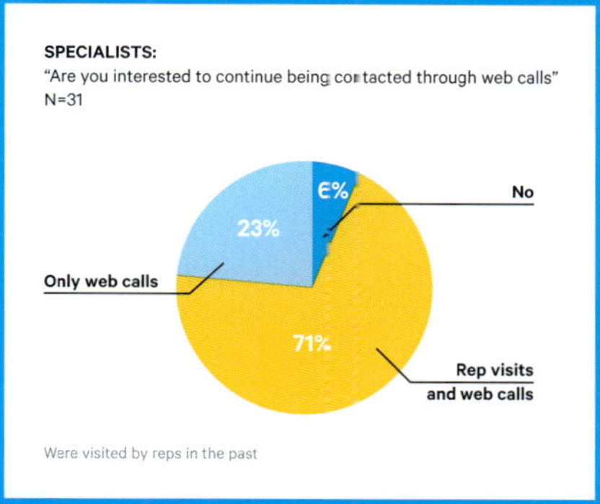


Initially, the sales reps were very sceptical about teledetailing, but after taking the training course and having seen the customer satisfaction numbers, rep enthusiasm increased rapidly.

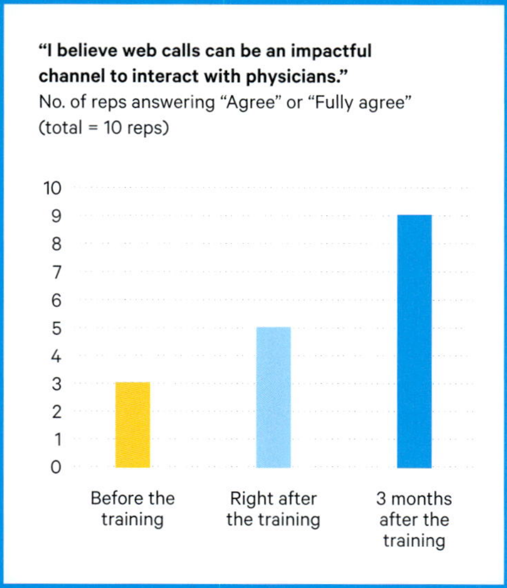


I did not really believe in it, even after 2 days of training. I was convinced I was going to miss the personal contact with the HCP. But after 3 days of web calls, I felt the enthusiasm of the physicians. Now I enjoy my "web call day", it is a nice variation compared to our usual field rep work.

During teledetailing, physicians are much more focused on our messages, and interactions are typically a lot more scientific in nature.

I am happy that I have acquired a new skill that I can put on my CV. I feel ready for the future in pharma.

# Web calls in a medical context

While the adoption of remote detailing in a promotional context in pharma is only 14% today, it is even **lower in a medical context**.

This is surprising for 2 reasons:

1 Research indicates that the **interest of physicians** to talk remotely with MSLs is higher than their willingness to talk to sales reps (36% versus 22% respectively). So, from a customer point of view, web calls executed by MSLs make sense.

2 Also, from an internal point of view, equipping MSLs with web call technology is the sensible thing to do. Companies have a lot more reps than MSLs. As a result, **fewer MSLs have to cover much bigger territories to address customer needs**. This should make the value proposition of web calls more apparent for MSLs, as it can significantly **reduce their travel** time while **shortening the time to fulfilment**.

Web call technologies for MSLs usually take one of the following 2 forms:

**1. eMSL on-demand**
Offering an e-MSL service on a pharma-owned website. Physicians with a medical question can **connect directly online with an MSL**, or schedule a time slot using a calendar functionality.

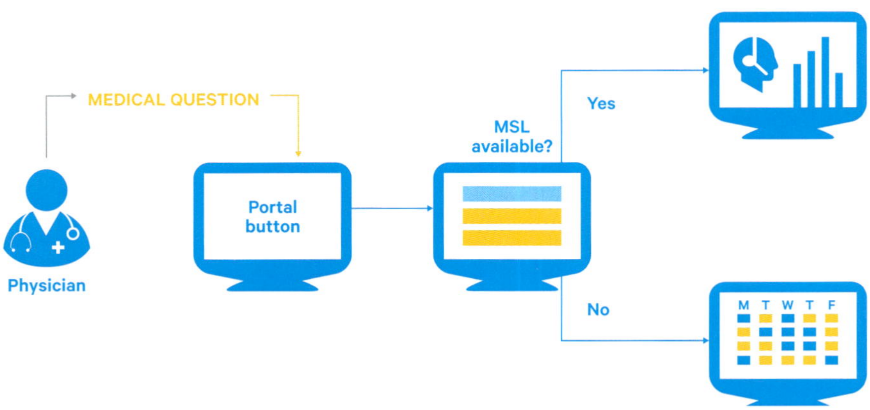


**2. In-office e-MSL activation**
Imagine a sales rep in a physician office, confronted with a medical question. They can then **check via a tablet** the availability of a remote MSL who can address the question immediately or suggest a slot when the physician can be called back.

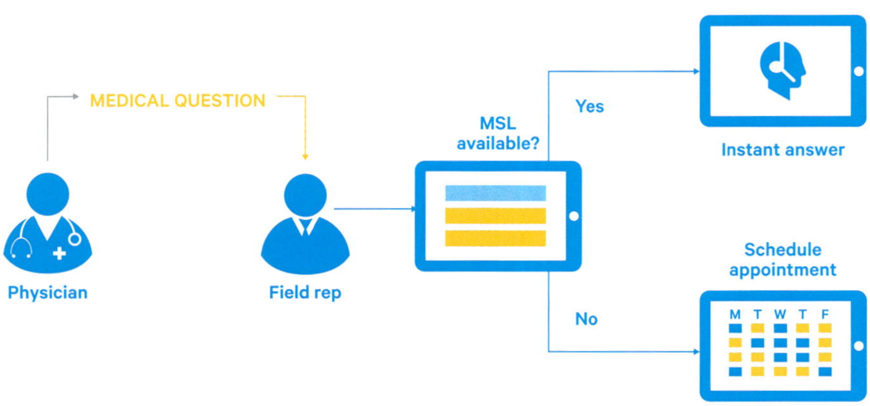


## Tip

### How to use the webcam?

Although both the rep and the HCP can switch on their webcams, in most cases it is only the rep who will do this.

Some reps will not feel comfortable with switching it on during the entire conversation. In that case, a solution can be to only switch it on during the introduction and then switch to a static picture for the rest of the discussion. This also helps to keep the focus of the HCP on the content of the presentation.

# Measuring the impact of teledetailing

As is the case for any channel, the impact of a teledetailing project too should be closely monitored, both quantitatively and qualitatively. The qualitative dimension can be added by triggering **a default evaluation survey** at the end of each web call. The evaluation survey should collect feedback on 3 dimensions: content, technology and presenter.

Additionally, there are a lot of quantitative things that can be tracked. Some KPIs to take into consideration:

**Internal KPIs**

- % of the field force that is **actively performing web calls** versus target
- % field force **productivity increase** in reach and/or frequency versus baseline

**Customer satisfaction KPIs**

- **Technology NPS:** to what extent is the HCP willing to recommend remote detailing to a peer?
- **Repeat intention:** would a HCP agree to be contacted again in the future via a web cal ?

**Impact KPIs (apart from financial metrics)**

- % of doctors **accepting** a remote call invitation
- % of doctors **participating** in a remote call versus those invited
- % of target customers having done **more than 2 web calls**
- Intent to Rx / brand NPS versus other HCPs

# The importance of training

Training is **a critical factor**. As the physician is not physically sitting in front of the sales rep, this requires **a new form of interaction,** which many reps initially do not feel comfortable with.

Training should be done on **3 levels:**

**1 Content**
Just like when presenting with a tablet, so too must the field force be trained on **how to present content in a remote setting,** and which messages they should focus on.

**2 Technology**
For reps who are unfamiliar with technologies like Skype, training on how to use the technology correctly is essential. This can range from manipulating the webcam, using the audio headset, and giving physicians access to the meeting room to sharing content in a secure way.

**3 Remote communication**
Reps will often not be able to see the physician with whom they are interacting. They should therefore be taught **how to communicate well remotely.** E.g. how can you ensure that physicians are paying attention to the presentation instead of doing something else ?

A good way to conduct a training is by using **role play in a group session.** It is also best to do at least three **remote simulation sessions** before reps try it out for real. Simulations can be done with a trainer or reps can practice with each other. It is also strongly advised for reps to do their first real sessions with physicians they know really well. They will feel more at ease and possible mistakes may be more easily forgiven.

# The maturity level of teledetailing

**Only 14% of pharma marketers** state that teledetailing is a standard practice in their company. With a 19th place on the list of the 25 most commonly used pharma marketing tactics, it clearly is not yet a top tactic for many pharma companies.

And this low adoption rate drops even more for **eMSL** (#20 on the list): only 12% of pharma staff indicate that this is a standard practice.

With more and more digital native physicians entering the workforce and remote technologies becoming common practice, the case for teledetailing in a promotional as well as a medical context seems clear.

## The adoption of teledetailing tactics by pharma

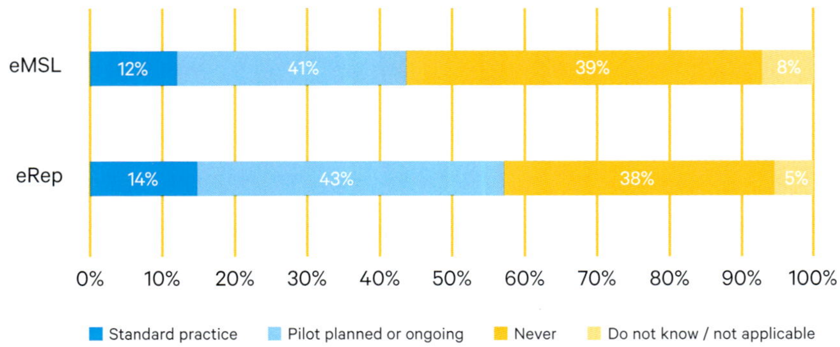


Source: The Across Health Multichannel Maturometer 2017 | N = 221 | EU scope

# Which HCPs engage in teledetailing?

Across Health research (2016) has shown that there is a strong relationship between teledetailing participation and the following factors :

- **Age**: in general, HCPs who engage with teledetailing are slightly younger compared to the general population (mean age: 45).
- **Device ownership**: physicians who own a tablet or smartphone are more likely to accept a teledetailing invitation.
- **Relationship**: physicians are 3 times more likely to accept a remote call if they already have a good relationship with the rep.
- **E-savviness**: physicians who visit pharma-owned websites or who are active on social networks for professional purposes are twice as likely to accept a teledetailing call compared to those who don't.
- **Specialists** are more open to teledetailing than GPs.

Having insights into one of the above factors for your target audience can help you make the recruitment process more cost-effective. This is especially the case when teledetailing is a new tactic where you don't know which customers will accept your invitation.

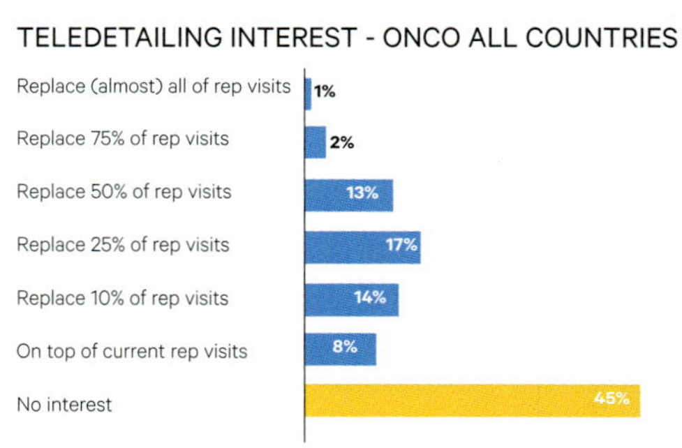


Source: Across Health Navigator 3.0, 2017 EU5 oncologists, N=367

*Over 50% of EU5 oncologists would like to engage in remote detailing*

## Teledetailing: reach and impact in Europe 2017

| Teledetailing | | Rep |
|---|---|---|
| 15% | ... reach versus... | 63% |
| 5.9 | ... impact versus... | 5.8 |
| 1.03 | ... MCQ versus... | 1.00 |

The Across Health Navigator studies the impact and reach of 57 off- and online channels amongst HCPs. From this, the multichannel equivalent (MCQ) is derived: a measurement of relative impact, which makes comparing between channels possible. Find out more on the Navigator data in chapter 1.

Source: The Across Health Navigator 2017 | N = 3,185 | EU5 scope (DE, ES, FR, IT, UK) | Specialists

## To conclude

**While the business case for remote engagement is very strong, adoption levels have remained low throughout the years. Teledetailing remains a big opportunity for most pharma companies and a good alternative or complement to F2F visits. Indeed, access to physicians is becoming increasingly difficult and more and more customers are becoming familiar with remote technologies.**

**Customers tend to report high satisfaction levels. But most customers also indicate that they prefer a combination of remote calls and F2F visits.**

**While internal adoption of teledetailing can be a lengthy process, proper training and solid change management will lead to sustained success.**

‘ … adding digital impact to your F2F conversations. ’

# 8 Tablet Detailing

## The #1 digital tactic in pharma

Only 7 years after the introduction of the iPad, tablet detailing became **the number 1 digital tactic in the industry** (2016). 84% of companies are using tablets to support their sales reps in their daily face to face (F2F) conversations with customers. And almost all companies have selected the iPad as **the 'device of choice'.**

Despite this rapid uptake, tablet detailing had a rocky start. Many sales reps felt **uncomfortable** using the device, as they were not immediately convinced that it would add impact to their F2F conversations.

Many doctors too failed to see **the added value** in using the iPad as they were confronted with sales reps who were struggling to plough through detail-aids containing dozens of screens, causing them to lose focus of the actual conversation.

But these early teething troubles are now a thing of the past. In recent years, we have seen a clear new direction in pharma, with tablet detail-aids being **drastically reduced in size** and focusing much more on the **interaction** rather than spelling out specific points.

The industry has learned some important lessons. After all, tablet detailing will only be used when sales reps are convinced it adds **immediate value and impact** to the conversations they have with healthcare professionals (HCPs).

## The metrics of tablet detailing

**84%** ... of EU pharma marketers say that tablet detailing is a standard practice. (Source: Across Health Maturometer)

**61%** ... of HCPs (in EU5) say they have been visited by a sales rep who used an iPad. Tablet detailing is closing in on the traditional rep (63% reach). (Source: Across Health Maturometer)

**5.8** The impact score of tablet detailing amongst HCPs, the same for reps without tablet. (Source: Across Health Maturometer)

**<20%** ... of the cases the iPAD is really used to support a F2F conversation of the sales rep. (Source: IQVIA)

### Tip

**Will the salesforce use my tablet detail-aid?**

Ask your salesforce to anonymously rate your screens using just one key question: 'will this screen add impact to your F2F conversation?' If the answer is YES, go ahead and launch. If the answer is MAYBE or NO, then it is **back to the drawing board.**

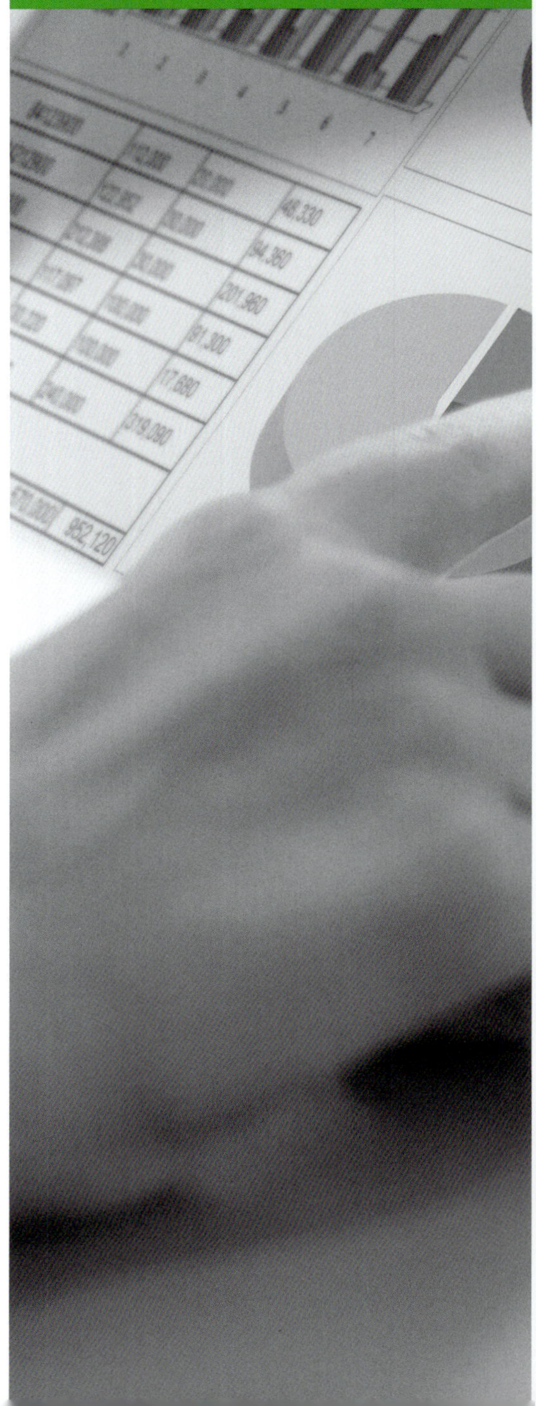

## Some common mistakes

There are two very common mistakes when tablet detailing is first launched in a company:

1. **Creating a digital copy of a paper detail-aid.** The first tablet detail-aids were **exact copies of the paper detail-aids,** without any additional functionalities or data capturing capabilities. The potential added value of the device was not used and many reps, who were used to their old paper versions, felt less comfortable using the tablet. This made it hard to convince the salesforce to switch.

→ When you introduce tablet detailing, make sure it offers **clear added value** from the very start compared to paper.

2. **Adding too much content.** The tablet made it possible to **add an almost infinite stream of documents.** But, however tempting it is to equip the salesforce with so much content that any objection can be handled and any question answered, this can ultimately quickly result in sales reps no longer having an idea where to find the content they are looking for. **The more content that is added, the harder it becomes to find specific content.** In reality, most reps use only three to five pages of a tablet detail-aid to support their conversation. When a brand manager needs to add additional content items, make sure it is not part of the main navigation stream, but instead, available as side steps. Otherwise, a sales rep may end up searching for two minutes to find a content piece which is buried under a pile of pages, slides and flows.

→ When you introduce tablet detailing, make sure the main flows are short, to the point and **directly available.** Place all secondary content under a sub-menu.

## Country differences in tablet adoption

While most countries are heading towards a digitally enabled fieldforce, this is not necessarily happening at the same pace everywhere. Research from IQVIA (published in 2017) shows significant divergence between countries in the use of tablet detailing. There are certainly many factors involved, ranging from regulatory barriers, to customary HCP/rep interactions, to the preferences of the HCPs themselves. However this does suggest that, when rolling out this tactic, local considerations, as well as company policies, should be considered when setting goals.

**Use of tablet detailing support by country** Top 15 countries - FY2016

% of face to face calls using a tablet as detailing support

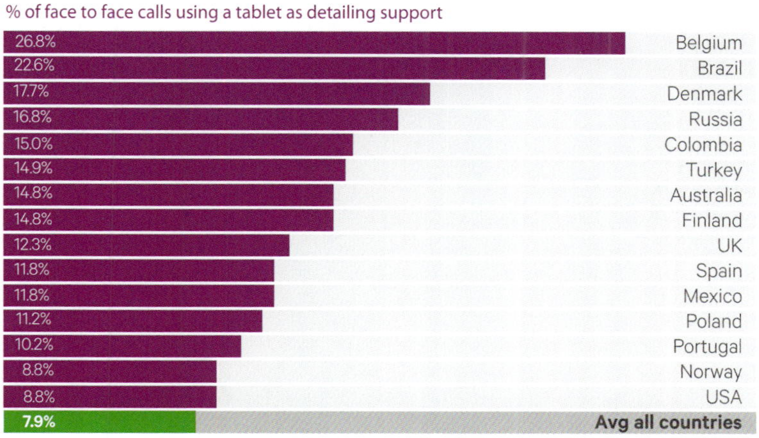


Source: IQVIA ChannelDynamics Global Reference, 2017

## Setting up for success

A simple test to see if you are setting up for success, is to ask a sales rep the following question: "Is this part of the tablet detail-aid adding **impact** to your verbal conversations?".

Extending the impact on conversations via the tablet detail-aid can be achieved in 3 ways:

**1 Use the detail-aid to support the verbal conversations of the sales rep, do NOT spell out everything for them.** Spelling out everything not only leads to an overload of slides, it is also demotivating for them. In the past, the experienced sales rep hardly ever used the text in the traditional printed detail-aid and a switch to tablets will not change that. A good tablet detail-aid helps the sales rep strengthen their message delivery by providing structure, examples and cases to support the verbal story. At all times, the sales rep needs to lead the conversation, not the tablet.

**2 Invite the HCP to interact: create more engagement and capture relevant market data.** The tablet is an ideal way to capture data on treatment practices and brand perception of HCPs. The data can immediately be used in the call, by making statements based on the input, or by drilling down to filtered information based on the individual HCP's responses or perception.

Over time, the brand manager can use this data to monitor the sentiments and needs of customers and develop additional tailored content to address these.

Continual content refinement and development will also increase the motivation of the sales rep to capture this kind of data. This is often referred to as 'closing the loop'. **Closed loop marketing** captures interaction information via all possible channels and acts upon it accordingly with each new interaction, regardless of the channel being used. Tablet detailing can be an excellent channel to start the closed loop marketing experience, whith additional channels being integrated later.

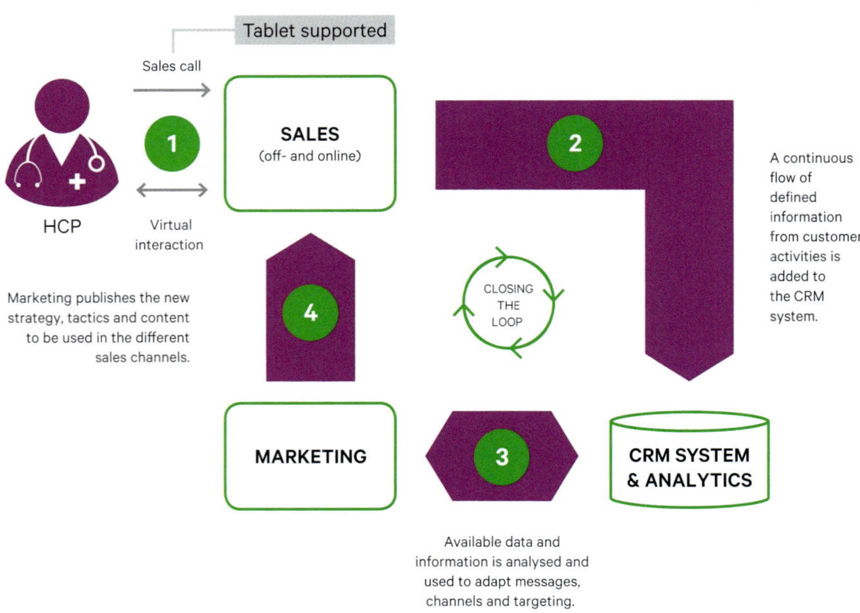

> 'The sales rep is leading the conversation, not the tablet.'

**3 Maximize the graphical opportunities of the iPad to strengthen the marketing message.** The possibilities of the tablet extend well beyond just text and images. You can include, for example, treatment class or product animations, peer video statements, patient cases, and much more. The tablet enables you to turn the content into **an interactive and lively experience!**

A word of caution though: never use animation for the sake of animation. Use animated graphics and video content only when they are clearly strengthening the key message. Consider, for example, the difference in impact of a written quote on the screen ("Professor Jones stated at the congress last month...") versus a 30-second video clip in which she actually delivers this quote.

## Anatomy of a high-impact tablet detail aid

Here you can see a good example of a tablet detail aid screen.

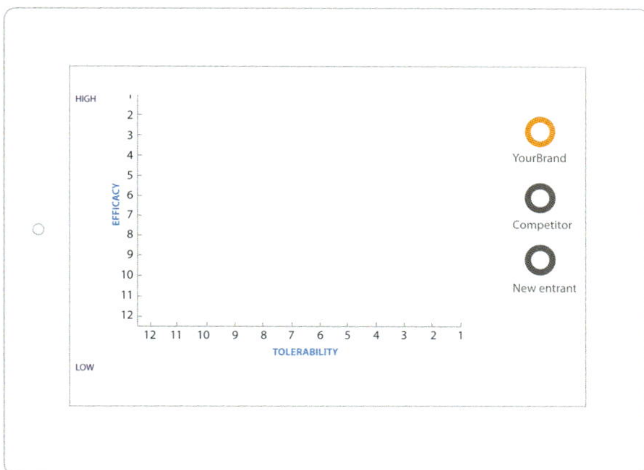


**1.** During a conversation about the relative tolerability and efficacy of different treatment options for a condition, a rep can ask the HCP to drag the different options onto a chart.

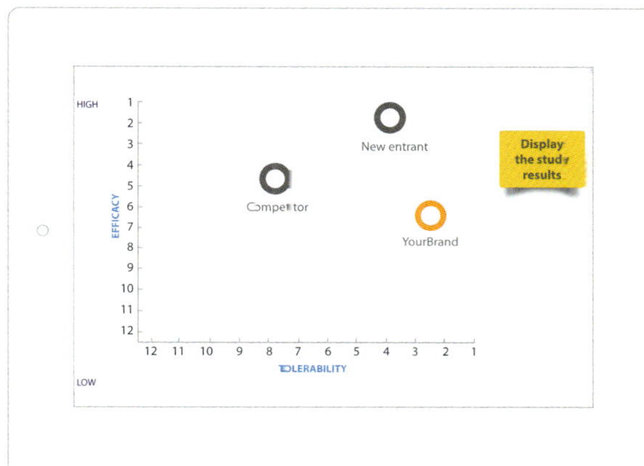


**2.** The HCP will position them according to their view of each's relative benefit. This will reveal valuable information on the perception of your treatment, which can be used not only for that conversation, but also in the implementation of a closed loop marketing strategy.

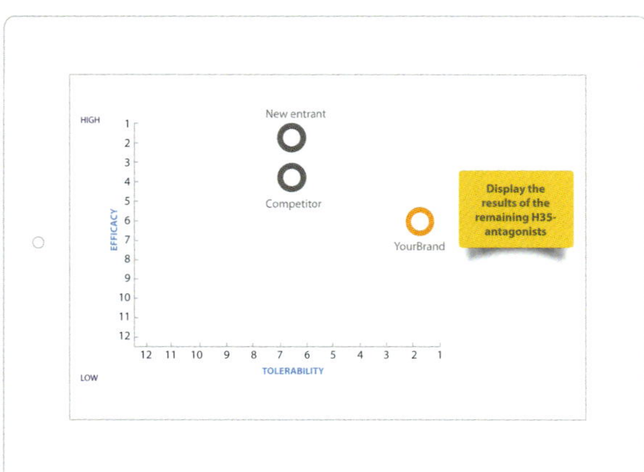


**3.** After all options have been placed on the graph, the 'true' position of different drugs can be revealed. This will show HCPs the reality of the available evidence, and can prompt conversations about why they held previous beliefs, and allow the rep to present information to counter areas of concern.

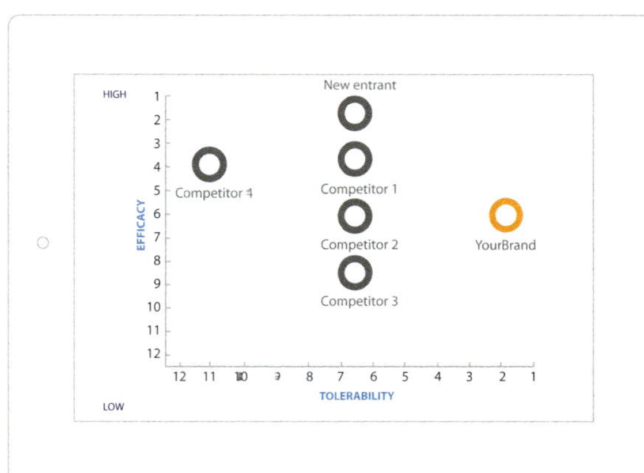


**4.** In order to comply with regulations on information display, it is then vital to show the full range of competitor treatment options.

# How to set up your tablet detail-aid

Brand managers are usually responsible for creating the tablet detail-aids that will be used by their salesforce. The following 4 steps are recommended:

**1 Segmentation**

Your detail-aid typically covers 1) all **the segments** you have defined in your brand plan and 2) all the possible **ladder-of-adoption positions** you have identified. During their calls, the salesforce will try to find out on which ladder-of-adoption step the HCP currently is. Best practice suggests structuring different story lines according to these different steps. This allows sales reps to quickly access the right information and screens. Without segmented content, you must rely on the sales reps to do this exercise during the call, which may make it harder for them to use the tablet.

**2 Tailoring content per segment**

Once you have defined the segments and ladder-of-adoption positions, it is important to tailor all information according to the **behavioural objectives** and the **messages** that need to be delivered as defined in the brand plan. Try to limit the number of messages to between two and five per segment, as more messages can make it confusing for the sales rep. Tailored content increases the interest of the HCP and motivates the sales rep to use the detail-aid correctly.

**3 Adding different content types**

Tablets allow you to move beyond text and imagery and be **creative** with various content types. When doing so, bear in mind the different likes of HCPs: while some may prefer scientific content—e.g. guidelines and publication downloads—some may be more interested in references to peers—e.g. interviews, webinars and peer statements—while others may be more patient-oriented—e.g. patient cases and support programmes. The key is to differentiate in such a way that reps can quickly choose a content piece that is most in line with **the HCP's communication style and preferences.**

**4 Closure**

Finally think about a good closure, as many sales reps find this **the most difficult part of the call.** A good closure screen can be of great help here. For instance, consider ending with 1) a presentation of various patient profiles and 2) a suggestion to agree on starting to prescribe for a specific profile and discuss the results during the next call. It is also possible to summarize the call content or create an invite for a follow-up activity. The overall idea of a good closure is to **set up the next interaction** or to define future discussion topics.

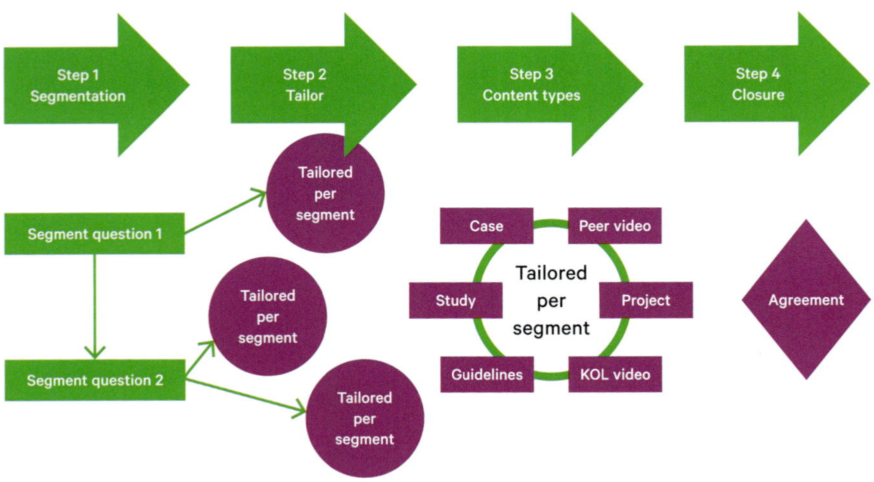


## Tip

### Ladder of adoption

The 'ladder of adoption' is a stepwise overview of the possible stages a doctor can be in concerning a brand. Typical steps are:

- **unaware** of the treatment or brand, not treating at all or with a different therapy/brand
- **first prescriber,** starting with the first patients
- **regular prescriber,** with Rx experience
- **brand advocate.** A high-volume prescriber who proactively promotes the brand to peers

Per ladder-of-adoption step, a brand manager defines specific behavioural objectives in the brand plan.

# Involve & train the salesforce

When tablet detailing is being launched, it is important to **include the salesforce from the very beginning,** well before the start of the development of the first version. As reps have to use the device and the detail-aids every day, they are best positioned to provide valuable input on what is required to maximise the chances of success.

Firstly, you have to convince them that using the iPad detail-aid will add immediate call impact. The best way to do this is to leverage their call expertise and show how this can be supported and improved further by using **tablets for interaction and data capturing.**

When they feel part of the creation team, they will also be more motivated to try it out and suggest improvements.

Secondly, you need to **train the reps on how to use the tablet.** Make sure to schedule at least half a day of role-playing exercises on top of the standard training time normally reserved for launching a new detail-aid. Best practice suggests recording these exercises and show the reps how they are using the tablet in their conversations. Most reps don't even realise how often they look at the tablet instead of at their customer, and showing them this can be quite eye-opening.

Specific training scenarios on tablet presentation skills and device usage should be developed. These can include:

- When to use the iPad (and when not)?
- How to **segment** HCPs?
- Which **message** to address first/best/preferably per segment?
- How to properly use the iPad (rules of conduct)?
- How to **close** the conversation?
- What to do if no **segmentation** can be determined?
- What to do if you only have 30 seconds?

# The maturity level of tablet detailing

Practically **every pharma company** is deploying or plans to deploy tablet detailing. With 84% of European pharma marketers stating that this tactic is a standard practice and another 10% stating a pilot is planned or ongoing, tablet detailing is **the absolute number one tactic** amongst the 25 researched tactics.

In comparison, the promising teledetailing tactic still has a steep potential growth curve (see related chapter).

## The adoption of tablet detailing and teledetailing by pharma

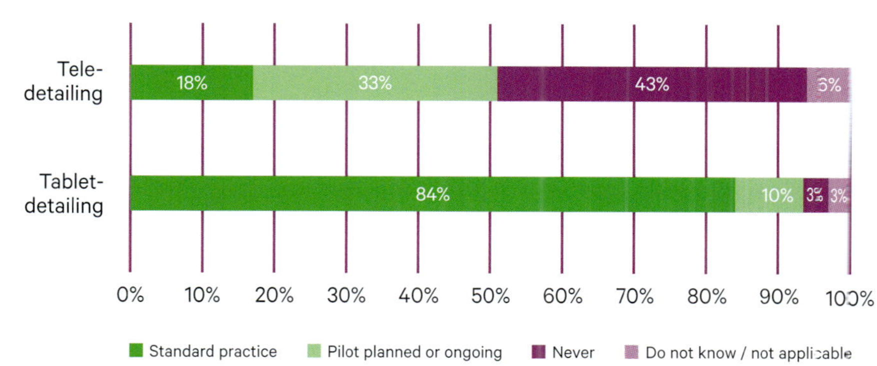


Source: The Across Health Multichannel Maturometer 2017 | N = 221 | EU scope

# The KPIs of tablet detailing

Many sales reps feel somewhat uncomfortable about the fact that the tablet platform can monitor if and how much the detail-aid is being used in the field. But, in reality, as it is the **brand manager** who created the detail-aid, the latter is much more exposed.

For the first time since paper detail-aids were introduced, pharma companies can now track exactly which sections of the tablet detail-aid are used. If some areas are not used at all, this could mean that there is no interest from the customers in that story, or the salesforce sees no value in using that part in the conversation. In both cases, the brand manager needs to **take corrective actions.**

It is important to agree from the start on the success indicators, which should cover both behavioural and communication indicators:

1. **Behavioural indicators** – when and how often do you use the tablet? Not every call needs tablet support, but it's important to ensure that there's a high level of comfort in using the device. Certainly at the start, it is recommended not to set performance levels too high. It's better to go for a softer start with an agreement on intent to use as they become more familiar with the tool. In later stages, you could become more ambitious.

2. **Communication indicators** – which sections do we plan to present and how often? What data would we like to capture and how do we use it? For a sales rep, it needs to be crystal clear how the brand manager has structured the detail-aid and how it is set up to support verbal conversation.

Some relevant KPIs and metrics to consider for tablet detailing:

| EXPOSURE | INTERACTION / ENGAGEMENT |
|---|---|
| • **Reach of target** (% of HCPs receiving tablet detailing)<br>• **Frequency** (of tablet detailing per HCP) | • HCP **uptake & message recall** (e.g. with interactive content)<br>• Content **coverage**<br>• **Collection** of information (e.g. % of answers given to a questionnaire)<br>• **Planning** of a next step (e.g. email to send, another call, etc.)<br>• Net Promoter Score **(NPS)** |

# The context of tablet detailing

Of the digital tactics that are available to the rep, tablet detailing is the **most widespread.** However, they are not as systematically used as one would expect... Depending on the market and specialty, on average tablets are **used between 25 and 50% of rep visits.**

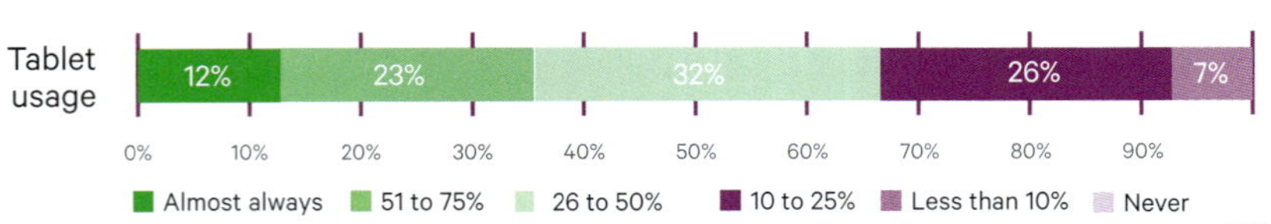


Source: The Across Health Navigator, EU5 Specs, 2017, n=1869

Tablet detailing is not universally loved by HCPs, however. The most important criterion for them is reps **knowing when (and when not) to use them**. The two most impactful ways of doing this is to ensure that reps have been trained extensively on the best times to use them, and that content on them is as engaging as possible.

## Content is king - also in tablet detailing!

**Rep tablet topics** - Oncologists, all countries

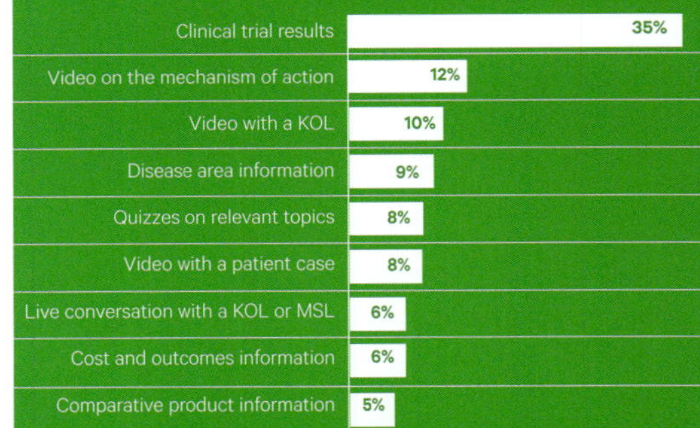


*HCPs were asked to distribute 100 points to no more than 3 options*
*Score=sum of points scored over total possible points (ie #HCPsx100)*

Source: Navigator 3.0 2017, EU5 oncologists, N=367

> "If the tablet is not part of an authentic, closed-loop strategy, it simply replaces a glossy presentation with a shiny one. It's like replacing a traditional hammer with an auto-hammer. It's cool, it's electric but, in the end, it still does the same thing."

**David Ormesher**
**CEO Closerlook**

## Tablet detailing: reach and impact in Europe 2017

| Tablet detailing | | Rep |
|---|---|---|
| 61% | ... reach versus... | 63% |
| 5.8 | ... impact versus... | 5.8 |
| 1.02 | ... MCQ versus... | 1.00 |

The Across Health Navigator studies the impact and reach of 57 off- and online channels amongst HCPs. From this, the multichannel equivalent (MCQ) is derived: a measurement of relative impact, which makes comparing between channels possible. Find out more on the Navigator data in chapter 1.

Source: The Across Health Navigator 2017 | N = 3185 | EU5 scope (DE, ES, FR, IT, UK) | Specialists

## To conclude

**Tablet detailing is the number one digital tactic in pharma. To be successful with it, pharma companies must concentrate on the following:**

- **Create content that supports the sales rep. The detail-aid should add immediate value and impact to the conversation.**
- **Involve the salesforce from the very start to ensure you are creating the right supportive material.**
- **Divide the content in line with the ladder-of-adoption stages and different customer segments. Be sure to include multiple content types.**
- **Limit the story flow to a maximum of three to five slides per segment, and offer quick access to this main content. Place all other supportive content in submenus where it will not distract the rep from the key conversation elements.**
- **Maximize the opportunities for closing the loop, i.e. collecting relevant customer insights to improve subsequent customer experience and engagement.**

'... building customer relationships through online conversations.'

# 9 Social Media Engagement

# The network always wins

Social media marketing combines a wide variety of social media tools and platforms to establish conversations with physicians, patients or other stakeholders. Through online conversations, customer relationships are built. Through electronic word of mouth, brand messages are spread.

Nevertheless, social media adoption by pharma has had quite a bumpy ride for many reasons. The fear of adverse events being reported keeps most pharma companies away from social media, as it could require 24/7 monitoring. And those engaging with social media often did it for the wrong reasons. Some, for example, launched Facebook groups with no ability to comment, which misses the purpose and opportunities presented by social media. In other cases, the rules of engagement established by pharma companies are so strict that it is hardly feasible to have meaningful discussions.

If you want to engage with your customers on social media, it is important to establish your objectives first. The Groundswell Social Media Framework from Forrester can help you with that (covered later in this chapter). Conversations help to build understanding and trust with customers and prospects. While traditional marketing tactics are mostly one-way, social media marketing is two-way and leverages the power of the network.

## Tip

### Social success

The succes of social media is built on:

1) **Interaction:** patients and physicians can interact directly with companies and each other, making the relationship more personal.
2) **Engagement:** users become publishers, either by creating their own posts or by sharing and reposting content from others. Keep track of your social media engagement through the number of comments, shares, mentions and likes.
3) **Network effects:** almost every web user has one or multiple social profiles, almost everyone is within reach.
4) **Mobile:** online social activity has shifted largely to smartphones and tablets, making social media even more "anytime, anywhere".

## The metrics of social media marketing

**68%** ... of all online consumers in Europe use social media for health-related purposes. But only 6% are also actively contributing. (Source: Manhattan Cybercitizen Europe)

**18%** ... of European physicians are actively using social media for professional purposes. (Source: Manhattan Research)

**<1%** ... of all product-related mentions in social media concern adverse events. (Source: Ciision)

**5%** ... of European physicians use Twitter for professional purposes. (Source: Across Health Navigator)

> People don't share facts, they share emotions.
>
> **Oxford University Research**

### Tip

#### Social story-telling

The best approach to social media is **telling lots of stories**, from very **short tweets** over **mid-long blog posts** to **long articles** and **e-books**. Many **different stories combined** then build a comprehensive and consistent overall story about your pipeline, guidelines/publications or therapeutic area. It clarifies who you are and what you stand for.

The punchier the story, the more likely it will be shared by others. This way, you can **turn employees into marketers** and **customers into advocates.**

## Social media platforms: what happens in 60 seconds?

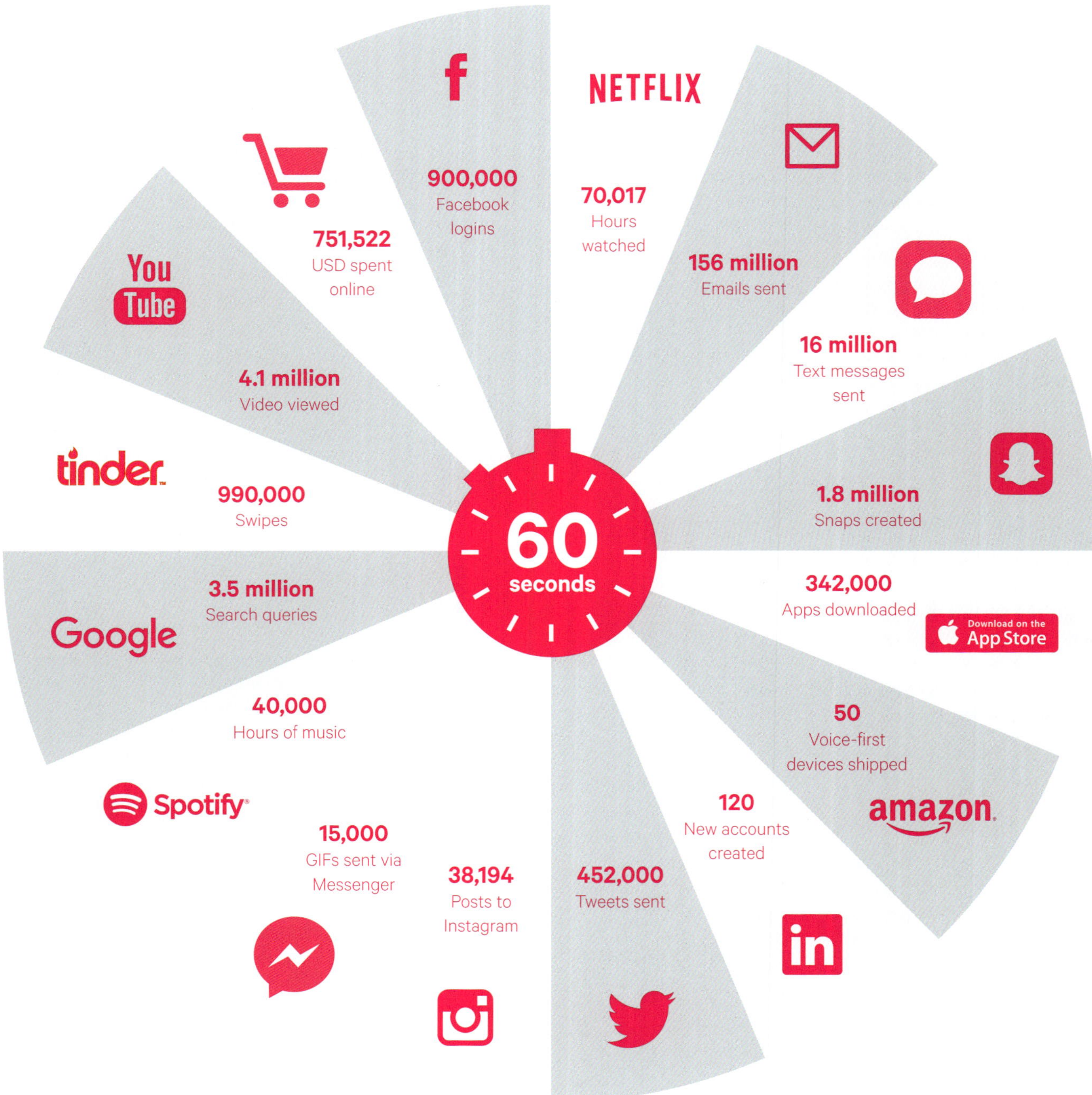


Source: Cumulus Media and Westwood One, 2017

# A social framework

The groundswell framework, as developed by Forrester, ties together **corporate functions, objectives, social tactics** and **success metrics**. When combined, different roles within the organization can see how social adds value for them and the organization as a whole. (Note: Since 2011, several new social channels have emerged; Forrester has not provided an update of the below chart).

| Corporate function | Typical groundswell objective | Appropriate social applications | Success metrics |
|---|---|---|---|
| **Research** | **Listening** – gaining insights by listening to customers | • Private communities<br>• Brand monitoring | • Insights gained<br>• Comparable costs of surveys or focus groups |
| **Marketing** | **Talking** – using conversations with customers to promote products, services or provide disease education | • Blogs<br>• Communities<br>• Social networking sites<br>• Video or user-generated sites | • Awareness<br>• Online "buzz"<br>• Time spent on sites<br>• Sales |
| **Sales** | **Energizing** – identifying customers and using them to persuade others | • Brand ambassador programmes<br>• Communities<br>• Embeddable widgets | • Community membership<br>• Online "buzz"<br>• Sales |
| **Support** | **Supporting** – making it possible for customers to help each other | • Support forums<br>• Wikis | • Members participating<br>• Questions answered online<br>• Avoided support calls |
| **Development** | **Embracing** – turning customers into a resource for innovation | • Innovation communities<br>• Suggestion boxes | • Usable product ideas<br>• Speed of development |

Source: Forrester Research, 2011

# Social tidal wave

There's a multitude of social media sites and applications available. Most of them are free of charge so it is tempting to use many channels. However, be aware of hidden costs:

1. Managing your social media presence is **time-consuming and resource-intensive**.

2. **Failing** to manage your social presence well may cause more harm than not being present at all.

Choosing the right combination of social media channels depends on your **resources** and your **objectives**. The Forrester framework can help you establish those goals.

# 1. Listening to customers: social (buzz) monitoring

When you lack the resources to actively engage with customers on social media, or your company policies prevent you from doing so, the least you can do, is listen to what your customers say about your brand or disease area.

Following what's being said about your brand or therapeutic area on social media is **impossible to do manually**. Various automation tools can help you keep an eye on social media. They track a wide variety of social media platforms such as social networking sites (Facebook, Linkedin, ...), blogs and user-generated content in general.

Social media monitoring enables you to ...

- **Monitor** the overall **visibility of a brand or disease**
- **Measure** the impact of **marketing campaigns**
- **Identify opportunities to engage** with prospects and customers
- Keep track of **the sentiment of online conversations** about your brand or therapeutic area
- Generate **valuable insights** from patients or physicians that can be used for finetuning content of future marketing campaigns
- **Assess** the **competitor activity** and share of voice
- Be **alerted** to impending drug related **crises.**

## Tip

### Market research through social media

Social media's direct link with healthcare professionals and patients enables organizations to **1) test out new ideas** in a small group of interested prospects / customers, as well as **2) perform market research** by searching for **hot discussion topics** within your target groups. It should be added, however, that this group is not representative of the entire population - you typically "hear" about the 20-30% most active and engaged customers.

## Healthy snack

### The use case for social sharing among consumers

**The situation:** a top-10 pharma company created an awareness campaign to activate expecting parents and grandparents to see a doctor and request a vaccination against pertussis.

**The challenge:** create awareness and activate consumers to see a doctor.

**The approach:** the company created an activation site where the targeted audiences could take a 'myths and facts' quiz on pertussis. To increase the impact of the campaign, quiz participants were invited to share their result on Facebook and Twitter afterwards, in order to attract more visitors to the site. A talk-to-your-doctor factsheet could be downloaded to support patients in their discussion with a doctor.

**The result:** 17% of all participants shared their results with their social network, generating substantial additional awareness and traction for the campaign.

## 2. Talking to customers: social marketing

When it comes to disease-related **discussions with patients and their carers,** the two most relevant social media platforms are **Facebook and YouTube.** A large part of the general public is already aware of or active on these platforms and they offer a wide array of possibilities to engage with people based on specific socio-demographic criteria. For healthcare professionals, Facebook is less appropriate. Channels like LinkedIn, Twitter and dedicated HCP online networks are better suited for this target audience.

Regardless of whether you want to talk with patients or healthcare professionals, it is always important to generate sufficient **awareness** around your initiative in order to build **a critical mass of fans or followers.** Without this, it is almost certain that your initiative will have little impact.

For example, for patient/caregiver campaigns, it is good practice to invest in Facebook ads to help you build a significant fan base for your Facebook page. If you want to do something on YouTube, it also helps to embed your disease videos into your own website to generate as many clicks as possible. This will also help you obtain a more favourable ranking on YouTube when people are searching.

Many companies have tried to talk with customers by launching Facebook pages in the past, but **many became disillusioned** as either the pages were suboptimally promoted (leading to a lack of critical mass) or the rules of engagement they set themselves were so strict that it was impossible to have meaningful discussions. The fact that these initiatives needed to be monitored 24/7 has also led to a decline in Facebook activity.

Nevertheless, successful examples do exist, for instance the VIH-SIDA (now 'Stop au SIDA') Facebook from Janssen France. This page has over 81,000 members. Most of them have been recruited by Facebook ads. At regular intervals, interesting 'myths & facts' about HIV are posted, which generates awareness on the topic and allows people to talk about it and/or share with their own network. Furthermore, the page also drives traffic to the company's HIV disease awareness website.

**76%**

**... of social media crises were preventable.**

Source: the Altimeter Group.

"In the age of uncertainty, the best hope for organizations is to learn how networks operate, so that they can become more like networks themselves."

**Peter Hinssen**
**Thought leader, author and entrepreneur**

## 3. Energizing customers: social selling

This social practice focuses on identifying **influencers and advocates** related to your product, therapeutic area or services, and helping them become ambassadors of your company in the social media space.

As soon as your organization succeeds in 'talking' to customers and the initial phases of 'know-like-trust' (cfr. infra) are completed, the moving process towards 'energizing' the customers becomes more natural. 'Social selling' can therefore become a meaningful addition to the traditional sales process.

Social selling is built upon:

• **Listening and learning**: map out the relevant stakeholders for your disease area or drug. Determine which decision makers and which influencers should be targeted.

• **Word-of-mouth:** this is probably the oldest and most effective marketing channel out there and today it is still very much alive, especially in the online space. Initiatives such as TripAdvisor have become a daily part of our lives. Word-of-mouth can be stimulated through two marketing techniques: 'viral marketing' and 'social sharing'. Both are ideal to energize customers and turn them into ambassadors for your company.

• **Research**: once you have identified who would be an ideal ambassador, it is important to understand their aspirations and link these to 1) your content assets and 2) the solutions your business offers.

• **Engagement**: provide useful and relevant information to your ambassadors. Engage in conversations with your prospects to demonstrate your expertise and relevance.

• **Collaboration**: take the conversation to a different medium (email, phone, face-to-face, ...) when needed. Demonstrate continuity in delivering a real solution without being pushy.

• **Partnership building**: continue the conversation beyond the first recommendation. Build loyal customer relationships. Look out for up- and cross-selling opportunities.

> 'Marketing is no longer about the stuff that you make, but about the stories you tell.'
>
> **Seth Godin**
> **Marketing guru**

## Healthy snack

### The use case for setting up a LinkedIn community to energize customers

**The situation:** a leading medical device company already had a portal aimed at stimulating awareness among the medical community about the latest technological advancements in their core therapeutic areas.

**The challenge:** the company wanted to broaden the scope and reach of their awareness activities.

**The approach:** a closed community on LinkedIn was launched. Multiple objectives were set forth:
- Build thought leadership
- Engage with the target audience
- Facilitate peer-to-peer discussions
- Gain greater customer insights
- Detect product issues earlier

Besides active endorsement by the company's sales reps, LinkedIn advertising tools such as InMail and targeted ads were used to drive membership.

The following KPIs were used to monitor performance:
- Number of members
- Number of discussions (engagement)
- Number of insights generated
- Net Promoter Score (recommendation power).

**The result:** the LinkedIn group currently has over 145,000 professional members.

## 4. Helping customers: social support

In some cases, your strategy may not be aimed at getting patients to see a doctor, but rather to make it easier for patients to **connect with each other.** This can be very useful, particularly in an orphan disease context.

A good example of this is **PatientsLikeMe.com** ('making healthcare better for everyone through sharing, support, and research'). This patient support initiative was launched in 2005 by two brothers, Jamie & Ben Heywood, who wanted to create a support platform for patients. This is something that they felt was missing when another brother of theirs, Stephen, was diagnosed with ALS. The site has become so successful that it now has dedicated support communities for several therapeutic areas, many of which receive sponsorship from pharma companies. Besides supporting patients, PatientsLikeMe is also a great insights tool. In exchange for sponsorship, pharma companies get useful insights in the needs of patients, which allows them, in turn, to become more patient-centric.

**Pharma involvement in MD communities** - Rheumato EU5

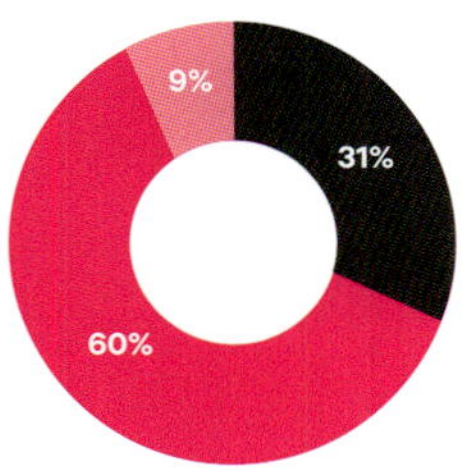


NO
YES, but pharma needs to declare itself as such
YES, and pharma can lead

Source: Navigator 3.0 2017, EU5 rheumatologists, N=371

> The ability to dictate the conversation with customers is fading quickly. Markets have transformed themselves into networks of intelligence, which behave under different rules and observe different behaviour patterns.
>
> **Peter Hinssen**
> **Thought leader, author and entrepreneur**

## 5. Embracing customers: crowdsourcing

In several instances, it pays to involve your customers in your innovation efforts. A well-known example outside of the pharma industry is that of Dell, which uses **the wisdom of the crowds** to continuously improve their products and services. Also in life sciences, more and more initiatives can be identified. A good example is that of Cancer Research UK, which turned to the public to help identify specific biomarkers in 2 million photos of breast cancer cells. Participants received a short tutorial before they began and 5 independent reviews were needed before an image was categorised. By crowdsourcing this initiative, Cancer Research UK saved a lot of time and money in progressing their research.

Gamification can be another way of involving the crowd. Eyewire, for instance, is a citizen science game aiming to map the brain. This human-based computation game challenges players around the world to map the neurons in a retina. There's absolutely no scientific background required so anyone can play. Over 200,000 people from 145 countries have participated. More than 150 neurons have been mapped, leading to new insights and even the publication of scientific papers. Eyewire has become the quintessential model of engagement in open science.

In recent research, HCPs have indicated that they are fine with pharma participating in communities, as long as they declare it transparently; 9% even states pharma can lead such online discussions.

## Social media marketing in action

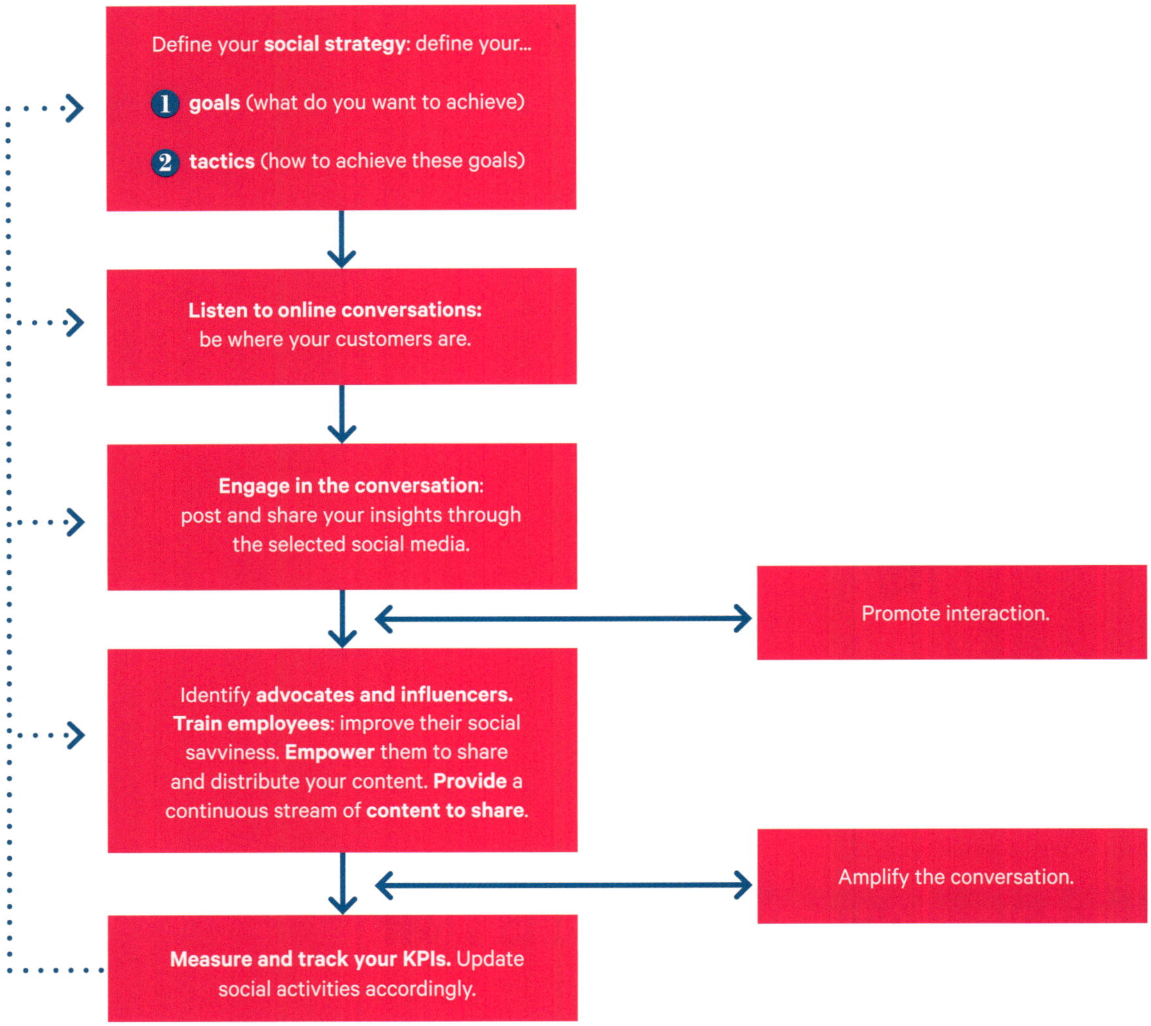

# Viral marketing

Through sharing, content can start to go **viral**. In his book 'Contagious: Why Things Catch On', Jonah Berger explains that **there is no wonder formula** to generate electronic word of mouth (eWOM). But following the **6 'STEPPS' principles** can take you a long way:

❶ **Social Currency**: we share things that make us look good. When you make people feel special and give them a feeling of being an insider, they'll tell others - spreading news of you by word of mouth along the way. This is why people brag about their thousands of Twitter followers, why golfers boast about their handicaps and key opinion leaders boast about their publications.

❷ **Triggers**: what is at the front of the mind gets talked about. If your brand is not at the front of the mind, see how you can be associated with something which is to spur conversation. For example, the flu or hay fever season can be ideal triggers if you are marketing a product in this context.

❸ **Emotion**: when we care, we share. **High-arousal emotions** like awe, anger and anxiety lead people to share. **Low-arousal emotions**, like sadness or contentment, are less likely to prompt sharing. So consider how you can package your content in an uplifting, emotional format. If you want to activate patients to share experiences about their disease, it is better to focus on positive emotions such as hope, support and daily functioning.

❹ **Public**: what we talk about and how we behave is influenced by what we see others do. That's why customer reviews are considered highly credible. Collecting customer reviews on your website may represent a challenge as these would need to be closely monitored. An alternative could be to add a 'star rating' to your key content items.

❺ **Practical Value**: useful things catch on and are spread. Your products and services are solving a problem, so highlight the usefulness of them in your content.

❻ **Stories**: stories are like Trojan horses and people of all ages relate to stories. That's why a great customer service story is better than any advertising.

The more aligned your content is to the STEPPS principles, the higher the chances of it being spread by word of mouth. But **predicting** this – and planning for it – is almost impossible. What goes viral is often very unpredictable. A content piece may even go viral years after its first publication.

# Social sharing

Social sharing is one of the most **influential and impactful** elements of social media. Research on social sharing by social marketing technology provider SocialTwist showed that out of a total of 3.2 million people who participated in a series of B2C social referral campaigns...

- 19% (600,000 people) became **influencers**, meaning they shared messages
- Each influencer reached on average **15 people**. A total of 9 million new people were reached via these social referral campaigns.

Although social referral is highly successful at reaching new people, **the conversion rate is still low**: of the 9 million new people reached through these referrals, only 3% (300,000 people) become paying customers.

As with any marketing tactic: combining multiple channels delivers the best results:

- 41.8 % of influencers preferred **Facebook** for sharing
- 55.4% of influencers preferred to share messages **via email**
- 85.1% of **new consumers** were reached via Facebook versus 12.4% for email. Hence, Facebook was more effective in reaching large numbers of people.

## Tip

### 1% The 1% rule

Social media is hugely important. Or isn't it? In the genre-defining book 'Crowdsourcing', Jeff Howe makes mention of **the 1:10:89 rule:** 1% of visitors will actively **produce content**, 10% will vote or like the content, 89% will simply consume it without real interactivity. Hasn't the web changed much then?

Looking at Facebook's 1.7 billion+ audience and their activity rate the web has definitely changed enormously. But likewise, not every visitor to your content will interact with it. Having 11 out of every 100 people react (by commenting, voting, liking) might already be pretty good. But it also makes clear that the 1% of highly interactive people might deserve some **extra special attention** from you.

The 1% rule also applies to European HCPs: only 3% are very active, and 20% active.

**Participation level in MD communities - Rheumato, EU5**

Source: Navigator 3.0 2017, EU5 rheumatologists, N=371

## Your 'know – like – trust' factor

In today's social world, it's important to build a networking attitude which encourages "sharing information in a reactive and proactive way without expecting anything immediately in return". This description may initially sound counterintuitive, but as you communicate with passive customers and prospects, knowing, liking and trusting comes before buying. It's about 'paying it forward'.

• The **Know factor**: what do people know about you? What is your background? How easily can you be found online and how is that information presented?

• The **Like factor**: people like other people who are helpful, kind and not pushy. So be willing to respond to questions and remarks without being overly commercial. Consider how you can help this person, before calculating how much money they can generate for you.

• The **Trust factor**: consider your trust equation in every conversation:

$$\frac{\text{credibility + reliability + intimacy}}{\text{self-orientation}}$$

• Credibility: are you a credible expert on the topic?

• Reliability: can people depend on you to do what you say you will do?

• Intimacy: can people trust your discretion and can they sense your empathy towards them?

• Self-orientation: is your focus primarily on yourself (or on your company) or on the other person? People have low trust in people that only care about themselves.

The 'know – like – trust' mentality is a crucial stepping stone to conversion.

> ‘All things being equal, people do business with, and refer business to people they know, like and trust.’
>
> **Bob Burg**
> **Business author & network expert**

## Customer communities

Customer communities are **interactive open spaces** where people can have conversations about your therapeutic area, products and services. Customer communities are always on and connect customers to...

1. one another,
2. your company,
3. the answers they're looking for.

As such, they're very strong **loyalty-building** assets, stuffed with relevant and trustworthy content.
With customer communities...

- Customers **help themselves**,
- **Conversations** happen in a more natural manner,
- **'Helping out'** comes before 'selling',
- **Market research** becomes continuous and real-time.

Customer communities complement your support centre and **improve efficiency**.

Customer community platform provider GetSatisfaction found that implementing a customer community helps to ...

- **Reduce the time** a customer care agent spends on a support call by 33% on average (a reduction from 6 to 4 minutes)
- **Handle more customer support requests** with the same staff.

Beware: maintaining a customer community takes effort. Customers will only visit the community if there is sufficient value – content and other customers – there to be found.

Another challenge is to get a critical mass of community members for engaging and frequently updated discussions to happen. In pharma, HCPs or patients also might be reluctant to have conversations on a platform that is owned by your company. That's why it might sometimes be better to just tap into a community initiative that is already out there and which is independent from your company.

A good physician example is Doctors.net.uk, a network of over 225,000 UK doctors, educating, interacting and collaborating together via clinical forums. For patients, the communities set up by several MS companies are excellent examples (for instance, the MS Gateway offering by Bayer).

"Our social tools are not an improvement to modern society, they are a challenge to it."

**Clay Shirky**
**Author of 'Here Comes Everybody: The Power of Organizing Without Organizations'**

# Policy or police

Develop a policy to ensure **consistent use of social media** across the company. Cross-functional participation–from executives, subject matter experts, sales, customer support, ...–generates more diverse insights and helps to extend your social media expertise. It also greatly enlarges your **social media footprint!** In most pharma companies, clear guidelines exist at global level on the use of social media.

Train and prepare **everyone within the organization** to use social media properly. The **'Always – Sometimes – Never' framework** can be a helpful starting point for training:

• **Always**-guidelines must be followed for every social media update. E.g.: 'always understand that your social media content lives forever', 'always support the brand'.

• **Sometimes**-guidelines are for instances that happen occasionally. E.g.: 'if wrong information about your brand is posted that is potentially harmful to patients, you can rectify it.'

• **Never**-guidelines are for posts that should never occur. E.g.: 'never provide medical advice and discuss off-label information or adverse events for your brands.'

Besides training, you must also provide **a clear policy**. Make sure these topics are covered:

1. Clarify that the policy is applicable to all multimedia, social networking websites, blogs, ... for **both professional and personal** use.

2. Postings should never **disclose** any information that is confidential or proprietary.

3. When people comment on the organization's business, they must **clearly identify themselves** as an employee.

4. When posting online, a **disclaimer** should be included clearly stating that "the views expressed are mine alone and do not necessarily reflect the views of [your company's name]."

5. Do not include **company logos** unless permission was given to do so.

6. Always respect **copyright**, privacy, fair use, financial disclosure and other applicable laws.

7. Always be respectful. Consider proper **netiquette**.

8. Employees should neither claim nor imply that they are speaking on the company's behalf. Only **authorized spokespersons** for the company can do that.

9. The company has the **right to request** that 1) certain subjects are avoided, 2) certain posts are withdrawn, and 3) inappropriate comments are removed.

A clear policy can help protect your organization, your staff members and your customers.

You should not only have clear policies for company employees. Clear rules of engagement should also exist for patients or physicians having discussions on your company-owned social media platforms.

Make sure that community members are advised not to discuss the following topics:

• product **side effects** and/or **adverse events**
• **off-label usage**
• **medical advice**
• **unbalanced product discussions** or product promotions.

## Tip

### Wikipedia

When people search for diseases or drugs, chances are high that Wikipedia will show up in the top 3 of Google search results. For many, patients and HCPs alike, Wikipedia is the go-to platform for health related information. 45% of European physicians use Wikipedia at least weekly. Nevertheless, it represents a challenge for pharma companies to make edits on their drugs and/or therapeutic areas. In most pharma companies, clear policies exist on doing Wikipedia edits. Should you consider doing this, it is good practice to work with a key opinion leader or independent scientific third party to guarantee objectivity and a well-balanced edit.

## Tip

### From off- to online

Social media is omnipresent in many people's lives and **offline experiences** increasingly find their way to social media. The conversation may start off in real life, but it can easily continue online. An increasing number of bad customer experiences are being voiced through social media. As an organization, **you always have to be ready** to react, quickly and openly.

# The maturity level of social media

While social media has become omnipresent in most industries, within pharma its usage remains limited. **Social media marketing** is a standard practice for only 19% of pharma marketers. Social media monitoring (capturing the sentiment of social media posts on for instance a therapeutic area) is a standard practice for 18%. Still, this low number is a missed opportunity, as the monitoring activities could be constructed so that they stay clear of the typical pain points of social media marketing.

## The adoption of social tactics by pharma

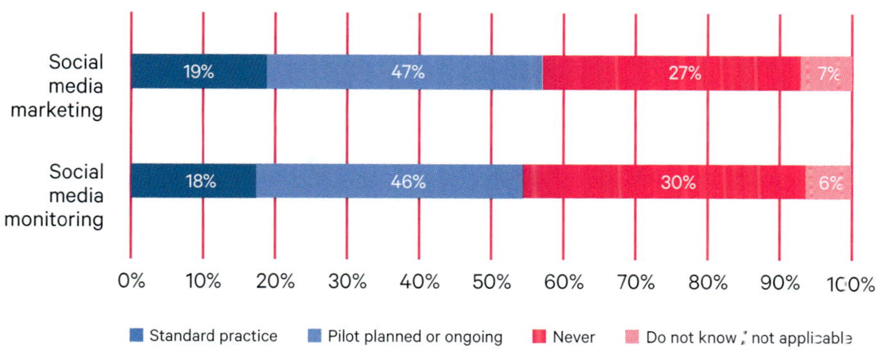


Source: The Across Health Multichannel Maturometer 2017 | N = 221 | EU scope

# Social Media: reach and impact in Europe 2017

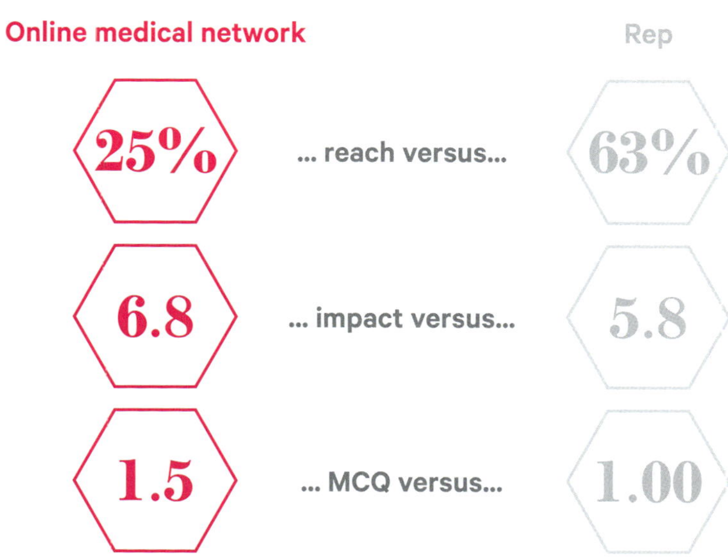


The Across Health Navigator studies the impact and reach of 57 off- and online channels amongst HCPs. From this, the multichannel equivalent (MCQ) is derived: a measurement of relative impact, which makes comparing between channels possible. Find out more on the Navigator data in chapter 1.

Source: The Across Health Navigator 2017 | N = 3,185 | EU5 scope (DE, ES, FR, IT, UK) | Specialists

## Tips for novices

> Marketing is about telling good stories. Social media marketing is about getting your customers to tell them for you.
>
> **Corey Eridon**
> **Marketer at HubSpot**

**Start small**: set up social media company accounts on the main social network sites. Join existing communities rather than trying to create your own community from scratch. Limit the number of channels based on your **available resources** (people and time) and **marketing objectives**. Only set up company pages when you are sure you are able to maintain them. It's better to manage your presence on 1 social website well, than to poorly manage 4!

**If you start on Linkedin**, start by building a company profile page. Add a ...

1. **Company overview and description**: describe clearly what your company does and how you can be reached.
2. **Logo + banner**: create an enticing banner that highlights what you do and what you're about.
3. **Careers page:** a strong employer brand can cut cost per hire by over 50%. Consider using rich media to strengthen your company's profile.
4. **Company updates**: let the world know what you're up to. Make sure to post relevant content, don't just toot your own horn. Post regularly! Make sure your own staff 'likes' and 'shares' your updates.

### Tip

#### Social by nature

**People are social by nature** and we have always forged relationships through communication. It's **impossible for humans not to communicate**: even when we don't say anything, we're communicating! Although the technology to communicate has changed dramatically throughout history, the human condition itself has not changed as quickly. **Basic human behaviour** continues to drive communication, also on social media. **Technology is just a means** to facilitate this communication. Social media is just a means to build stronger customer relationships, it's not an end in itself.

## Challenges of social media marketing

| Challenges ☹ | Solutions ☺ |
|---|---|
| **How to manage the breadth of social media marketing?** | • Assign a **conversation manager**: a dedicated **expert** who actively manages the different social media outlets and who **facilitates social adoption across the entire organization.** |
| **How to manage adverse events being reported on my brands?** | • **Monitor** what's being said about you and your products on social media. Set up flows for **prioritization** and always **react** in a **timely** manner. |
| **How to avoid sensitive discussions on Rx products, side effects, medical advice, etc.?** | • Whenever possible, inform customers of the **rules of engagement** before they start conversations on your social media initiatives. This can help in avoiding unwanted posts and it allows you to explain why certain posts might not get published afterwards. If you do restrict the topics that customers can address, it is good practice to inform them of the channels that are appropriate to discuss these issues. |
| **How to avoid employee conversations that are not aligned with your company objectives?** | • Most companies have clear policies on the use of social media by employees. It is important to **make employees aware** of this and train them. |

## To conclude

**So far, social media has not not been widely adopted in pharma. Social channels and networks, however, are not disappearing; they're only getting stronger over time.**

**A social media strategy is therefore key to ensure that it isn't just an 'add-on' or an afterthought. As a tactic, it should be integrated in your overall engagement strategy. You can create substantial leverage through social media. At the same time, because of its omnipresence, social media also challenges old-school silo-thinking in organizations.**

**Although not all social media activities have the same impact, by integrating them throughout the entire communications mix, social media can boost the reach and impact of your efforts and help you improve customer insight and engagement.**

> "The reality now is that more marketing messages are created by the public than by marketing departments."
>
> **Grant Leboff**
> **Author of 'Stickier Marketing'**

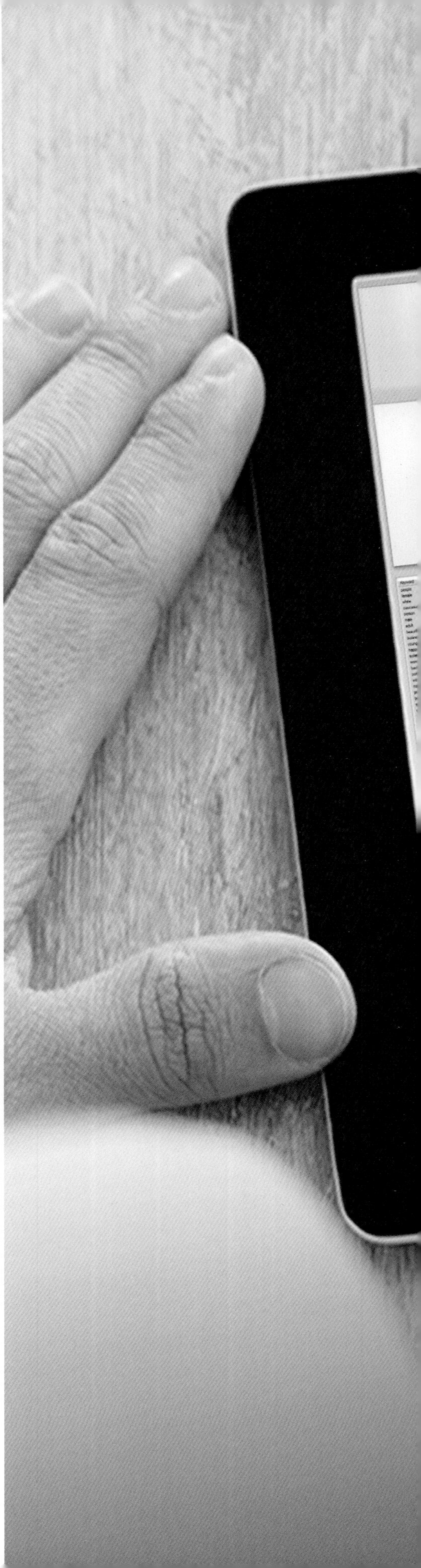

# 10 eMedical

"...there have never been better ways to reach the always-on HCP with medical education."

# eMedical: the next big thing for pharma?

While pharma marketers have quickly adopted digital, their medical affairs colleagues have continued to rely on traditional methods of customer engagement, including publications, congresses, scientific meetings and in-field MSLs. The increasing demand from HCPs to receive medical information "anytime, anywhere" combined with increased limitations on in-person congress attendance, as well as the interest of other stakeholders beyond prescribers, means the requirement for digital alternatives in medical education is rising rapidly. The arrival of 'disruptive' trends such as real-world data, wearables, sensors, advanced analytics and physician communities will further accelerate the strategic importance of eMedical programmes across the product life cycle.

> 'We are moving from 'share of voice' to 'share of science'.'
>
> **IQVIA**

## Medical & eMedical across the product life cycle

**Pre-launch**
The stage where medical education has the most impact. Multichannel medical education can be started during phase II/III to establish unmet needs, thought leader advocacy, a strong medical platform and the core scientific positioning of the product to maximise uptake at launch.

**Launch**
Maximize data and message dissemination for optimal product awareness, via the full range of multichannel vehicles.

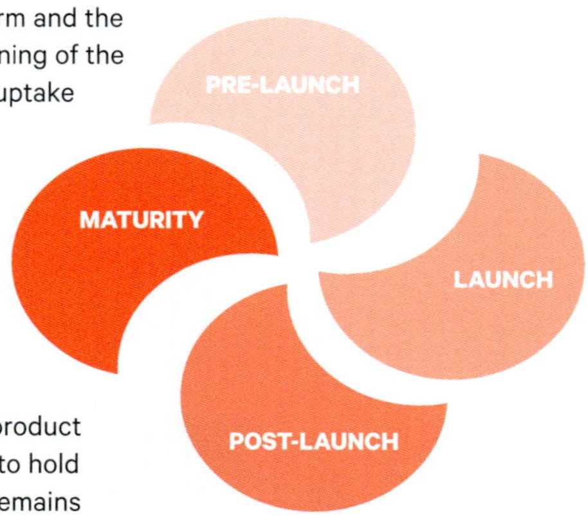


**Maturity**
As the life cycle of a product progresses, the need to hold on to early adopters remains while the importance of moving other stakeholders along the ladder of adoption increases. Digital can also support new clinical trials to pave the way for future indications, line extensions or formulations.

**Post-Launch**
Use educational initiatives to target a broader range of audiences, including nurses, GPs, pharmacists and other groups, all of whom have increasing influence on the prescribing and decision-making process.

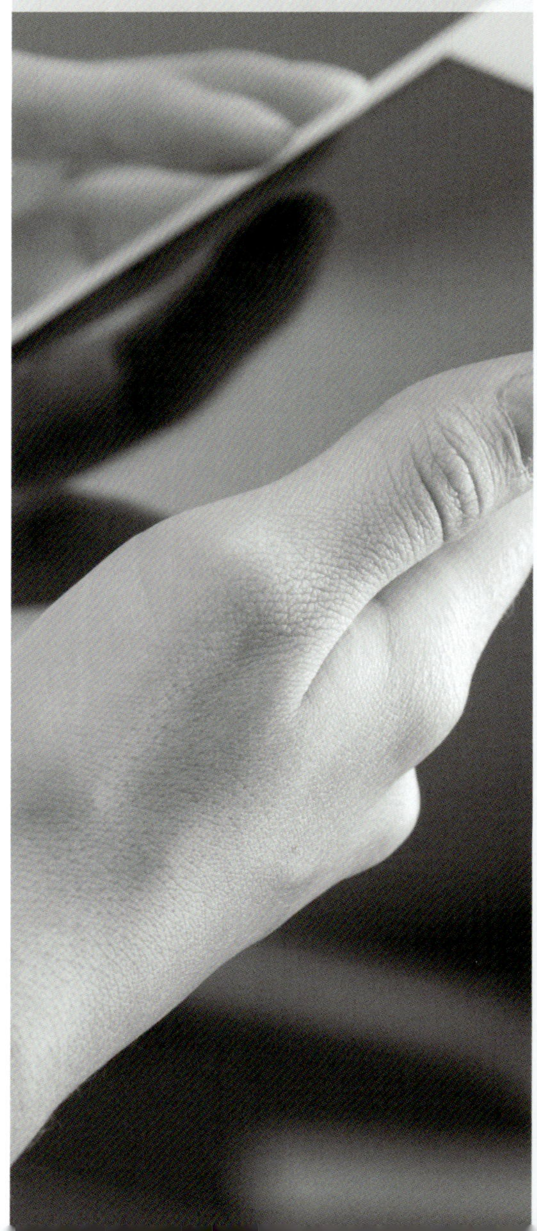

# The metrics of eMedical

**12.7%**
The average spend on digital by Medical Affairs in Europe (vs. 19% for marketing). (Source: Across Health Maturometer)

**20%**
The average reach of the top 3 eMedical channels in EU5 is only 20%, vs. 28% for the top 3 e-marketing channels. (Source: Across Health Navigator)

**50+%**
... of EU5 physicians prefer a mix of online & offline or purely digital medical offerings. (Source: Across Health Maturometer)

**77,494**
The number of tweets sent during ASCO 2016. (Source: ASCO)

**x2**
The number of virtual participants to ASCO 2016 doubled in only two years from 8K to over 17K. (Source: ASCO)

**12%**
... of pharma companies are offering e-MSL approaches to HCPs in Europe. (Source: Across Health Maturometer)

> ‘In the future, only companies that use real-world data to demonstrate superior outcomes for new drugs will generate attractive returns.’

Bain & Company, 2015

# The 'always-on' education seeking HCP

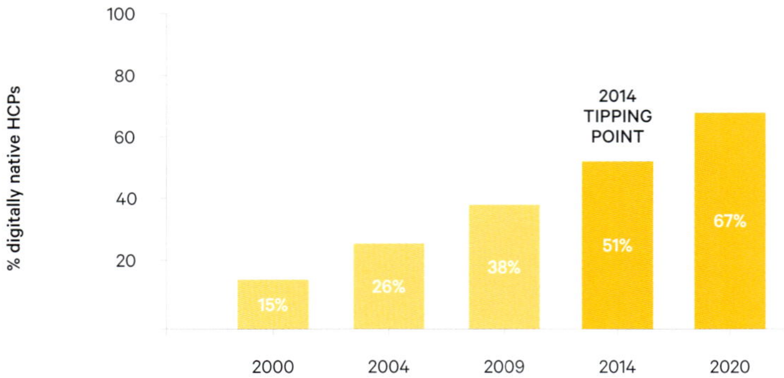


We are witnessing the rise of the digital native HCP – defined as those who completed their studies in the digital age. These HCPs have very specific learning requirements driven by their experiences through medical school and very specific channel preferences. Given that 67% of the total HCP population will consist of digital natives by 2020, we need to clearly understand how these new HCPs want to learn, assimilate the mountain of data and apply it effectively to benefit the health and wellbeing of their patients.

### Normalized channel reach by age group

| | WEBSITE | E-NEWSLETTER | TELEDETAILING | ONLINE MD NETWORK | WEBCAST |
|---|---|---|---|---|---|
| Digital native HCP Age <35 | -- | -- | ++ | ++ | ++ |
| Digital immigrant HCP Age 35-50 | + | - | - | + | - |
| Digital immigrant HCP Age >50 | + | ++ | -- | -- | -- |

Source: The Across Health Navigator

For example, we see that digital natives have a much greater affinity for newer, innovative channels such as webcasts, teledetailing, and HCP social networks; while older 'digital immigrants' are happy with email and the occasional static website page. Also, when you look at the time spent online for professional purposes there is also a clear cut-off at the age of 50yrs.

### Average minutes online per day for professional purposes

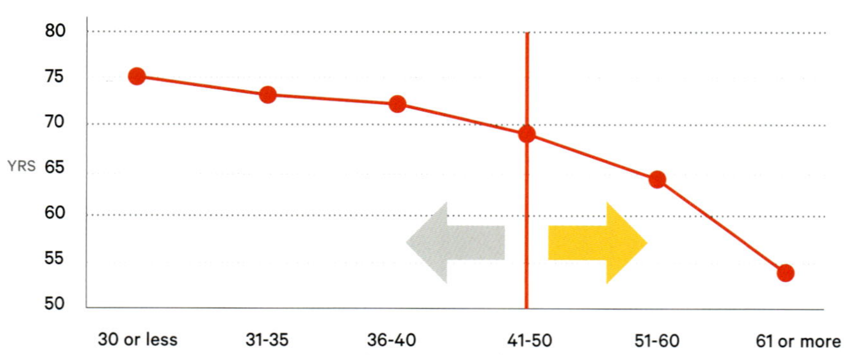


Source: Across Health Navigator EU5 SPEC; 2016-17; n = 1654

This trend continues when we look at the number of HCPs who would like to communicate digitally with pharma (the 'demand'), and the amount of those who already do (the 'supply'). We call the gap between these two numbers the 'digital divide', and there is a glaring difference when you compare digital promotional information and medical educational information.

### The digital divide

Digital divide = (% Preferring digital or mix) - (% ePharma reach)

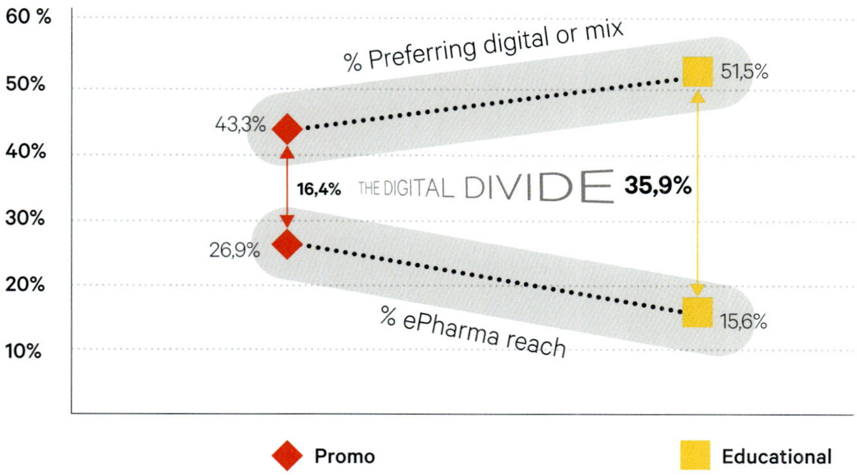


Source: Across Health Navigator EU5 SPEC; 2016-17; n = 1654

Looking at this by age group for EU5 specialists, you see the digital divide for education is high for all age groups, but highest for the youngest group. The promo divide, on the other hand, is much smaller for digital immigrants...
Hence, the opportunity for digital in eMedical is simply amazing...

### The digital divide by age group

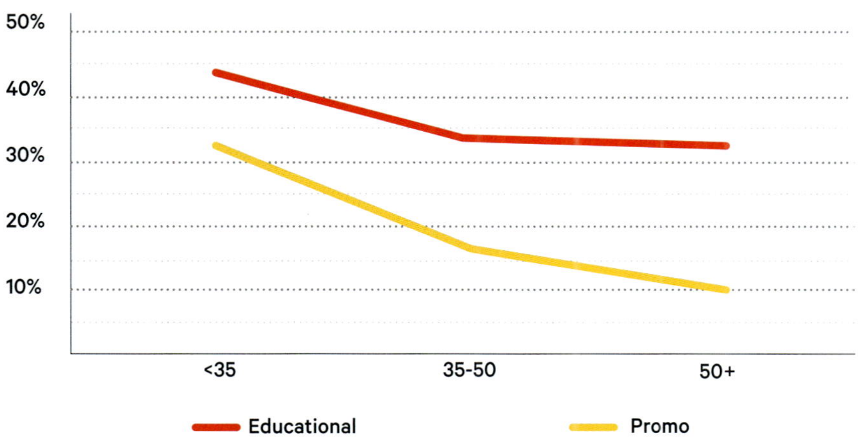


Source: Across Health Navigator EU5 SPEC; 2016-17; n = 1654

> 'Medical education must finally step up to meet the expectations of empowered patients, the needs of busy physicians, and the use of disruptive technologies'
>
> **Dr Bertalan Meskó, The Medical Futurist**

To better reach the always-on HCP, pharma needs to understand their information-seeking behaviour before engaging with them.

GPs and specialists access medical information at different times throughout the day (US, 2015):

| | Cardiology | Endocrinology / Diabetology | General practice and family practice | Internal medicine | Neurology | Oncology | Pediatrics | Psychiatry | Urology |
|---|---|---|---|---|---|---|---|---|---|
| Early morning (before morning hours) | 25% | 23% | 26% | 23% | 20% | 29% | 23% | 14% | 21% |
| During weekday office hours | 20% | 40% | 31% | 27% | 35% | 40% | 43% | 43% | 28% |
| **Evening (after office hours)** | **59%** | **69%** | **56%** | **67%** | **71%** | **59%** | **53%** | **58%** | **60%** |
| Weekends (during office hours) | 8% | 10% | 8% | 5% | 8% | 13% | 10% | 9% | 8% |
| Weekends (during time off) | 40% | 54% | 39% | 37% | 38% | 30% | 36% | 45% | 35% |

Source: CMI/Compass 2015

**Take home:**

1. HCPs are more than 3 times more likely to access medical information outside than during office hours.
2. Evenings are the most popular time for HCPs to access medical information, for instance educational webinars.
3. While HCPs access most of their medical information outside office hours, pharma tends to focus its efforts on HCPs during the day, which creates opportunities for multichannel.

# The maturity of eMedical channels

With around 43% of EU pharma leaders stating that **online medical education** and **webconferencing** are standard practice in 2017, and between 30–40% stating they are experimenting with these channels, the maturity level of eMedical is still relatively limited. However, the high proportion of planned pilot programmes indicates that these channels may be ready to make a big leap forward in the next few years.

The trend for e-MSL's is clearly just emerging, with only 12% of pharma leaders stating it is a standard channel and 39% saying they 'never' use it.

These findings are in line with the low reach of these 3 channels in the Navigator data. This illustrates the enormous potential of these and other eMedical channels going forward.

## The adoption of eMedical tactics by pharma

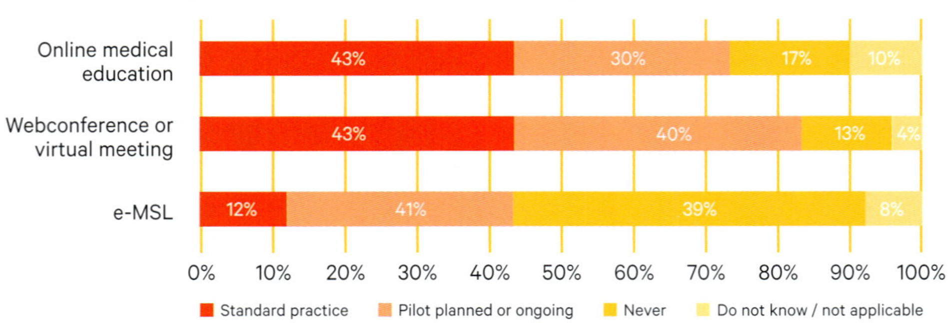


Source: The Across Health Multichannel Maturometer 2017 | N = 221 | EU scope

## Tip

### 3rd Third-party vs pharma-owned eMedical channels

Even more so than in marketing, medical affairs programmes tend to focus on **third-party channels,** as they are perceived to be **more credible** for physicians. Indeed, third-party channels, e.g. scientific websites, newsletters, online journals, and virtual congresses. have a stronger impact than pharma-owned medical channels, as the Navigator data consistently confirms with between 20% and 50% greater impact for specialists in EU5/US. In addition, pharma companies often do not have the required channel behaviour data for their customers (email address and digital affinity) to reach out to them directly.

However, in an omnichannel world, **both pharma-owned and third-party channels should be leveraged** to maximize reach, frequency, relevance and impact. For instance, third-party channels can be used to maximize reach and trigger customers to further engage with pharma-owned content or events (website, webinar etc.). In this way, the loop can be closed, follow-up (offline or online) can be given where appropriate, and individual customer journeys can be identified and acted upon.

# Virtual congresses

2014 was not only the year when **'digital natives' first outnumbered 'digital immigrants'** but also the year when the number of people virtually attending the European Society of Cardiology Congress outweighed those attending physically.

| | | |
|---|---|---|
| ESC Congress | **2013** | 17,567 virtual attendees |
| | **2014** | 25,178 virtual attendees (43% increase over 2013) vs. 24,622 physical attendees |

Why is this happening? Several factors explain the drop in physical attendance at congresses:

1. COST: the cost of hosting satellite symposia, exhibit booths etc. is going up.
2. REGULATION: HCPs are reducing attendance or speaking engagements at conferences, because of increasing compliance pressures; at the same time, pharma is inviting fewer HCPs.
3. DIGITAL-SAVVY HCPs: digitally native HCPs increasingly access medical events online – anytime, anywhere – while satisfaction with traditional medical congresses is dropping.
4. TECHNOLOGY: it has never been easier to attend a virtual meeting as software and broadband speed, robustness, and cost-effectiveness improve significantly year on year.

So what does all this change mean for tomorrow's medical congresses? Firstly, medical societies are quickly realising that their conferences are not the primary reference for new data/evidence that they once were. To maintain their prestige and revenue streams they need to change their model to provide year-long engagement, deeper personalised immersion and more opportunities for social and professional networking.

**There are 3 types of popular virtual congresses to consider:**

**1. Virtual congress highlights:** Platforms such as Vivinda TV allow HCPs to virtually access on demand and live congress sessions from home.

**2. Sponsored sessions held on the official congress platform:** Allows pharma to provide medical information microsites to all official congress portal traffic.

**3. Independent virtual conferences extending the physical experience:** Educational and promotional portals providing HCPs with virtual congress content.

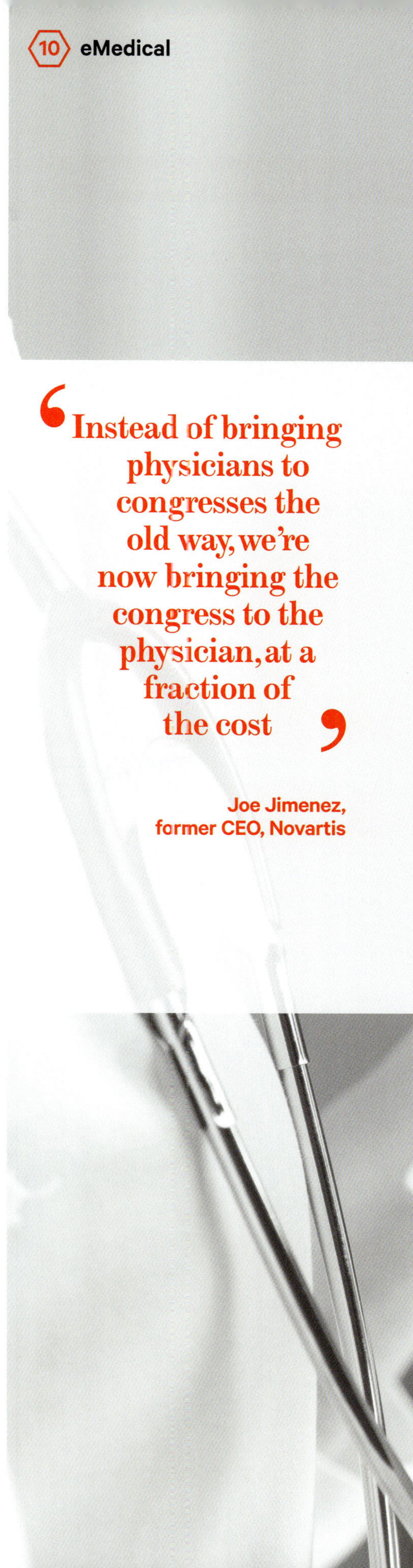

"Instead of bringing physicians to congresses the old way, we're now bringing the congress to the physician, at a fraction of the cost"

Joe Jimenez,
former CEO, Novartis

# Pharma webcasts

**Virtual meetings**, i.e. webcasts, webinars, and virtual symposia, present pharma with an excellent opportunity to not only deliver medical content but also build customer engagement as they can:

1. **extend reach** beyond the limited group of in-person participants
2. **increase frequency of contact**
3. **reduce cost** per engagement
4. **improve customer preference** (convenience)

However as the Maturometer & Navigator data show, pharma is not yet fully embracing this opportunity. In terms of practical steps, the following key elements are recommended for optimal eMeetings:

1. Get early buy-in from legal and regulatory on the concept and its approval requirements
2. Appoint an experienced project lead internally
3. Define target group and behavioural objective(s)
4. Select a robust platform vendor and an experienced content agency
5. Select compelling content aligned with the objective and consider whether CME accreditation should be added
6. Ensure speakers will allow their presentations to be put online
7. Define where the session(s) will be hosted (internal vs. third party)
8. Define and execute the cross-channel promotion plan
9. Follow a multi-channel, multi-week webcast reminder process
10. Agree on follow-up item(s) with delegates (closing the loop with MSLs/reps)

Next to – obviously – content and process, one of the often underestimated key success factors of virtual meetings is recruitment. A combination of third-party and pharma-owned recruitment channels is optimal, and the maximum impact is reached if both offline and online channels are used.

## Multichannel recruitment for webinars

‘If you broadcast it, they will not come.’

Once the recruitment process is finished, delegates need to be regularly reminded of the upcoming event, without spamming them.

The following multichannel event process has proven its robustness in recent years:

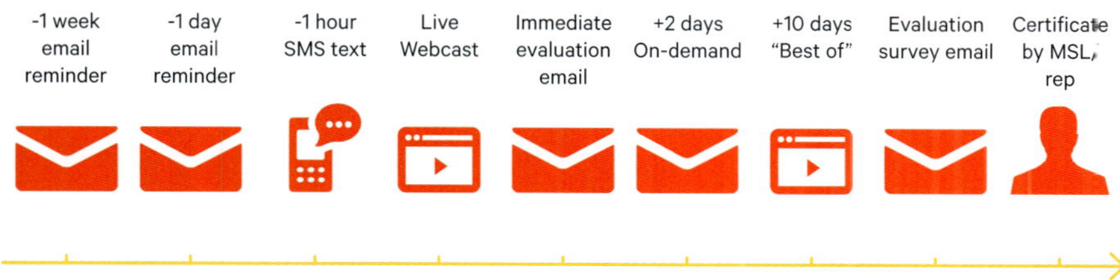


## Tip

### Time is money

There are good and less optimal moments to send out an invite or host an online session. Capturing this data can help you drastically increase the effectiveness of your programme. Test the timing of all your activities. A different time of day can mean a doubling in responses and participation.

The on-demand, or 'watch later', version is key to the reach of the programme, as this version often gets 50%+ of the total viewers. This should be taken into account beforehand, as the on-demand version may pose several regulatory hurdles (leading to long delays or even non-publication). The on-demand version should ideally also be shorter than the live one and allow viewers to go to sections relevant for them via 'chapterization'.

## How to maximize reach, engagement, conversion and advocacy for virtual meetings

### 1 Reach

**Registrations**

- Run recruitment and invitations internally and externally
- Invites should be signed off by the appropriate scientific committee
- Ensure registration is as easy/short as possible
- Leverage your database for future communications (e.g. reminders, new programmes)
- Maximise the cross-channel reach programme (acquisition, reminders, non-responders)
- Monitor views vs. registrations and follow-up with the no-shows
- Optimise timing around the best days and times for live broadcasts

**Viewers**

- Ensure you can identify your participants individually for follow-up opportunities
- Monitor the % of your target group who attended and boost if you can
- Make an on-demand version available immediately after the event
- Ensure your offering is compatible with multiple platforms and browser types
- Avoid platforms that require a plug-in download or other set-up complications

## ❷ Engagement

**Visit duration**
- Assess when participants drop out and apply these learnings for future programmes
- Ensure stated webcast duration is in line with expectations (around 30 mins. for live, 15-20 mins. for on-demand)
- Completes vs. starts
- Ensure content is in line with the objectives and participant expectations
- Continuously engage the audience interactively
- Test new experiences/formats regularly
- Consider 'incentives' at the end (e.g. CME, educational material)

## ❸ Conversion

**Number of calls-to-action (CTAs) completed**
- Ensure CTAs are clearly defined
- Ensure the CTA is compelling to participants
- Make certain the CTA can be accessed at all times

**Number of valid leads**
- Ensure colleagues have been briefed on how to execute the follow-up action
- Review the timeline and hand-over process to make certain follow-up actions can occur quickly

The trend towards webcasts and virtual congresses will only increase. 65% of EU5 neurologists say they will decrease their attendance of traditional congresses (Navigator 2017). Conversely, only 25% never attend virtual congresses.

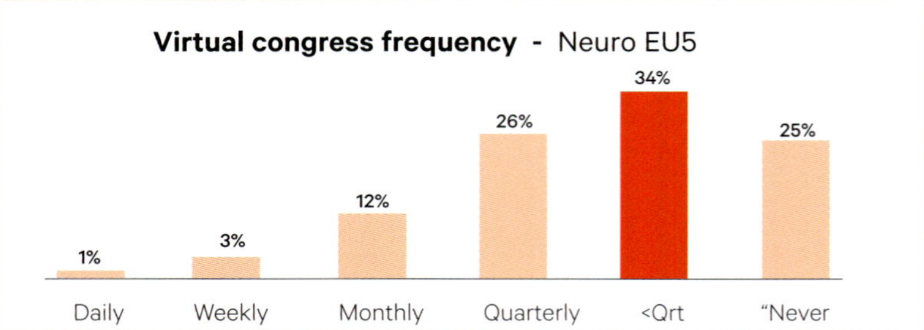


Source: Across Health Navigator 3.0 2017, EU5 Neurologists; 2016-17; n = 375

Importantly, the ideal length for EU5 neurologists is significantly below what currently is being offered: 15-30 minutes vs 1+ hour (see also the limit of length concept in the next section).

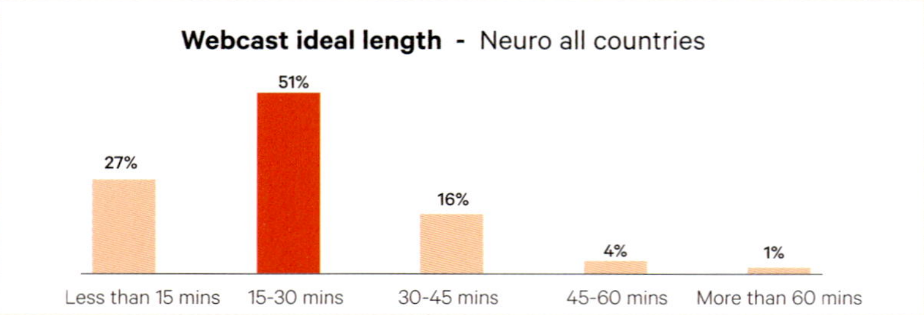


Source: Across Health Navigator 3.0 2017, EU5 Neurologists; 2016-17; n = 375

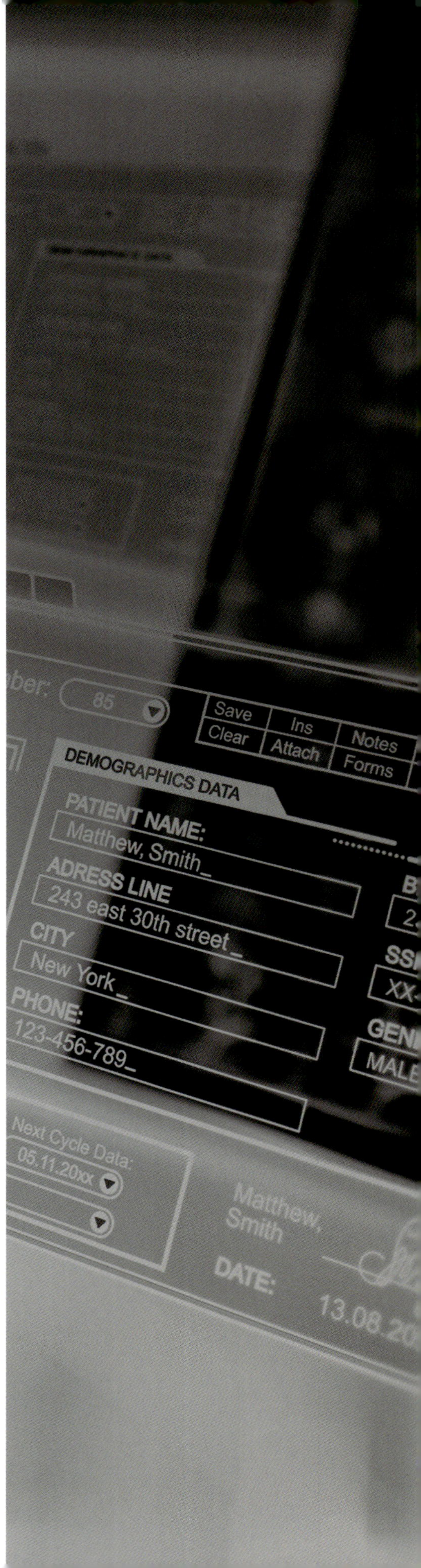

# The omnichannel MSL (eMSLs)

MSLs provide a very important service to HCPs, being **the main face of pharma at national scientific and medical education levels**. A survey conducted by the MSL Society in 2013 shows MSLs are involved in the following important engagement areas:

1. KOL relationship management
2. Attending medical conferences
3. Delivering scientific presentations
4. Educating KOLs/other healthcare professionals
5. Training/supporting the salesforce

(n = 275 MSLs, across 29 countries)

The MSL is seen as **a valuable resource** as they can quickly react to thought leaders' disease or product information needs. MSLs can also help with cascading global educational content down to local HCPs. In particular, they can invite local experts, determine the educational content needed and then help disseminate it.

As a result, the **reach of MSLs has rapidly increased** over the past couple of years, reaching 50% in Belgium, and over 20% in 4 out of 5 EU5 countries (IT, SP, FR, UK) (Across Health Cross-Channel Navigator 2017, SPECs; n =3661)

However, there is a clear opportunity to boost the reach and frequency of scarce MSL resources by leveraging digital channels. In Japan, the reach of an eMSL almost equals that of the MSL (23% vs 29%) - notably, Japan is also the country where remote rep activity is one of the highest in the world (1 out of 3 calls are done remotely there). And markets like Spain and Turkey also exceed this 10% threshold. Overall, though, this is still **an emerging field** at best. Importantly, HCPs value this kind of interaction highly - close to 50% of specialists want to engage with MSLs for a scientific or medical exchange via videoconference or call.

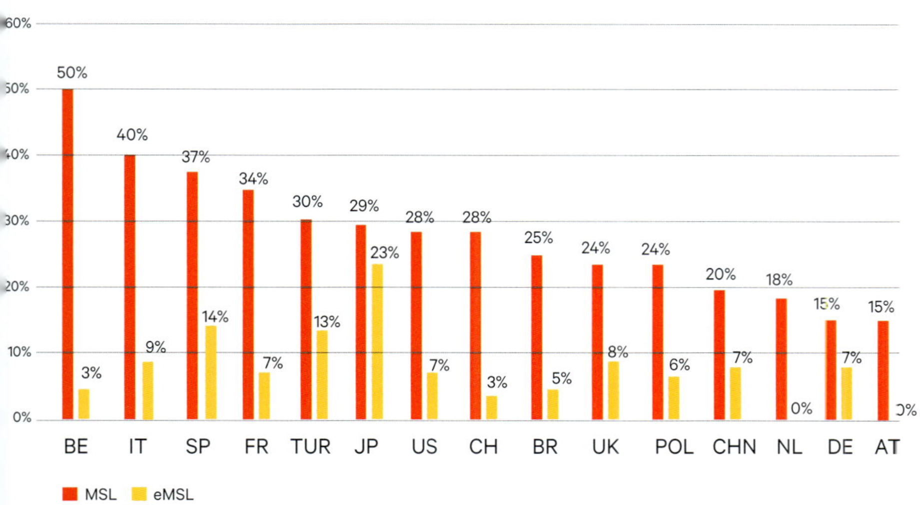


Reach of MSL and eMSL (Navigator 2017)

The Navigator data shows that pharma has been slow in adopting this new customer-centric approach (only 12% of the 2017 EU Maturometer respondents see it as standard practice, while 41% has a pilot planned or ongoing (N=221)). It is clear that eMSLs will create a robust competitive advantage and customer preference going forward, particularly in highly dynamic therapy areas like oncology and neurology.

**eMSL TIPS**

- Remote MSL (eMSL) calls should be an integral part of your multichannel strategy.
- Decide on whether a full eMSL service or hybrid approach is needed based on current resource availability and physician interest.
- Position the remote MSL (eMSL) service within the medical information section of the HCP self-service portal – using intuitive customer journey mapping.

**eMSL process**

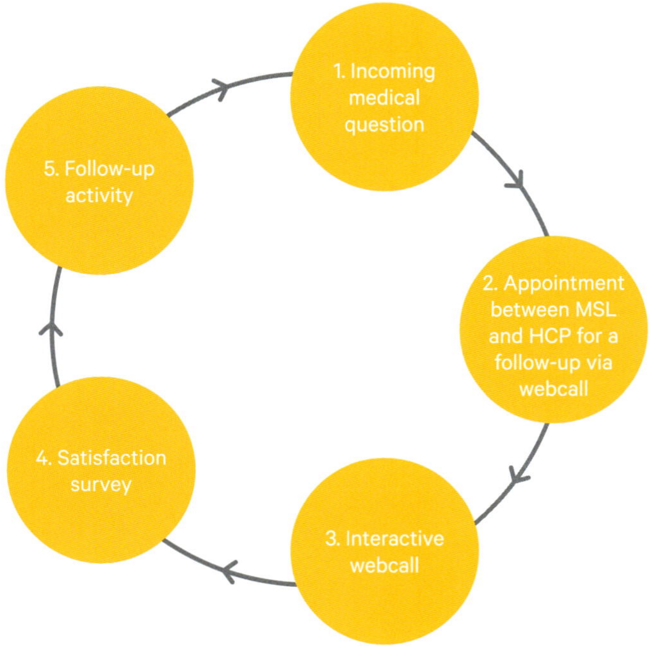


> ‘Implementing best practice is replicating yesterday. Innovation is designing tomorrow.’
>
> **Paul Sloane**
> **Author**

# What kind of educational content do HCPs prefer?

Digitization has made it so simple to search, retrieve, store, post and forward information, that we have ended up in a very curious situation. The amount of information customers get 'hit' with every day is staggering, the number of channels that 'aim' at them has exploded, yet the amount of information that they really 'digest' is shrinking.

**The limit of length = zero**

In what can be termed the 'attention economy', the problem lies in **getting and holding the attention** of information-overloaded customers. You need to grab their attention instantly and convincingly, not by presenting them with the full story straight away, but with short teasers. And these messages are getting shorter and shorter – from an executive summary, to an email, to a 140-character tweet, to an infographic/image, to...

As a result, the limit of length of messages is rapidly becoming zero in this attention economy.

**The limit of depth = infinite**

However, once you have the attention of the customer, their capacity to access digitized information is truly **limitless.** Wikipedia, Google, online communities, news websites, online journals... The solution is at their fingertips, anytime anywhere. So, the limit of depth is... infinite. The more companies can help to reduce complexity and enhance filtering and increase personalization once customers are "hooked", the more likely their message will be heard.

These limits also hold true in medical education, where supply is abundant, but very often **not adjusted to digital natives' interests**. Traditional multi-day medical congresses are often used more for networking purposes than for obtaining new insights (which customers can receive pre-congress or via real-time Twitter). The same applies to local scientific meetings and even to traditional webinars: the limit of length should more approach zero. So, rather than 1-hour long webinars, interest may be higher in short and focused anytime/anywhere sessions, with Q&A at the end (to fully leverage the depth of expertise offered by peers and presenter).

HCPs have needs for medical information relating to conducting their job, i.e. assessing, informing, treating and managing patients. Essentially, **they seek information to inform, and perhaps even influence, their medical practice on a daily basis**.

## Tip

### Attention span

The abundance of information and channels has caused a decrease in attention span. The average attention span of a person in 2012 was only 8 seconds. For comparison: the average attention span of a goldfish is 9 seconds. We used to read books, today we are bombarded with multiple messages every minute. Your message will only be noticed if it respects your customers' time!

> "Understanding and managing attention is now the single most important determinant of business success."
>
> **Thomas H. Davenport**
> **Data guru**

> "The problem is not information overload, but filter failure."
>
> **Clay Shirky**
> **Author**

Therefore, when planning your eMedical content strategy it is important to ensure the plan delivers information that meets the following essential content criteria:

1. **Findable** – make it easy for HCPs to find what they want, when they need it
2. HCPs have expectations of **truly interactive content** that allows them to dive deeper into topics
3. **Help HCPs stay up-to-speed** in a world of constant alerts to help them empower patients - engage them with the latest information in their areas of interest
4. **Help HCPs answer their questions** at the point of care
5. Physicians want **information on demand** that meets their evolving learning styles
6. Digitally native doctors have different expectations of content delivery – always consider how content can be 'multichannelled' to them

> 'People will give you their time and attention if you give them more of what they want.'
>
> **John Lavine**
> **Professor, Kellogg School of Management**

Also nearly all HCP surveys show that physicians prefer to read medical content that has been **endorsed by recognised leading therapy area experts**, and/or peers from within their network.

'Optimized content' means **creating relevant content** for **each target audience**. The more relevant the content, the more likely it will engage, inform and inspire to the level where it will be passed on to others, leading to higher engagement and advocacy. Additionally, relevant eMedical content meets both HCP need and medical strategy.

## Tip

### Some quick tips

- Make content easy and rapid to find – no complicated links or access details
- Include interactivity to deepen engagement and keep HCPs coming back
- Update medical information regularly so HCPs receive the latest information
- Provide options for HCPs to access content from experts/peer network
- Create various digital formats to suit differing learning styles

# Consider learning styles

HCPs, like all of us, have different learning styles. Similarly like us, they prefer to learn at different times of the day to suit their work and home schedules.

When seeking to disseminate medical content, it is important to consider that individual content items should form part of **an overall medical 'story'**. This 'story' will only be adopted and passed on to others if it is memorable. To optimize this memorability, it is important to consider that different HCPs will engage with educational 'stories/content' based on differing learning preferences. These are influenced by multichannel delivery, as indicated here:

| Left/right brain differences | Preferred learning styles | Multi-channel story adoption |
|---|---|---|
| 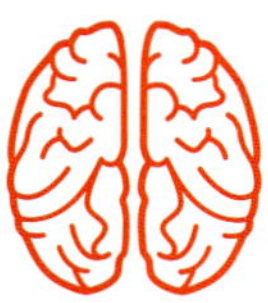 Analytical Creative | Kinesthetic<br>Musical<br>Logical<br>Visual/spatial<br>Naturalistic<br>Linguistic<br>Interpersonal<br>Intrapersonal | How we learn / How much we remember<br>5% Lecture<br>10% Reading<br>20% Audio-visual<br>30% Demonstration<br>50% Discussion in group<br>75% Practice by doing<br>90% Teaching each other |

Unsurprisingly, analysis into preferred medical information sources for HCPs also confirms they prefer to learn medical content in different ways – i.e. audio, visual, verbal, practice, through discussion.

**Learning preference take-aways:**

**Specialist-preferred content**

- Focused on guidelines, evidence, disease info, innovation/medical research
- Written summaries and presentations are important – can be delivered online
- Panel debates are popular for hearing clinical opinions
- Videos and case studies are popular for clinical procedures and innovations

**GP-preferred content**

- Prefer summarised, concise information for all areas of education
- Case studies popular, video content less so (this is more difficult to consume during working hours)
- Barriers & myths type content also popular
- Multi-page pharmaceutical material unlikely to be read

This shows the vital importance of not adopting **a "one size fits all" approach** when creating eMedical programmes. Indeed, applying insights into the variation of information preferences when designing future eMedical plans and campaigns will secure maximum retention, adoption and advocacy.

When all HCP preferences for times, content and formats are brought together, an eMedical campaign can be created that reaches HCPs both inside and outside working hours, is engaging and memorable, and leads to 'customer loyalty' and onwards advocacy.

## Tip

### The RIBS test

Caryn Marooney, Head of Technology Communications for Facebook, advises people to test the stickiness of their content with the RIBS test (i.e. does it stick to your 'ribs').
Is your story...

- **R**elevant (is your company solving a problem they care about?)
- **I**nevitable (is your content part of a trend? Does it make intrinsic sense to the audience?)
- **B**elievable (is your content credible?)
- **S**imple (what is the one line you want your audience to remember?)

# Healthy snack

## HCP archetypes and their educational preferences

**To get a clearer picture of the evolution of the HCP landscape, we also need to look at the relationship they have with Pharma. A good lens is McKinsey's Archetype segmentation.**

**INDEPENDENTS**

- Do not place much value on interactions with pharmaceutical companies
- Rely on evidence-based materials
- Tend to be slower to try new medication

**TRANSACTIONALS**

- Only value samples from pharmaceutical companies
- Cost conscious
- Most receptive to patient's preferences
- Tend to be slower to try new medication

**KNOWLEDGE SEEKERS**

- Interested in educational programmes offered by pharmaceutical companies
- Do not value informal talks or samples
- Least receptive to patient's preferences
- Tend to be early adopters and pro-pharma

**RELATIONSHIP SEEKERS**

- Look forward to interactions with reps and pharmaceutical companies, and other clinicians
- Value samples and education from pharmaceutical companies
- Tend to be earlier adopters of new medication

Source: McKinsey's Archetype segmentation model & Across Health Navigator 2016-2017, n = 1654 EU5 Specialists

When we look at the preferences of HCPs over time, we see a clear trend throughout the EU. The conservative, fact-based 'independents' as well as 'knowledge seekers' are on the rise, and together comprise over 65% of all EU specialists, while the traditional target group, the rep-friendly 'relationship seekers' are generally in decline. While this is probably not in itself a huge surprise, this has a profound effect on how the industry should think about sharing data and information.

For instance, while conservative independents do not place much value on pharma interaction but rely on evidence-based materials from third parties, knowledge seekers hold educational programmes provided by pharma in high esteem. As the blend of archetypes changes, so should the blend of channels and content.

# Overall medical MCM/content tips

- Create **various digital** formats to suit different HCP access times and learning styles
- Produce content that is concise, easily adaptable to format variation, **interactive**, and **engaging**
- Clearly define **objectives** from medical strategies and patient pathways, align content with these
- **GPs** prefer shorter summarised/ concise information across all areas of education
- Develop a range of **measureable KPIs** for different medical channels
- **Specialists** prefer guidelines, evidence, disease info, innovation, case studies and panel debate
- Make sure content is **relevant** – i.e. it meets both HCP needs and medical strategies
- Seek **expert endorsement** of content where possible and appropriate

# How to measure eMedical programmes?

A key benefit of an eMedical programme is the ability to measure a **range of KPIs across different channels** to judge overall outcomes.

Areas of eMedical activity measurement include:

**Quantitative** (reach & cost-effectiveness)
- Via web analytics: #contacts, #open rates, #click-throughs, #downloads, #views, #questions received, #viral mentions,...
- Cost/reach/channel

**Qualitative** (customer engagement and conversion)
- Via online (or offline) surveys: net promoter score (NPS), medical message clarity and endorsement, intent to change behaviour, ...
- % of audience engaged
- Cost/engagement/channel

# eMedical: reach and impact in Europe 2017

| eMedical education | Webinar | eMSL | | MSL |
|---|---|---|---|---|
| 17% | 22% | 9% | ... reach versus... | 32% |
| 6.2 | 6.1 | 6.3 | ... impact versus... | 6.5 |
| 1.19 | 1.16 | 1.24 | ... MCQ versus... | 1.38 |

The Across Health Navigator studies the impact and reach of 57 off- and online channels amongst HCPs. From this, the multichannel equivalent (MCQ) is derived: a measurement of relative impact, which makes comparing between channels possible.
Find out more on the Navigator data in chapter 1.

Source: The Across Healtl Navigator 2017 | N = 3,185 | EU5 scope (DE, ES, FR, IT, UK) | Specialists

## To conclude

True cross-channel medical strategies remain rare in pharma. This is despite the increased need for medical education, the 'digitisation' of HCPs, the arrival of massive and continuous real-world product and treatment evidence, and the reduced effectiveness of traditional medical channels.

To fully take advantage of the opportunities presented by eMedical, senior management buy-in is necessary, as is boosting digital skills and budgets. In addition, a rigorous approach to eMedical planning should be undertaken, which takes into account a clear understanding of HCP preferences for content, channel & context (such as access times and devices). Knowing which channels perform best within each therapy area can make an enormous difference to the performance and measurability of the overall medical education strategy. It also allows for a faster, fuller and richer cascade of information from global KOLs to regional & local KOLs, and ultimately to the prescribers and referrers who may change their medical practice.

Importantly, there is a real risk of siloed customer engagement approaches in pharma. Marketing, sales, medical education and medical information may all develop 360° strategies in isolation, resulting in sub-optimal disease education and product adoption by key decision makers. Although regulatory barriers are sometimes real, it is important to approach strategy formulation from a customer perspective rather than a (siloed) company perspective.

This co-ordinated, non-siloed, effort will not only boost customer engagement and preference but also optimize internal resource efficiency. If this is combined with fact-based planning and execution at scale, leveraging a mix of pharma-owned and third-party channels, and including continuous measurement, then fully digitized eMedical programmes will quickly become core components of successful launches and growth strategies in life sciences – all whilst delighting customers.

> 'Does marketing come from Venus and medical from Mars?'

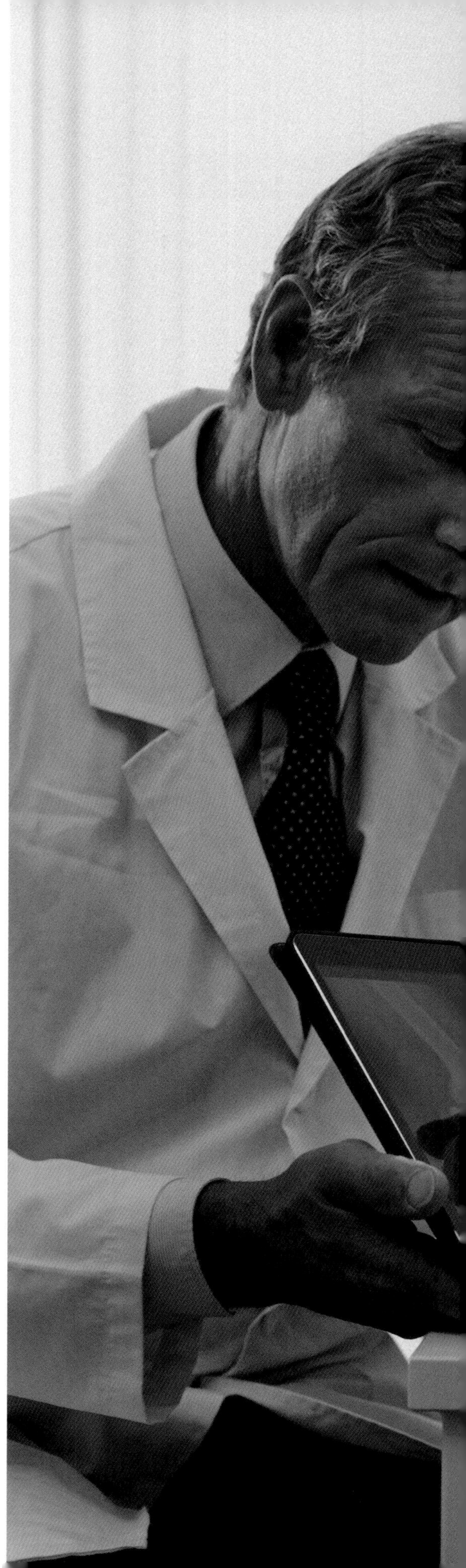

'… customer centricity along the patient journey.'

# 11 Patient-centric Multichannel Engagement

## Welcome to the age of the empowered patient

The weather is changing for pharma, as the industry moves away from its sole focus on HCPs towards a more diversified landscape with multiple stakeholders. Increasingly, attention is also directed towards nurses, pharmacists, payers and... patients. Thanks to the wide availability of information online, patients are much more empowered today than ever before. This is only going to accelerate with the increasing availability of real-world patient data and the explosion of web-based diagnostics and self-tracking devices. In fact, according to EY (Progressions 2017), the patient will become the most important stakeholder, followed by payers - and only then specialists and GPs.

Although the call for 'more patient centricity' has been heard for many years now, truly patient-centric approaches are still limited in pharma.

According to the WHO, increasing the effectiveness of patient support may have a far greater impact than any improvement in specific medical treatments. Despite that, today, an estimated 95% of budgets in pharma is still being spent on finding the next patient, while only 5% is spent on them after they have been found.

> ‘Patient engagement is the blockbuster drug of the century.’
>
> **Leonard Kish**
> **Health IT strategy consultant**

## The metrics of patient centricity

**85%** ... of pharma companies plan to increase their investments in patient-centric capabilities over the next 18 months. (Source: Across Health Maturometer)

**23%** ... of pharma companies are currently running patient adherence programmes, with another 40% planning a pilot. (Source: Across Health Maturometer)

**36%** The pharma industry misses out on 36% of potential sales because of a lack of patient adherence. (Source: Capgemini)

**73%** ... of pharma marketers identify a lack of ownership (i.e. the identification of a single dedicated person within the company) as the biggest hurdle for realising patient-centric initiatives. (Source: Accenture)

**41%** ... of patients are interested in support programmes from pharmaceutical companies. (Source: Across Health Patient Navigator)

**39%** On average only 39% of US HCPs are aware of patient services from pharma. (Source: Accenture)

## From pharma 1.0 to pharma 3.0

Over a decade ago, the focus of pharma was on **blockbuster drugs for primary care** (pharma 1.0). However, as a result of reduced growth in key markets, decreasing R&D productivity, patent expiry and squeezed margins, the focus shifted to diversified drug portfolios, emerging markets and more tailored commercial models (pharma 2.0).

Over the next 5 years, it is expected that the focus will shift again, this time to health outcomes, with focus on patients and payers. Combined with an exponential growth in technology, this will fuel pharma's next evolution (pharma 3.0).

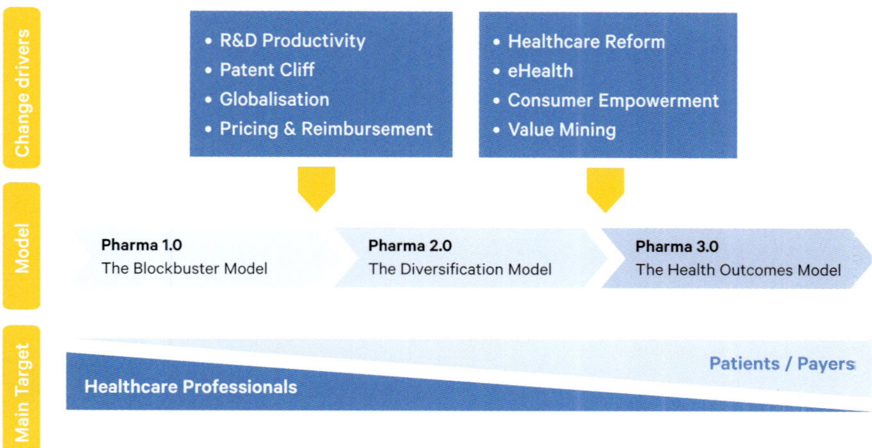


Source: EY - Global pharmaceutical industry report: Progressions Pharma 3.0

> *We spend around 95% of our budget on finding the next patient and probably less than 5% after we found them.*
>
> **Gary Walker**
> **Sr. Director Customer Innovation at Eli Lilly**

## Healthy snack: Patient Awareness

**The situation: A major pharma company wanted to increase patient awareness of migraine prevention options in a small European country, in support of a new indication for a drug.**

**The challenge:** To increase the number of patients seeking prophylaxis for migraine from their HCP, and the number of HCPs willing to prescribe it. However, there were two operational challenges:

- Migraine headaches have been traditionally treated acutely (ie, after their manifestation)
- The product was well known for another (totally different) indication, mainly with specialists

**The approach:** To develop the key message that it is possible to prevent migraine headaches, a number of different approaches were taken – with the aim of reaching all stakeholders at the same time (patients/carers, pharmacists and HCPs) – the so-called "triple marketing approach".

Firstly, a patient activation website was set up which contained disease awareness education and interactive tools, primarily for patients/carers (but which could also be used/recommended by HCPs and pharmacists). It contained questionnaires and quizzes which helped patients identify if they suffered from migraine, as well as whether prophylaxis would be appropriate for them. It was also possible to download a 'migraine calendar', which could help during discussions with their HCP.

To maximize qualified traffic generation, the website was supported by

1. banner advertising (both dynamic and normal, static banners) on popular health portals and women's magazines (the key audience)
2. search engine advertising (see Chapter 3)
3. PR: a broad-based 'migraine day' campaign, using newspaper, television and radio, with a focus on migraine prevention and the campaign website

Secondly, for HCPs, alongside the rep visits, direct mailings were used BEFORE the campaign started, providing information on the campaign as well as on migraine prevention. This would ensure full awareness and acceptance from HCPs when patients would refer to the campaign or migraine prevention during a visit. The same DM campaign was used to inform pharmacists.

**The results:**
Over a period of one year, there were 80,000 unique visitors to the website, and 30,000 quizzes were taken. Additionally 26,500 patient-oriented migraine calendars were downloaded. From an HCP perspective, 15% of GPs and 33% of pharmacists requested further information from the direct mail outreach. Finally, there was widespread media coverage, with 100% of radio stations and 70% of newspapers in the country, as well as the medical press, covering the benefits of prevention vs the more common acute treatment.

# 3 angles to patient-centric engagement

There are 3 angles pharma companies can take to become truly patient-centric:

1. Open innovation/health-tech partnerships
2. A 360° holistic patient view
3. Outcome-based healthcare

### 1. Open innovation/health-tech partnerships

Many pharma companies are exploring partnerships with non-traditional healthcare partners to bring—mainly technological—innovation into their traditional business model. This implies a shift from providing merely drugs to **'beyond the pill' thinking**. Value to patients must be provided by improving the management of their condition, and being omnipresent at all important touchpoints along the patient journey.

Some examples:

- Teva reinforced its leadership position in respiratory by acquiring Gecko Health Innovations.
- Roche formed an alliance with Voluntis to co-develop mobile-enabled therapies for breast cancer.
- Roche also bought oncology data provider FlatIron Health, and diabetes management platform mySugr.
- Boehringer Ingelheim formed a partnership with Propeller Health to help patients with respiratory diseases manage their conditions.

### 2. A 360° holistic patient view

True patient-centricity unites 3 key areas:

- **The patient journey:** a deep understanding of the patient journey and the important touchpoints in patients' everyday lives is crucial. It allows pharma companies to better understand where they can play a role in providing extra value to patients.
- **The patient experience:** good channel affinity insights can provide a more tailored experience to patients by reaching them through the channels they prefer.
- **The patient value delivered:** not all patients have similar needs. Hence, advanced patient segmentation is needed so that the tools and services that truly deliver value are available for the right patients.

To accomplish this, **centralised data management** will be necessary to gain a holistic view of patients.

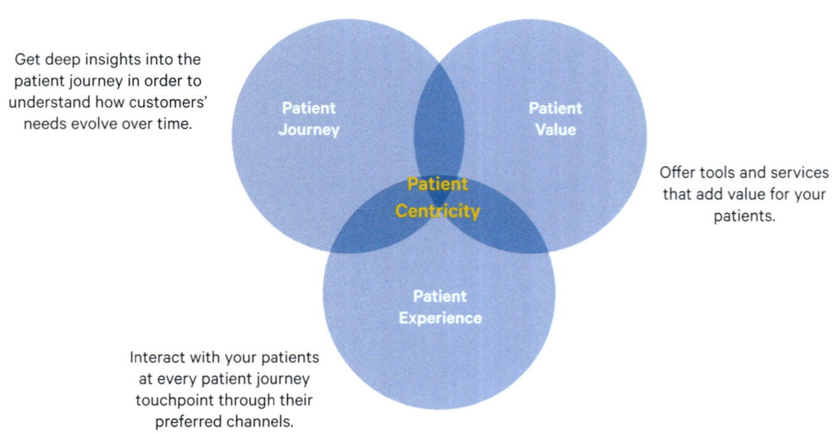

### 3. Outcome based healthcare

The rise of electronic medical health records (EMR) and the explosion of wearables, remote tracking devices and self-diagnostic tools, will enable payers to collect real world data that is clinically meaningful. It will become possible to monitor large patient populations and get deeper insights into the effectiveness of drugs.

Derived from this, it is expected that payment models will switch **from volume-based to value-based**.

| Open innovation/ health-tech partnerships | 360° patient view | Value-based healthcare |
|---|---|---|
| • Rapid prototyping (learn from technology peers)<br>• Outside-in, open approach (combine the competencies of multiple companies)<br>• Flexible control (quick response to new challenges and opportunities)<br>• Portfolio management (learn from each other) | • Execute MC strategies and use analytics for future decisions<br>• Centralised data management for a holistic view of the patient<br>• Flexible segmentation that can change according to market conditions<br>• Integrated campaign management to reach customers through their preferred channels with one-to-one messaging (MC surround sound)<br>• Realtime reporting to integrate learnings in the campaign cycle | • Switch from volume-based to value-based payment<br>• Reward models based on cost savings<br>• Big integrated patient data: ability to measure improvements in quality that are also clinically meaningful |

Source: Disrupting the Model - Patient Centricity. Pharmavoice

# The patient journey: starting point of patient-centricity

The figure below reflects **the patient journey in pharma**, from the moment a patient experiences first symptoms to receiving a diagnosis and staying adherent to a treatment regime.

When looking at the patient journey closely, a first observation is that **the patient is the dominant stakeholder**. In more than 50% of the stages, patients are either in control of or are influencing the journey. This is counter-intuitive to where pharma spends the majority of its budget today, being HCPs.

A second observation is that the journey requires companies to step back from a treatment focus (from making the correct diagnosis to brand choice), towards **a disease management focus**. This means omnipresence in helping patients (and their carers) manage their disease, from the moment the first symptoms arise, to (re-) evaluating the treatment outcome. One way to achieve this is by **establishing partnerships**. This could be done with both traditional healthcare partners, such as hospitals and patient advocacy groups, but also with non-traditional players such as health technology providers.

A last nuance is the fact that not all patients have similar needs for the management of their disease. Advanced **patient segmentation** will be needed to create a seamless omnichannel, patient-centric experience, including differentiated messages and services.

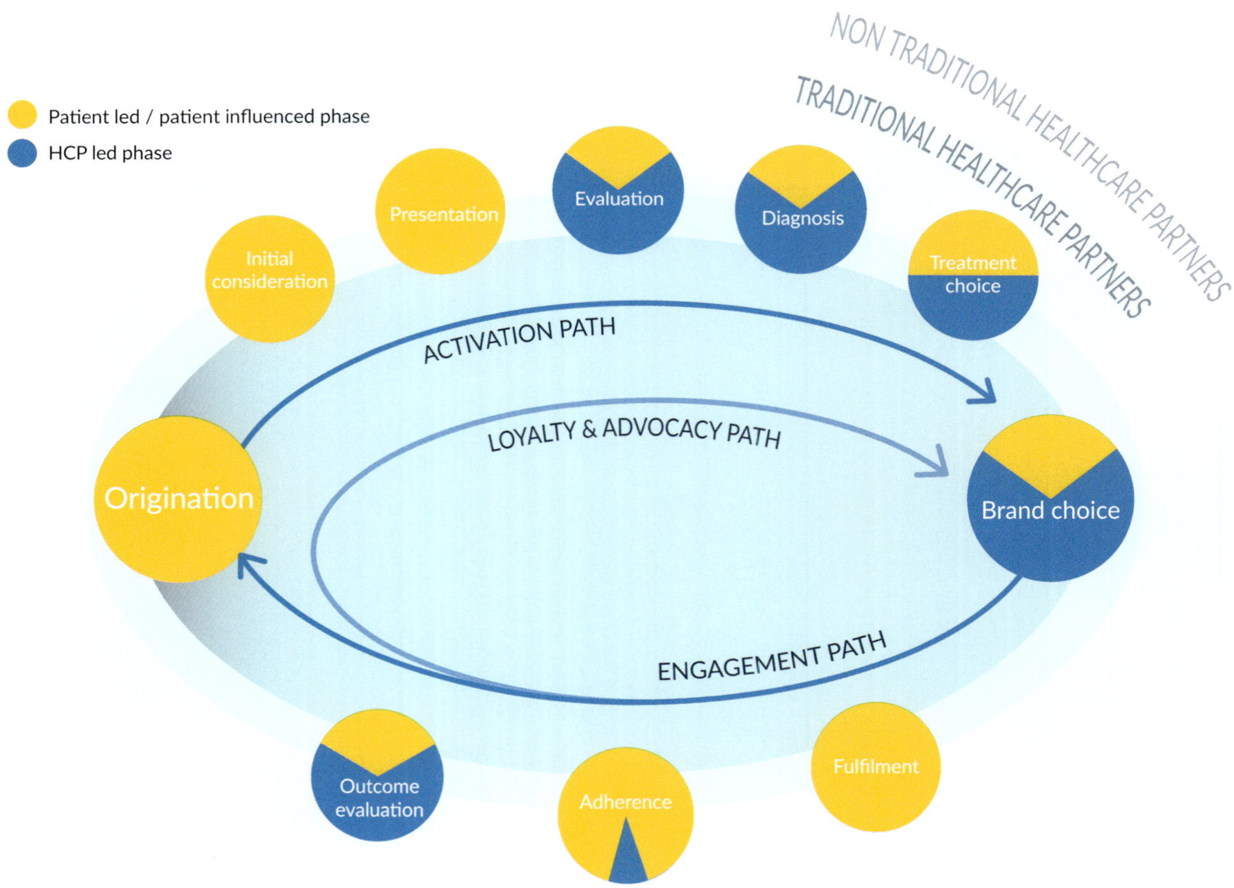


*The Patient-Centric Engagement Model*

# One size doesn't fit all: the importance of patient segmentation

No two patients are alike. So the better you can tailor your efforts to your specific patient (sub-)groups, the higher your chances of delivering a valuable experience.

A good starting point is the use of a **validated patient segmentation** model, like the one developed by Bloem and Stalpers (Nyenrode Business University and Johnson & Johnson).

Their model measures the subjective health experience of patients with a chronic disease based on 2 dimensions: their level of **disease acceptance** and **disease control**.

From these 2 dimensions, **4 patient segments** can be derived with different needs and expectations when it comes to the management of their disease, as illustrated in the model below.

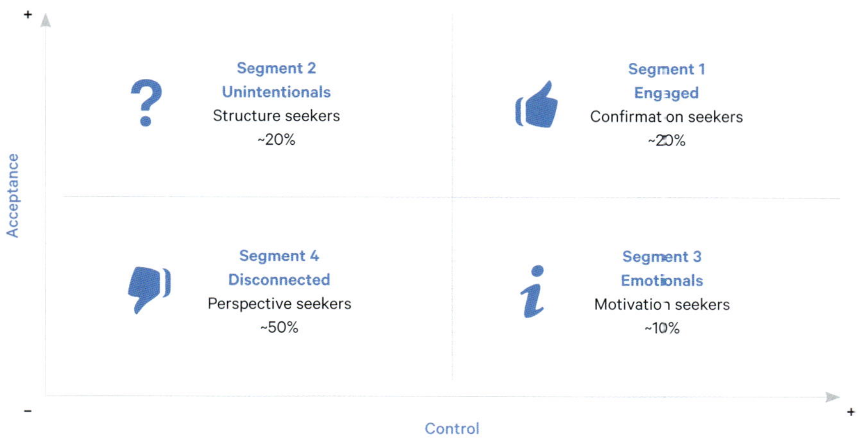


**Segment 1: Engaged (high acceptance – high control); average segment size ~20%**
This segment is characterised by patients who are managing their disease relatively well. It is the most adherent segment. What these patients are mainly looking for is **confirmation** that they are doing a great job and **additional information** related to the medication they are taking and/or disease they have.

**Segment 2: Unintentionals (high acceptance – low control); average segment size ~20%**
This segment is characterised by patients who in general accept their disease, but have issues with structure and planning. The type of outreach that resonates well with this segment are tools that help to **build a medication routine** (e.g. SMS medication reminders) or tools that help to **provide structure** in the management of the disease and the daily life (e.g. check-up reminders, condition tracker tools, ...)

**Segment 3: Emotionals (low acceptance – high control); average segment size ~10%**
This segment of patients considers their disease as their **enemy**. They struggle to accept it. What they mainly need is **motivation** to better manage their disease. When developing a programme for these patients, this should mainly contain **emotional support**, which could be personal in the form of e.g. a nurse, but also in the form of tools such as goal setting exercises. This segment also benefits from tools that help to improve or facilitate the relationship with their doctor/nurse.

**Segment 4: Disconnected (low acceptance – low control); average segment size ~50%**
This patient segment tends to be the least adherent of all segments and is characterised by patients who are **looking for perspective** when it comes to the management of their disease. Patients in this segment are best helped by someone who can **coach** them and who provides **personal guidance** and **a sense of hope**. In general, this segment also has a suboptimal relationship with their healthcare provider. Tools or services that help to improve this could also be beneficial.

The interesting thing about this segmentation model is that there is **a correlation between the way patients experience their health and their level of adherence**. The higher the level of acceptance and control over their disease, the better their adherence.

As a consequence, patient support programmes that demonstrate a segmented progression for enrolled patients, have a high probability that these patients will also show better adherence levels. You can measure this by repeating the same segmentation questions at different time intervals throughout the programme, with a baseline measurement at the time of patient enrolment. The segmentation questions are listed below.

## The patient segmentation questionnaire as used in the Bloem & Stalpers model

Patients only need to answer 6 questions in order to be allocated to one of the 4 segments. It is important that these questions are presented to patients in a random order on a 7-point scale ranging from 1 (= fully disagree) to 7 (= fully agree).

**The measurement of disease acceptance**

*Q1. I am at peace with how my health condition is.*
*Q2. The way in which I am functioning physically and mentally is acceptable to me.*
*Q3. I accept my health condition the way it is.*

The cut-off point for this dimension is 5.333 (average score (Q1+Q2+Q3)).

**The measurement of disease control**

*Q1. I have the feeling that I have a grip on my health condition.*
*Q2. My health condition is to a great extent in my own power.*
*Q3. I have a substantial amount of influence on my health condition.*

The cut-off point for this dimension is 5.666 (average score (Q1+Q2+Q3)).

# Reasons for non-adherence

One of the most common reasons why patient support initiatives are set up, is poor adherence levels. Unfortunately, as there is not one single cause of non-adherence common to all patients, it is not a simple problem to solve.

The table below provides an overview of the different factors that can play a role in patient adherence:

| Therapy | Patient | Healthcare System | Condition / Disease | Cost | Socio-Economic |
|---|---|---|---|---|---|
| Drug effectiveness and tolerability | Inability | Health system: team-related | Level of disability | Reimbursement related | Demographic variables |
| Side effects | Inadequate knowledge of disease and treatment | Access to providers | Perception of seriousness | | Lack of effective social support network |
| Previous treatment failures | Forgetfulness | | Symptoms | | Cultural beliefs |
| Frequent changes in treatment | Health beliefs | | | | |
| Duration of the treatment | | | | | |
| Complexity of the treatment | | | | | |

Source: Patient adherence: the next frontier in patient care. Capgemini.

Furthermore, adherence can be quite **dynamic** over time and the reasons might vary according to the patient segment you are dealing with. Initially, patients may 'drop out' because they are afraid of side effects, while later they might drop out because they stop experiencing symptoms and feel that medication is no longer needed.

## Case study: reasons for non-adherence for Type 2 Diabetes patients

In a recent study, Across Health looked at the reasons for non-adherence by Type 2 Diabetes patients (T2D).

A total of 200 T2D patients were surveyed and the Bloem & Stalpers segmentation model was applied. Next, reasons for non-adherence were investigated at treatment initiation and after some time.

Reasons per segment are listed in the figure below:

### Validation / Information
### Segment 1 – Engaged

**At the start:**
- Lack of trust in physician
- Complexity of treatment
- Side effects

**Longer term:**
- Clear improvement of condition
- Doubts about effectiveness
- Forgetfulness

Acceptance = high
Control = high

### Structure / Planning
### Segment 2 – Unintentionals

**At the start:**
- Lack of involvement in treatment
- Side effects
- Forgetfulness

**Longer term:**
- Side effects
- Forgetfulness
- Clear improvement of condition

Acceptance = high
Control = low

### Motivation
### Segment 3 – Emotionals

**At the start:**
- Clear improvement of condition
- Side effects
- Doubts about effectiveness

**Longer term:**
- Clear improvement of condition
- Doubts about effectiveness
- Side effects

Acceptance = low
Control = high

### Guidance
### Segment 4 – Disconnected

**At the start:**
- Side effects
- Forgetfulness
- Self-blame

**Longer term:**
- Forgetfulness
- Side effects
- Not compatible with lifestyle

Acceptance = low
Control = low

# Healthy snack

## Roll-out of an automated 6-month Type 2 Diabetes patient support programme

**The situation:** a leading pharma company wanted to create a tailored support programme for type 2 diabetes patients.

**The challenge:** get as many patients as possible on the programme. Questions to be answered at the start included:
- How to maximize patient enrolment?
- What should be the ideal length of the programme?
- What type of content and services should we offer, assuming that not all patients have the same needs?

**The approach:** the company opted for a multi-stakeholder recruitment approach. Not only relying on physicians to enrol patients, but also actively using pharmacists, who got a notification when they fulfilled a prescription of the drug.

Patients could also self-enrol online by means of a barcode on the packaging of the medication or use a call centre. The latter was included to support the enrolment process as the patients' average age was 55+ and some had difficulties enrolling themselves.

At enrolment, patients were asked to answer the 6 questions from the Bloem & Stalpers patient segmentation model in order to better understand their needs and tailor their support experience. Patients who decided not to fill out the enrolment questionnaire were entered into a default support programme.

A 6-month fully automated support programme was set up, including differentiated messages, tools and services, tailored to the specific needs of each patient segment. A couple of default channels (such as email, SMS, website) were included for all segments, but, on top of that, some specific channels (like remote nurse support, disease magazines, ...) were added for the segments where the biggest gains in adherence could be made.

A baseline measurement was made at the time of enrolment. To measure the impact of the programme, there were 3 feedback moments at month 1, 3 and 6 respectively. During these feedback moments, the same 6 segmentation questions were asked to measure the progress in the way patients perceived control and acceptance over their disease. Furthermore, an adherence scale was used and satisfaction questions were added to see if patients would recommend the programme to other patients.

**The high-level campaign overview:**

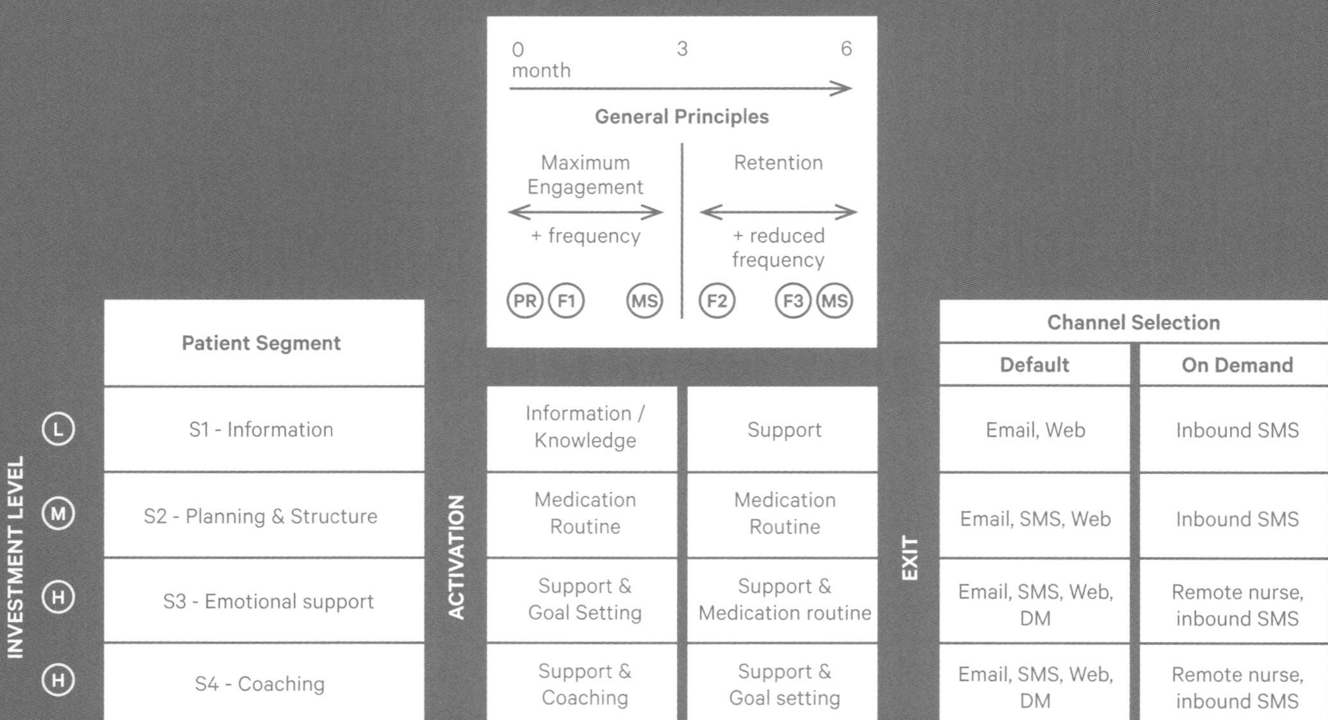


H = High, M = Medium, L = Low

PR = Product Info
F = Feedback Mechanism
MS = Message Reminder for Checkup

DM = Direct Mail

# Measuring the impact of patient programmes

Pharma companies that want to position themselves as truly patient-centric need to **find the right balance between patient value, scientific innovation and financial profit**.

A good framework for measuring the impact of patient initiatives is illustrated below:

| | Direct (channel-related) effects | Indirect (outcome-related) effects |
|---|---|---|
| Communication effects (qualitative) | **Q2 – Engagement**<br>- Likeability<br>- Knowledge improvement<br>- Attractiveness<br>- Channel satisfaction<br>- Ease of enrolment<br>- ... | **Q3 – Conversion**<br>- Morisky (self-reported adherence)<br>- Evolution of wellbeing<br>- Net promoter score (NPS)<br>- ... |
| Behavioural effects (quantitative) | **Q1 – Reach and Advocacy**<br>- % patient recruitment<br>- Number of responses<br>- Number of inbound calls<br>- Web activity<br>- Click-through rate (CTR)<br>- Viral referrals (word-of-mouse)<br>- ... | **Q4 – Cost and return**<br>- Medication adherence ratio<br>- Cost effectiveness<br>- Sales and MS change<br>- ... |

Patient focused KPIs    Commercial KPIs

## Tip

### Optimal length of a patient support programme

In a chronic disease context, research indicates that **the biggest drop-off** (on average 33%) is to be seen **during the first 3 months after treatment initiation**, with a further decrease of up to 50% within the first 6 months. As a result, the highest impact of patient support programmes can be expected within the first 6 months after treatment initiation for most chronic diseases.

A starting point are the quantitative metrics in quadrant 1, which can be directly derived from communication channels. In general, these metrics can be measured quite easily through tools such as Google Analytics. They provide good insights about the **reach**, number of **interactions** and **advocacy** of programmes. Examples of such metrics are: the number of patients enrolled in a programme, response rates on the channels that are deployed, number of patients sharing content with others, website activity, ...

The next quadrant (2) looks at **engagement**. As is the case for quadrant 1, these metrics can also be directly derived from programmes themselves. The only difference with quadrant 1 is that, in this case, qualitative insights are collected such as the ease of programme enrolment, likeability of programmes, improvement of patient knowledge levels, etc. This type of information can be collected through **feedback surveys** at regular time intervals throughout a programme.

Quadrant 3 looks at the **qualitative outcome or conversion** of programmes. In order to measure the outcome, it is advised to start with a baseline measurement at the time of enrolment. KPIs that could be considered in this case are the Net Promotor Score (NPS), which measures the extent to which patients are willing to recommend a programme to other patients, and the Morisky-scale, which measures self-reported adherence. When the Bloem & Stalpers patient segmentation model is applied, a good KPI is 'the evolution of wellbeing'. By asking the 6 **segmentation questions** at regular intervals, the level of acceptance and control of individual patients can be measured, as well as whether they move from one segment to another over time. This is a strong indicator of improved functioning and adherence.

> "Everyone assumes this is sort of a soft science, but we can measure patient activation just as rigorously and scientifically as other things in health care."
>
> **Judith Hibbard**
> **Senior Researcher**
> **University of Oregon**

When the KPIs in quadrant 1, 2 and 3 evolve positively, it can be expected that eventually, commercial KPIs will also be positive. This is seen in quadrant 4. In general, when patients are more adherent, not only will there be an increased prescription fulfillment ratio, there will also be an indirect effect on brand equity as health outcomes improve. As a result, both HCPs and patients will likely have **a more positive perception** of your brand. An alternative way of looking at business impact can also be through the lens of cost. By looking at the cost per supported patient over time, the economic viability of the programme could be assessed and fine-tuned: programme length and/or channel choice can then be adjusted.

## The patient-centric organisation: key dimensions

Making patient-centricity the focus of the organisation requires a fundamental transformation from how pharma companies are organised today.

Four dimensions should be taken into account to embed patient-centricity in the organisation.

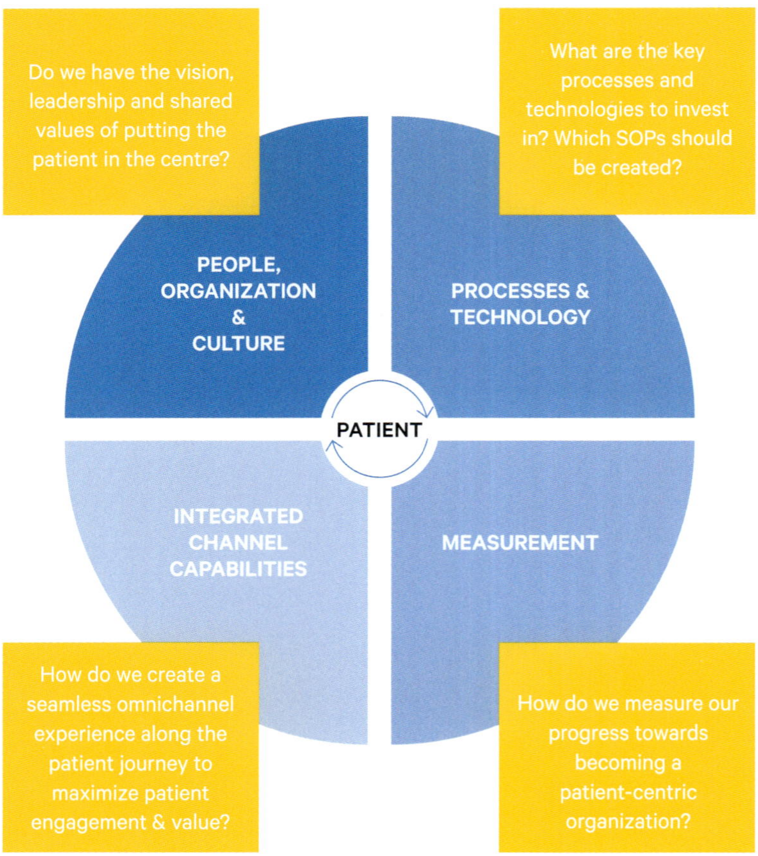

**People, organisation & culture**

Any patient-centered organisation should start with a **patient-centric leader** who pushes the patient agenda and identifies the right resources to truly embed a patient-centered culture. For example, by setting up reward systems that look at the patient value created instead of the number of rep interactions.

As many functions in the organisation are directly or indirectly affected by patients, cross-functional collaboration, rather than silo-thinking, is required.

Another good practice is to put the patient at the top of the pyramid; start by identifying the needs of patients and then work your way down by translating these needs into concrete objectives for every layer in the organisation. Start with the layer that is directly in contact with patients.

**Processes & technology**

In order to get a **360° holistic view of patients**, the technology that allows centralised data management needs to be in place. Just as many companies are centralising their HCP data collected through different channel interactions, the same needs to happen for patients. For compliance reasons, collecting identifiable data on patients may present a challenge, but it could still be worthwhile to collect aggregated data at the patient segment level as a basis for further improvement of patient offerings. In addition, it is worthwhile to look into "digital therapeutics" software platforms, which are focused on enabling behavioural change leveraging MCM concepts (Pear Therapeutics, Omada Health, Evidation Health, ...)

**Business processes** too need to be redefined. For example, it's possible to set up **incentive schemes** for commercial staff around patient satisfaction as opposed to only financial targets, or centering service design around patients rather than vice versa. An example of this is a remote patient monitoring programme **that better informs HCPs** about how they should treat patients, and as a result improve patient outcome.

**Integrated Channel capabilities**

Patient-centricity requires a deep understanding of the patient journey and its most important touchpoints ("moments of truth", or MoT) where pharma companies can really make a difference. It is much more than just hiring a market research agency to map the journey. It requires real, direct and regular interactions with patients to get a deep understanding of their needs and expectations, and how pharma can meet and exceed these. Virtual patient focus groups are an efficient way to get in contact with patients. Also, social media listening can help to regularly get an unbiased opinion on how patients are managing their disease and to uncover their key pain points.
It also requires a differentiated communication mix. Not all patients have the same needs and expectations. Therefore, it is important to segment patients. Some patients might benefit from personal coaching sessions, while others may simply need a planning tool that reminds them to take their medication. The Patient Navigator—a quantitative assessment on the reach and impact of 40+ patient channels, developed by Across Health—can help create the right communication mix for each patient segment.

**Measurement**

A good way to measure how patient-centered a company is, is through the selection of a few KPIs per measurement quadrant, to ensure a balanced set of leading and lagging, qualitative and quantitative metrics (see above).

## Tip

### Chief Patient Officer

To emphasize the fact that the patient is becoming a much more important stakeholder overall, some pharma companies have assigned a chief patient officer (CPO). One of those companies is UCB, which also created 'patient value teams'. These cross-functional teams are built around a therapeutic area, and ensure **the patient's voice is being heard**.

Impact measurements of these teams is threefold:

- Are they offering relevant services for the patient?
- Are customers satisfied?
- Is employee engagement high?

## The Patient Navigator: a quantitative channel mix assessment tool

The Patient Navigator 3.0, developed by Across Health, assesses the reach, impact and frequency of 40+ channels on the health decision-making processes of patients with a chronic disease. It compares the impact of different channels to the impact of a GP visit

The research looks at the full channel spectrum, taking into account both on- and offline channels, as well as owned, paid and earned channels. Furthermore, the Bloem patient segmentation model is implemented, providing detailed information on channel needs by segment. In addition, it looks into emerging areas like health tech and digital therapeutics, as well as preferred content, 3d-party destinations and offers extensive company benchmarking.

The Patient Navigator is a robust tool for optimising the communication mix towards different patient segments.

# The maturity level of patient-centric engagement initatives

Apart from the traditional disease awareness website, pharma companies haven't yet widely adopted patient-centric tactics. While many 'talk' about it, few actually 'walk the talk'.

- **SEO/SEA**: today, only 37% of companies are optimising their websites to be more visible in search engines. And only 1 out of 3 companies is actively engaging patients via search engines. That's surprising, knowing that search engines are by far the most frequently used channel by patients when it comes to making health-related decisions. Even when experiencing their first symptoms, patients are likely to search online prior to seeing a doctor.

- **Social media**: a good way to collect patient insights in a spontaneous way is to listen to what patients say about a disease online. Although there are a great variety of tools available to monitor online patient discussions, less than 1 in 5 companies is actually making use of them.

- **Patient compliance / adherence tools**: one way to improve the outcome of treatments, is by ensuring that patients adhere to treatment guidelines. Tailored support programmes can be of great help here, although only 23% of companies are executing these programmes today. Nevertheless, it is promising that 43% are planning pilots in this space.

- **'Quantified self', self-tracking devices** and **remote patient monitoring** are further ways to capture even more accurate patient data, but hardly any pharma marketer currently deploys these tactics as standard practices (3% and 5% respectively).

## The adoption of patient centric tactics by pharma

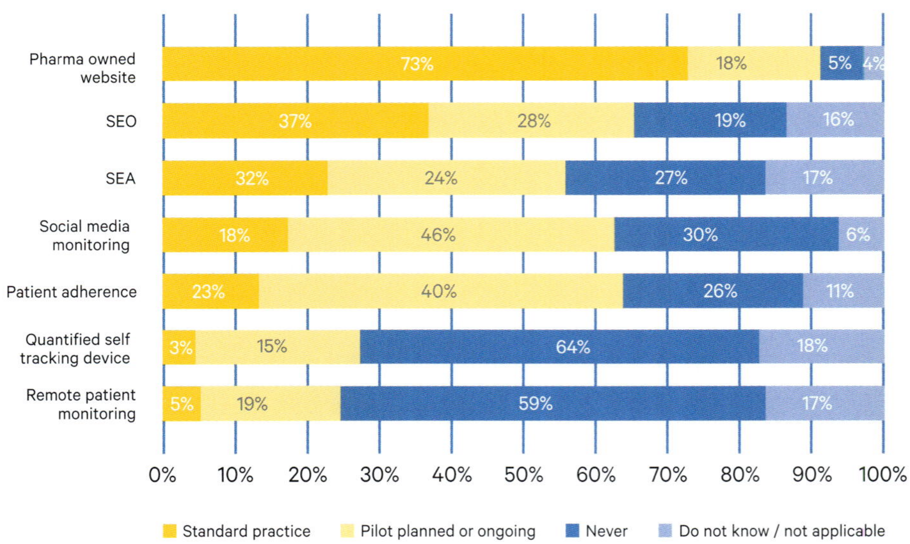


Source: The Across Health Multichannel Maturometer 2017 | N=221 | EU scope

## Tip

### Listening to patients

As the focus in pharma shifts from HCPs to patients, it makes sense to also listen to what they have to say. Engagement through social media can be a way to achieve this. In reality however, it is standard practice for only a minority of pharma companies (18%). Proof perhaps that patient centricity still has a long way to go.

There are various ways to more actively engage with patients through social media:

**Listening to patients**: social (buzz) monitoring can enable you to keep track of the sentiment of online conversations about your brand or therapeutic area.

**Talking to patients**: besides just listening, you can also actively engage in conversations. Many pharma companies, however, still see too many risks in doing this.

**Supporting patients**: patient communities are often a great support channel. Being actively involved in, or sponsoring, such initiatives can be a good way of getting to know patients better.

**Embracing patients**: taking things even further could be done by involving patients in some parts of your 'disease management' activities, for example in developing 'beyond the pill' services.

## Challenges of delivering on the promise of more patient value

According to two recent studies*, there are three key hurdles to becoming more patient-centric:

- **Lack of ownership.** 73% of respondents indicated there is no single role that has the primary responsibility for patient services in their organization.
- **Lack of awareness.** 81% of respondents said that their company relies on healthcare professionals to make patients aware of their services. But fewer than one in five patients (19%) is familiar with them. While most patients rely on healthcare professionals as their primary source of information, unfortunately, activating HCPs to provide your information and services to patients can be challenging. In a 2017 study, Accenture found that less than 40% of US HCPs are aware of the patient services offered by pharma.
- **Lack of precise measurement.** 40% of the executives surveyed cited an inability to precisely measure the impact of patient services on outcomes.

* Sources: Accenture 2016: The patient is in, and Accenture 2017: Lost in Translation.

## Patient Multichannel: reach and impact in Europe 2017

| Patient request | Patient adherence programme | | Rep |
|---|---|---|---|
| 33% | 18% | ... reach versus... | 63% |
| 5.9 | 6.2 | ... impact versus... | 5.8 |
| 1.06 | 1.21 | ... MCQ versus... | 1.00 |

The Across Health Navigator studies the impact and reach of 57 off- and online channels amongst HCPs. From this, the multichannel equivalent (MCQ) is derived: a measurement of relative impact, which makes comparing between channels possible. Find out more on the Navigator data in chapter 1.

Source: The Across Health Navigator 2017 | N=3185 | EU5 scope (DE, ES, FR, IT, UK) | Specialists

# Patient-centric multichannel engagement in action

1 **Map the patient journey** and identify leverage points where you can make a difference.

↓

2 **Build the business case.**
For each leverage point, define who the **target audience** is (the patient or carer segments ) and what **type of behaviour** you expect from them. Next, define **the conversion elements** (services, messages, tools) that will trigger the desired behaviour.

↓

3 **Select the appropriate channels per patient segment.**
Assess **impact**, **reach** and **cost** of different channels and define **the optimal channel mix** to support your messages. Think about a balanced mix of owned, paid and earned channels, both off- and online.

↓

4 **Define KPIs.**
Consider both channel based and outcome based KPIs. Measure quantitative (reach, conversion, cost, ...) and qualitative (satisfaction, NPS, ...) effects.

↓

5 **Run** the campaign.

↓

6 **Track** results continuously.
**Finetune** your programme where needed.

## To conclude

It will be hard to find a company or industry that doesn't state it puts its customers centre stage. But the pharma industry is somewhat special in this. Due to its nature, the many regulations and the complex business ecosystem, shifting focus from drugs to patients is even more complicated.

Patient-centricity will therefore require several important changes.

First of all, companies should find the holy trinity of delivering patient value, scientific innovation and financial profits. This needs to be deeply embedded within the DNA and culture of the company, which requires strong empathic leadership and a rethinking of many processes (such as incentivising reps based on patient satisfaction instead of the number of calls).

Secondly, it will require a shift away from marketing drugs towards managing diseases. In order to take on this role, pharma will need to form alliances with other healthcare partners, but also with health tech startups and/or the leading technology platforms (Apple, Google, etc), who are much stronger in the B2C space.

Lastly, it will require a shift from 'curing' to 'preventing'. While the focus today is very much on secondary care, the technology revolution—with wearables, tracking devices, remote monitoring tools, and electronic health records—will lead to more preventive medicine and self-diagnostics and, thus, place the patient as the key stakeholder.

> ‘Increasing the effectiveness of adherence interventions may have a far greater impact on the health of the population than any improvement in specific medical treatments.’
>
> R. Brian Haynes
> Professor, McMaster University Medical Centre, Canada

‘… using data to describe, analyze and predict engagement strategies and tactics’

# 12 Impact Measurement & Analytics

## Lost in analytics

The days of engaging with customers in 'Mad Men'-style are gone forever. Many marketing teams now staff up with analytics talent that previously used to reside in the business intelligence department. Today's marketer must be data aware, and understand the inner workings of data analytics. The bottom line is, getting lost in the data is as good as being fooled by it.

## The metrics of data analytics

**<1%**

Less than 1% of the world's data is analyzed. (Source: Business Insider)

**>80%**

... of the world's data is unstructured. (Source: IBM)

**5,247 GB**

By 2020, there will by 5247GB of data for every man, woman and child on earth. (Source: IDC)

**2017**

... was the year when CMOs began outspending CIOs on technology (Source: Gartner)

**15 to 20%**

... of marketing spend can be freed up by making better use of channel mix analytics. (Source: McKinsey)

**33%**

... of the digital universe will have Big Data value by 2020, if properly tagged and analysed. (Source: EMC)

## Metrics vs KPIs vs ROI

The beauty of digital is that almost everything can be measured. However, some of the terms are used very loosely and sometimes (wrongly) interchanged, which may lead to misunderstandings. Here's a useful way to differentiate between the 3 levels:

1. A **metric** is any standard of measurement : for instance the average visit duration, the number of tablet detail usages, or the number of email opens. However, it's definitely not recommended to treat every metric equally.

2. What should be highlighted is only what matters for the business. A Key Performance Indicator **(KPI)** is a metric that enables you to monitor your performance and can be used as a driver for improvement. In general, it is advisable to focus on just a handful of KPIs.

3. Return on Investment **(ROI)** is a specific KPI used to evaluate the effectiveness of an investment or to compare the effectiveness of a number of different investments. To calculate ROI, the benefit of an investment is divided by its cost. The result is then expressed as a percentage or ratio.

> 'A channel does NOT have an ROI! A full campaign can have an ROI over time, but this cannot be isolated down to the contribution per channel within the campaign.'

## A holistic approach to measurement

When measuring success, we can differentiate between two kinds of elements: the neocortex and the limbic elements.

1. **Neocortex elements:** the traditional (quantitative) numbers that drive information, such as costs, expenses, reach, etc. These are relatively easy to measure.

2. **Limbic elements:** the softer (qualitative) side of things, like conversion, engagement, advocacy and perception. These are more difficult to measure and quantify.

When we plan to measure success based on performance levels and KPIs, it's important to take both aspects into consideration.

**ROI =** f (**REACH**, ENGAGEMENT, CONVERSION, ADVOCACY, **COST**)

**ROI =** f (**NEOCORTEX** + LIMBIC)

# Data analytics in action

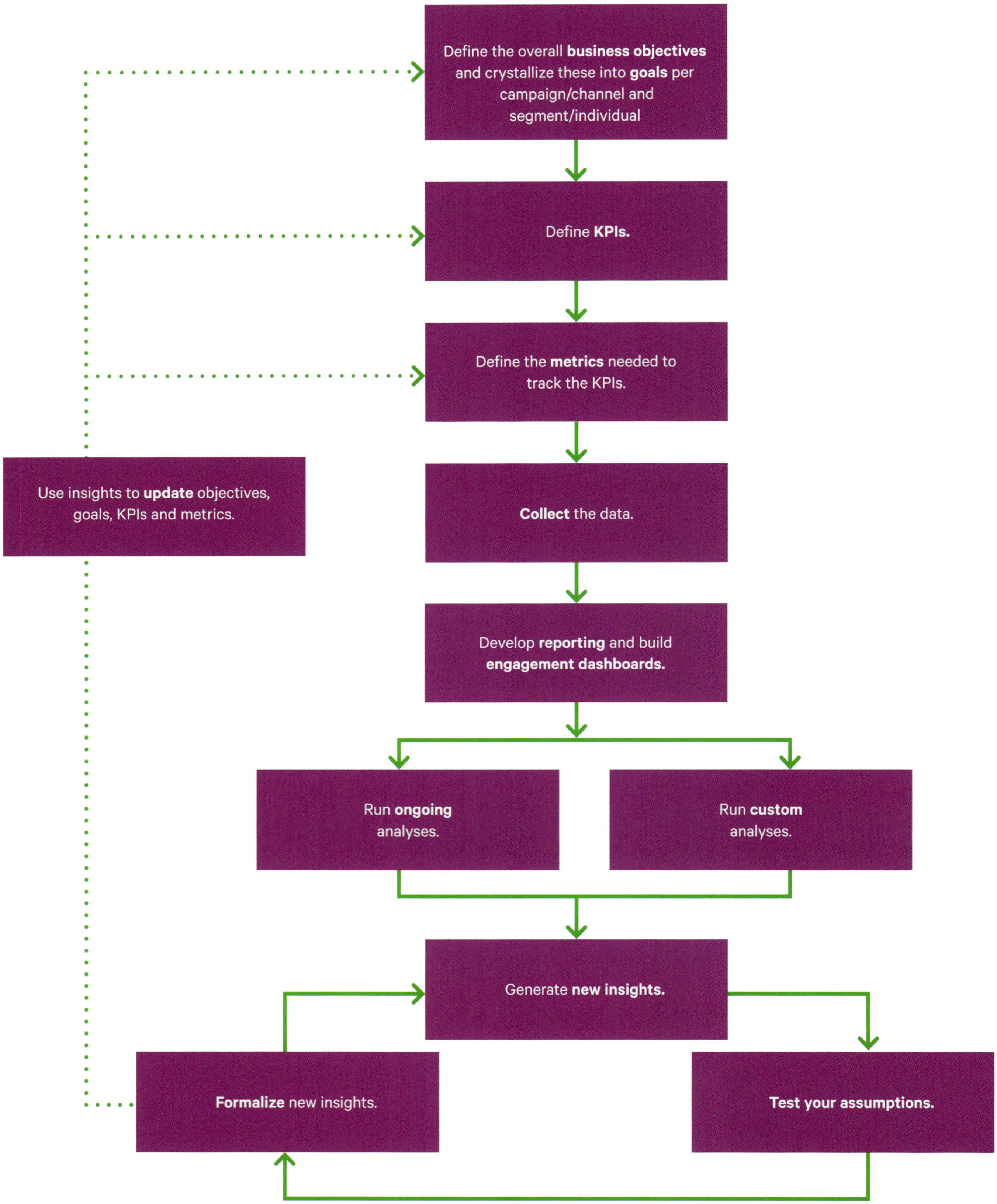

# 3 types of data

There are **3 types of data:**

❶ **Descriptive data** describes a situation or a problem. This is often referred to as reporting. It answers the question: 'what happened, and why did it happen?' In a sense, it's very much like a post-mortem analysis.
An example: a report on the total number and the percentage variation month after month, for the visitors to a website, or the number of new customers coming in every month.

❷ **Predictive** data uses past data **to predict future outcomes**. It answers the question: 'what will probably happen in future?'
An example: if a previous marketing campaign delivered X number of leads, with a similar set-up and investment, we can expect a similar number of leads to be generated.

❸ **Prescriptive** data uses **cause and effect analysis** to tell you **'what to do'.** It answers the question: 'what will happen, when will it happen, and why'. Prescriptive analytics combines structured and unstructured data, which is combined to deliver a series of options to choose from and what the likely impact will be for each option.
An example: if we hire 10 more salespeople, what is the expected impact on revenue and profit? If we raise our prices by 1 %, what will be the effect on 1) churn and 2) profit? What about a 2 % price increase?

Companies often start with descriptive data, and then move towards predictive and finally prescriptive types of data analytics. The most valuable insights can be found in prescriptive data analytics, as it gives a range of possibilities from which the optimal one can be chosen.

## Tip

### Top down and bottom up

Business objectives determine which metrics to use to build the right KPIs. But from the metrics come **new insights** which, in turn, **influence the business objectives**. This is comparable to social systems in human societies, where individuals are influenced by the social systems in which they live but the social systems, in turn, are also influenced by the individuals.

**Business objectives influence** the choice of **metrics** (top down), but the **metrics also influence the business objectives** (bottom up). This is **the yin and yang of data analytics.**

> 'Data is the new creative.'
>
> **Martin Le Sauteur**
> **CEO of Acquisio**

# The 4 maturity levels of data analysis

Companies go through different analytics maturity stages:

## ❶ No or limited data:

- The value of data is **not acknowledged.**
- Neither time nor resources are made available for data setup & analysis.
- Management focuses solely on running the **day-to-day activities.**

## ❷ Basic data:

- Some **basic data analytics** are used (e.g.: Google Analytics).
- Data is mainly used for **descriptive** purposes.
- Management uses data **retrospectively**, to affirm earlier decisions.

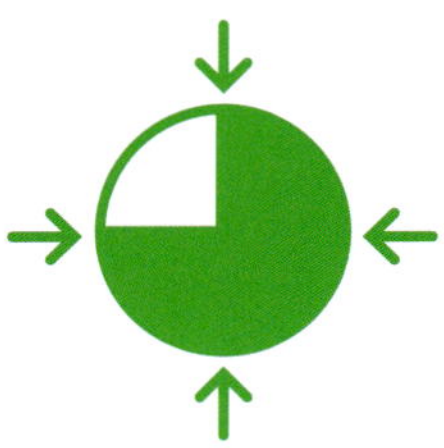

## ❸ Deeper data:

- Data analytics is **better developed** and is a business domain in its own right (e.g.: there is a Business Intelligence department).
- Different parts of the organization have access to data reporting, but only a limited number of functions are granted access. Data analytics is still **a separate silo.**
- Data is used mainly at **pre-defined moments** (e.g.: quarterly reviews, yearly plans), for both descriptive and predictive reasons.

## ❹ Democratic data access:

- Data analytics is **fully developed** and managed by a team of data experts.
- Data analytics are made **available to all stakeholders.** Every staff member has access to data analytics tools to run custom reports on the fly.
- The whole organization understands **the importance of data** for both day-to-day and long-term strategic activities.
- The whole organization is also empowered to actively use data analytics to describe, predict and prescribe strategies and tactics. **Data is omnipresent.**
- Decision-making without data analytics is considered **suspicious.**
- All stakeholders don't only use the data, they contribute to further **enrichment** of it.

> ‘If you torture the data long enough, it will confess.’
>
> **Ronald Coase**
> **Economist**

## Invest your time wisely

With so much data available and **more data pouring in every day**, it's easy to get **lost in data** Best practices suggest the following division of investment in time and resources to generate an optimal data ROI:

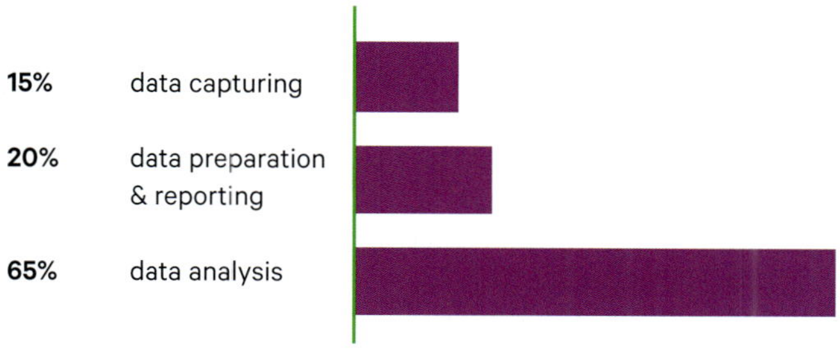


Source: bluehillresearch.com

**Automation** tools can greatly reduce the time needed for data capturing and reporting, while the **greatest value is to be found in the analysis.** Understanding exactly what the data means to the business and linking the data analysis directly to your strategic objectives, helps to fuel new insights generation, and in turn, aids in updating strategic objectives.

**80%**

**... of marketers think that silos within marketing – and the organization as a whole – prevent a holistic view from being formalized.**

Source: EMC

## Tip

### Continuous testing

A/B testing enables you to **test assumptions** before launching a full-blown programme. With schemes such as **discovery-driven planning and critical assumption planning**, small steps forward can be made with testable results at pre-defined milestones. Along the way, more insights are generated, showing whether the chosen direction is still correct. At every milestone, changes can be made or the complete programme can be halted. In this way, the **risk of failure and possible loss of investment can be minimized.**

> "When you're bringing in data from different channels or other areas of the company, the challenge is to put all those pieces of the puzzle together into one unified view of the customer."

**Mike Foley**
**Director of Data and Insight, EMC**

# Big ... bigger ... biggest

Data analytics has always been one of the key drivers for marketing and business innovation. Consider, for instance, the point-of-sale data boom in the 1980s, with scanner data and loyalty cards. Or the click and data tsunami at the beginning of the digital era a decade later. **The next data-driven evolution** will come from Big Data. Through the combination of myriad structured and unstructured data sources – including social media, mobile and sensor or machine-generated data - both companies and industries are being transformed.

As such, Big Data – typified by the 3 Vs, **Volume, Variety, Velocity** – requires a new generation of technology and IT architecture in order to (economically) extract value from these very large volumes of varied and constantly changing data. Classic data warehouses and business intelligence infrastructures will be inadequate to handle petabytes of structured and unstructured data in real time.

Business Intelligence (BI) is being replaced by **data science.** While BI is mainly focused on retrospective and descriptive analysis, data science extends this traditional view with **predictive analytics.** Companies embracing Big Data move away from a backwards view towards a forward-looking stance. All available data—both from within and outside the company—is assembled and processed in real time to optimize business performance.

When done right, Big Data enables organizations to...

- Increase sales and profit,
- Reduce costs,
- Better manage risks,
- Optimize process efficiency,
- Gain new customer insights.

| Traditional Decision-making | Big Data Decision-making |
|---|---|
| 'Rear-view Mirror' hindsight | 'Forward-looking' recommendations |
| Uses less than 10% of available data | Exploit all data from diverse sources |
| Batch, incomplete, disjointed | Real-time, correlated, governed |
| Business Monitoring | Business Optimization |

Source: Big Data: Understanding How Data Powers Big Business, By Bill Schmarzo

> Big-data computing is perhaps the single biggest innovation in computing in the last decade. We have only just begun to see its potential to collect, organize and process data in all walks of life.

**Randal E. Bryant, Randy H. Katz, and Edward D. Lazowska**

# Putting things into perspective... the FMCG approach

The FMCG industry has developed a great KPI measurement framework which can also be applied in the pharma industry. This framework differentiates between 4 quadrants, combining channel-related/brand-related and quantitative/qualitative elements.

1. **Channel-related** = any type of individual interaction in a specific channel that can be measured directly.
2. **Brand-related** = the overall result of the combination of individual actions on the brand's perception and positioning.
3. **Quantitative** = the numbers game. This tells you all about reach and frequency.
4. **Qualitative** = the relevancy game. This tells you all about relevance, engagement and likeability.

| | | Direct (channel-related) effects | Indirect (brand-related) effects |
|---|---|---|---|
| Qualitative | Communication effects | Engagement | Conversion |
| Quantitative | Behavioural effects | Reach and advocacy | ROI (cost and return) |

All 4 KPI blocks are related: when reach is good, channel experience is positive and brand perception is improved... then ROI should be positive. This also means you do not have to measure ROI each time. ROI is costly to measure and sometimes cannot be measured at all, such as in small pilots or medical programmes. The other three quadrants are easier and far less expensive to track, i.e. they are formidable leading indicators.

Let's take a closer look at the quadrants.

# Channel-related, quantitative

This is the quadrant in which pharma typically excels. It's important to measure these KPIs as they tell you something about your reach. And without good reach it's impossible to achieve a good ROI.

Typical KPIs in this quadrant include the number of visitors to a website, the number of participants in a webcast, the open rate of an email campaign, the number of inbound calls for a call centre, the number of fans on a Facebook page, or the number of downloads of an app.

## Tip

### Beware of GIGO

**The importance of data cleaning** and initial data analysis cannot be overstated. Flawed data will result in flawed outcomes. Data analysts refer to this issue as **'garbage in, garbage out'**, or GIGO.

In today's digital age, there's even the risk that GIGO becomes **'garbage in, gospel out'**: a less experienced interpreter of data may blindly rely on the analytics. Retaining **a critical stance** towards data remains important for every data consumer.

## Tip

### Online surveys to the rescue

**Online surveys** can help you identify if the goal of your content was achieved. This can be done by enriching the survey data with **quantitative interaction data**, and can be compared to the results of those who have not been exposed to your content.

## Channel-related, qualitative

However, measuring reach alone is not enough. The fact that a website attracts many visitors does not tell us whether they are actually the right type, or whether they appreciate the information on our website. In this second quadrant, we try to establish whether the information and interaction opportunities we offer are relevant and in line with expectations.

Typical KPIs in this quadrant are related to channel likeability and customer experience, for instance channel NPS, or channel satisfaction.

## Brand-related, qualitative

Over time and through continuous interaction across multiple channels and touchpoints, we strive to positively influence the way customers perceive our brand. As such, we hope to move the customer up the ladder of adoption. In this quadrant, the KPI data analysis examines how fast customers are moving up the ladder of adoption.

Quite often, it's easy to fit these brand-related qualitative questions into existing or scheduled market research, and combine it with qualitative, channel-related questions.

Typical KPIs in this quadrant are brand awareness, brand attitude, message recall, brand preference, intent to prescribe, and NPS for the brand.

## Brand-related, quantitative

Finally, we measure the brand-related quantitative elements. This is a return to the hard numbers game, moving from intent to actual behaviour. This is done by examining whether campaign efforts are translating into actual value.

Note, however, that measuring this is only 1 out of the 4 quadrants that you should be tracked. Ideally, you should reuse the KPIs and metrics from the previous quadrant(s), such as by demonstrating a link between the accelerated movement of some customer groups up the ladder of adoption and increased sales figures, for example.

Typical KPIs in this quadrant are changes in sales figures or market share, variations in cost effectiveness, increase in profit ratios and the ever-popular overall return on investment (ROI)!

> ‘We are drowning in information but are starved of knowledge.’
>
> **John Naisbitt**
> **Futurist and author**

### Tip

#### NPS before & after

When planning campaigns, **capturing NPS as a pre-campaign baseline** followed by **a post-campaign check-up** can give you valuable information about the quality of your campaign. While one-off NPS surveys give interesting insights, evolution over time is of far greater value.

# Net promoter score

The net promoter score (NPS) is a customer loyalty metric that was introduced by Reichheld in 2003. Today, more than two thirds of Fortune 1000 companies are using it. NPS measures the difference between the proportion of promoters (customers who highly recommend the company to colleagues or friends) and detractors (customers who advise others not to do business with the company). The NPS can range from +100 to -100.

**Net promoter score = % promoters - % detractors**

To get to these numbers, you ask 2 simple questions:

1. "On a scale of 0 to 10, what is the likelihood that you would recommend our company / product / solution to a friend or colleague?"

2. "Why?"

The first question, "would you recommend", generates a number which indicates **the overall sense of happiness of customers.** You can analyze the NPS results of different customer segments in order to correctly tailor marketing campaigns per segment. The second question, "why", gives you insights into why customers would recommend your company. From this customer feedback, **new insights** for service optimization and even **new product development** can be derived.

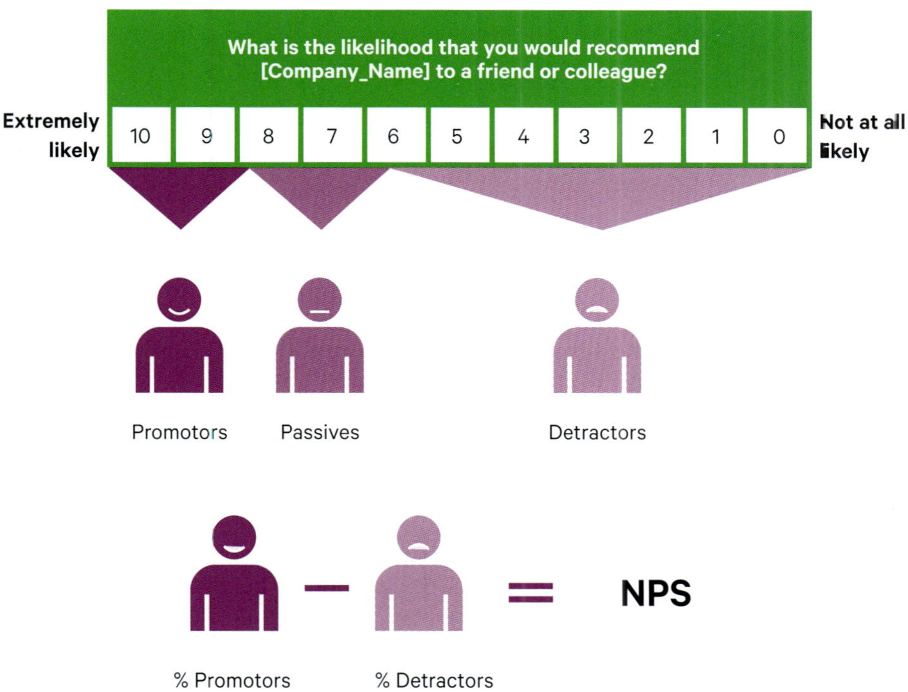


## Tip

### What's wrong?

It's always a good idea to follow up with detractors, for example, by asking them what **the main drivers** are for their (relatively) low score. This shows your customers that you take their feedback seriously and that you're continuously trying to improve your offering. It's not uncommon for a low NPS score or complaint to become **the starting point** for a great customer relationship later on.

**2x**

Companies that are net promoter score leaders in their industry grow, on average, at **twice the rate of their competitors.**

**3 to 8x**

The average customer lifetime value (CLV) of 'promoters' is 3 to 8 times that of 'detractors'. Promoters stay **longer** with the company, **buy more** products, **cost less** to serve and are **more likely to refer** the company to colleagues and friends.

(Source: Fred Reichheld: The Ultimate Question)

## Dashboard myopia

Dashboards are essential but some dangers do lurk:

- **Beware of tunnel vision.**
Over-emphasizing metrics may cause a loss of sight of the bigger picture. If you focus on the meters all of the time, you may miss out on what's happening around you.

- **Beware of metrics as the 'be all and end all'.**
Metrics are merely a means to an end, they're not the end in itself. Regularly review the relevancy of metrics and KPIs and make changes accordingly.

- **Don't automatically copy-paste KPIs year after year.**
Regularly re-investigate whether your KPIs are still correct. Ask yourself: "Were we to start from a clean slate, would we still build the same dashboard?"

- **Beware of experimentation apathy.**
Over-reliance on metrics may result in a **loss of experimentation and innovation.** As long as the meters move in the right direction, people may simply continue to do what they've always been doing, and lose focus on the need to try out new tactics and channels. This can lead to strategic drift.

> **He uses statistics as a drunken man uses lamp-posts - for support rather than illumination.**
>
> **Andrew Lang**
> **Scottish writer**

## The maturity level of measurement

Pharma is clearly in the early phases of measurement maturity. Indeed, measuring ROI is considered the **3rd biggest bottleneck for digital in pharma** and, as budgets and competition are increasing, its importance has been **growing over the years. Under 20%** of European pharma marketers are very comfortable with measuring the performance of all channels. Additionally, only **9% completely agrees that they measure HCP engagement**, which is at a three-year low. Finally, just **13%** of pharma marketers fully agree that they have a well-rounded mix of **qualitative & quantitative KPIs** in place. For the last 2 categories, the "completely disagree" group is bigger than the "completely agree", demonstrating the big (and increasing) gap between leaders and laggards.

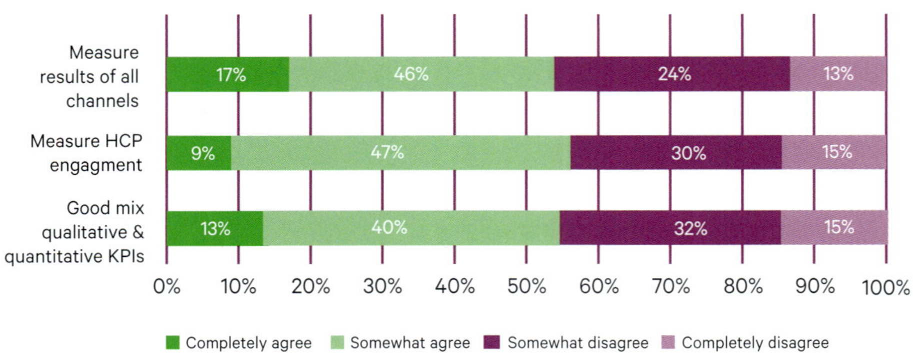


Source: The Across Health Multichannel Maturometer 2017 | N = 221 | EU scope

### Tip

#### Dust off your analytics skills

Correlation and causation, chi-square and paired-t tests, ... Maybe it rings a bell from the days when you were studying. Now's the time to dust off your analytical skills. In today's data economy, everyone must have an understanding of **statistical methods and logic**. Without this, it is difficult to correctly **interpret and scrutinize data.**

In a business context, we very often start from certain assumptions but often these **are insufficiently tested - or not at all**. Complete businesses have collapsed over assumptions that later proved to be wrong: what was thought to deliver great customer response turned out to be completely irrelevant. So make it a habit of identifying assumptions early on and apply **hypothesis testing** rigorously. Formulate a hypothesis, collect the data, run the analysis, then accept or reject the hypothesis.

## Different dashboards for different stakeholders

**Different roles** in the organization have **different dashboard needs**. Ideally, dashboards can be set up flexibly depending on the type of role accessing it.

Although different roles require different views of the dashboard, it's important that every stakeholder can drill up and down through them. Make sure the strategic level can **drill down to the tactical level** to see how a campaign contributes to overall business objectives. For the tactical level, it's important to be able to 'drill up' to understand how an individual campaign **contributes.**

Different views can create **new insights** and this can lead to new approaches.

| Level | Type of role | Focus | Goal |
|---|---|---|---|
| Executive level | CEO, CFO, ... | **Strategic** | Monitor and measure performance against **business outcomes** and marketing objectives |
| Operational level | Marketing Manager, ... | **Management** | Track the performance of overall **marketing strategies** and processes |
| Tactical level | Various marketing staff, ... | **Operational** | Analyze the performance at **project or campaign** level |

> **Always consider: What's the COI (Cost of Ignoring) vs the ROI?**
>
> **Anonymous**

## Learn from the past, optimize for the future

The data your campaigns generate do not only create value during or at the end of your projects. When properly managed, your data can be a goldmine for future campaign optimization, or to compare your current success against earlier initiatives. **Your data is your collective memory.** Anything you try is recorded and can potentially be reused: from finding out what the best day is to send out your emails, to which kind of messages work best, in which format, targeting which audience.

Next to deeper qualitative insights into channel impact, using benchmarking data tailored to your target audience can provide further insights into **which channels will work and which won't**. Certainly when covering regions with multiple countries, generalized ideas on channel performance rates may be inaccurate. Parameters like audience type, therapy area, and product lifecycle may all have an impact on channel performance, even within the same country.

Common sense will get you started, but never forget to assume nothing and question everything.

**14%**

**Did you know** that opening rates for emails differ as much as 14% between European countries? (Source: Across Illuminator, 2017)

# The human face of data

Should we leave decision-making to machines? Andrew McAfee, associate director of the Center for Digital Business at the MIT Sloan School of Management, claims that “as the amount of data goes up, **the importance of human judgment** should go down.”

The philosophical debate over **the role of man and machine** will continue for some time yet. In general, the consensus swings between **algorithm-driven** and **human-driven** approaches. Whichever position is taken, it’s clear that including data analytics in many more areas is clearly key to **future business** success.

> **Data are just summaries of thousands of stories – tell a few of those stories to help make the data meaningful.**
>
> **Chip & Dan Heath**
> **Authors of ‘Made to Stick’ and ‘Switch’**

*“We should turn many of our decisions, predictions, diagnoses, and judgments over to the algorithms.”*

Andrew McAfee

*“Intuition has an important role to play... Neither an all-intuition nor an all-analytics approach will get you to the promised land.”*

Tom Davenport

*“Human judgment is at the center of successful data analysis. Although these (Big Data) tools provide immense value, it is important to remember that they are just that: tools...”*

Jeffrey Heer

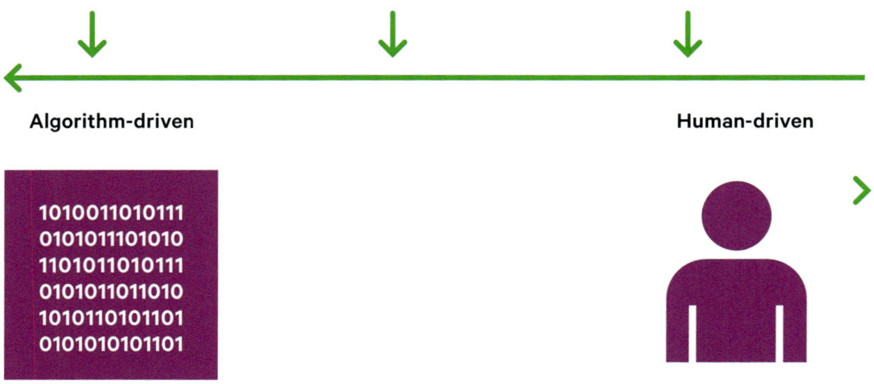


# Telling the data story

While data can generate tremendous insights, **data in itself does not generate action.** Departments must not only be able to handle and interpret data, they must also tell **the data story.**

As data appeals to reason, stories appeal to emotion. Every human decision is based on a combination of **reason and emotion.** Packaging data into persuasive stories helps facilitate decision-making. This is the ‘schizophrenic’ nature of today’s business professional: every person must fully deploy both **the analytic left and the creative right side of the brain.** As well as being able to crunch the numbers, people must also be able to tell great stories.

## Tips for novices

**Basic data analytics is better than no data analytics.**
One of the most common tools to get started with analytics is Microsoft Excel. Because of its relative simplicity, it is a great tool for 1) **basic analyses,** and 2) one-off analyses of campaign results. There are, however, drawbacks: 1) there's no connection with other systems so all **data needs to be imported** regularly to keep the reports up to date, and 2) as complexity increases, so does the **risk of errors.** For standalone projects or when you're in a startup mode, spreadsheets may work fine. But once complexity increases, it's better to deploy integrated analytics programs, like Tableau.

**88%** ... of all spreadsheets contain errors. (Source: Ray Panko, 2008)

**Measure only what you use.**
It's easy to **get lost in analytics.** Define the relevant metrics and measure only those. Revisit your choice of metrics regularly to make sure you still track the right things. Skip those that are not used by anyone in the organization and that don't provide much additional insight. Regularly revisit your measurement criteria: as your business evolves, so too must your analytics.

**Measure only what matters.**
Avoid **'vanity metrics'**: metrics that make you feel good about yourself but don't provide real insights into how your business is doing. For example: comparing the 'number of visitors' to your website against those of a competitor. This data may indicate who has the largest audience but it will not tell you much of how relevant and valuable your website audience is, or how this impacts revenue. Dig deep enough into the data and ask yourself: "Does this metric ..."

- ...tell me more about my business?
- ... clarify whether my business is moving in the right direction?
- ... explain ROI?
- ... help me to describe, predict or prescribe?

**Don't try this on your own.**
With more complex analytics, it makes sense to **get specialized help.** With regard to incorporating the right financial metrics, talk to the finance department. When setting up more complex marketing dashboards, talk to your platform provider for a proper and diversified set-up. It's better to ask for help and get things right then try your best and end up with incorrect conclusions.

> "In God we trust; all others must bring data."
>
> **William Edwards Deming**
> **Professor and author**

## To conclude

Digital is disruptive to many industries, and Big Data may very well be the next disruptive wave that separates the winners from the rest. The future of business is data-driven, but finding the right talent to manage it creates new challenges for all organizations. Bridging the gap between the enormous opportunities provided by (big) data and the ability to handle it, may very well be the greatest challenge of all.

In our data economy, competitive advantage will be generated by companies that optimally leverage real-time, robust, relevant data.

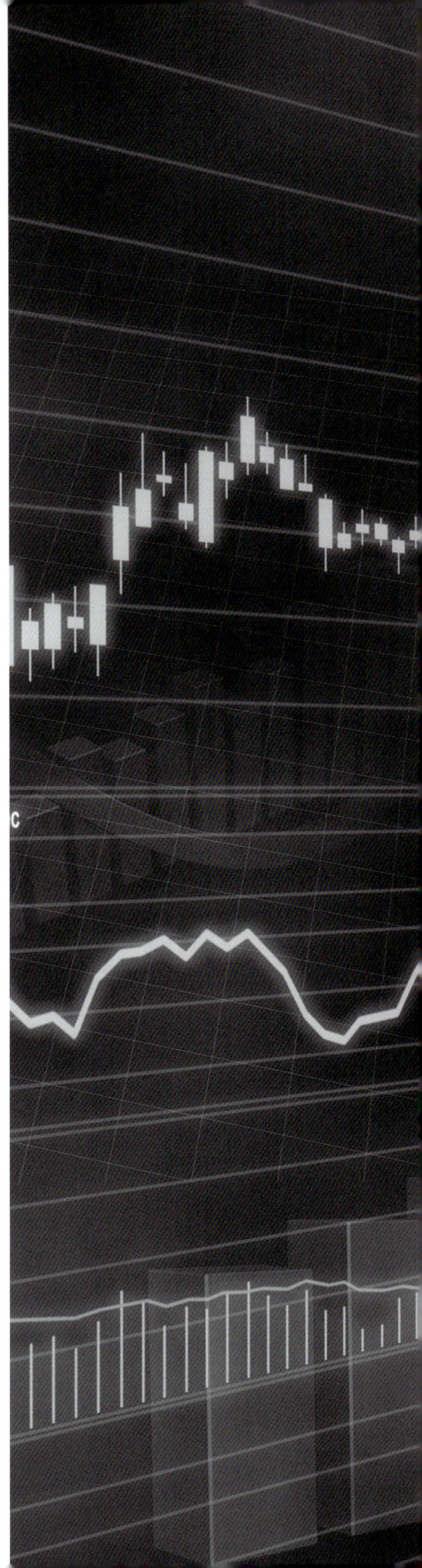

# 13 The Multichannel Rep

## The MC rep

More than ever before, HCPs have many choices for where they get their information, meaning non-favoured channels are unlikely to be used or accessed. Conversely, if these channels are considered high value (and fit around the busy lives of physicians), then it has become possible to continue conversations and engagement with doctors beyond what was feasible in the analogue era.

Developing new ways to empower the rep, for instance equipping them with a digital arsenal, allows them to become more effective and focus their face to face activities on where it really matters. This is also the kind of service which HCPs have come to expect. This means that the challenge has become to be there where, when and how physicians want – through the right channel, with the right content, in the right format and at the right time.

When reps are thus empowered, and placed at the centre of the multichannel journey, they are usually referred to as **Multichannel** or **Orchestrator Rep**. While in theory this concept could apply to any additional channels, it mainly refers to the usage of rep-triggered emails, customisable websites, remote detailing, and tablet detailing.
This transition is more than just the adoption of new technology, however. It requires a full-hearted re-alignment of key activities and concepts of the traditional rep model.

> ‘ High-value US physicians continue to be targeted once every hour of the workday via a variety of marketing channels ’
>
> ZS Associates, 2017

## The metrics of the MC rep

**46%** Only 46% of US physicians were “accessible” in 2017, vs close to 80% in 2008. (Source: ZS Associates)

**43%** ... is the current adoption level of rep-triggered email by pharma. (Source: Across Health Maturometer)

**>30%** Rep calls dropped 30% between 2014-16 (US). (Source: ZS Associates)

**37%** ... of HCPs is more likely to open a rep-triggered email than a company-sent one. (Source: Across Health Navigator)

**29%** % of HCPs have contact with two MC rep channels. (Source: Across Health Navigator)

**+300%** HCP emails more than tripled in the 2014-2016 period. (Source: ZS Associates)

**6%** Only 6 % of EU5 HCPs is experiencing the true MC rep (interaction with 3 rep-orchestrated channels). (Source: Across Health Navigator)

# The maturity level of the multichannel rep

While tablet detailing may well be the most popular digital tactic for pharma companies in Europe, other rep-orchestrated channels are at an earlier stage of adoption, particularly **remote engagement**. Adoption of rep-triggered email (aka "approved email") has strongly increased over a short time span, but is still considerably less often used than mass email marketing.

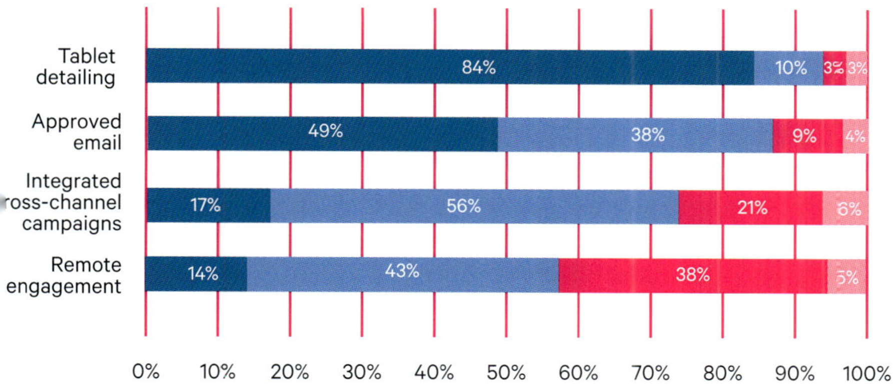


Source: The Across Health Multichannel Maturometer 2017 | N = 221 | EU scope

What pharma says they offer is only half the story. The real question is what physicians actually receive in terms of the multichannel rep. Well, **only 6% of specialists in EU5 experience true "omnichannel" engagement**, i.e. rep visits and two rep-triggered digital channels (vs 8% in the US). This is demonstrative of the low level of implementation of the multichannel rep...although it is perceived as the second most important digital topic to pharma.

## The "MC rep orchestrator": still early days

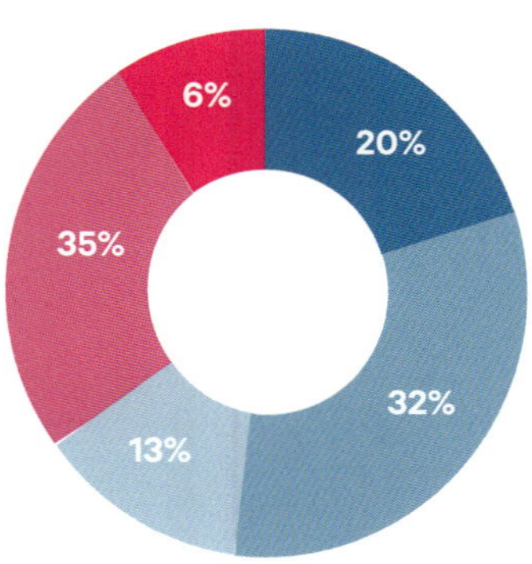


20% of specialists are not reached by any pharma channel

32% of specialists only receive rep visits

13% of specialists engage only through non face-to-face channels

35% of specialists engage through a mix of face-to-face and digital channels

**only 6% of these are experiencing the full multichannel rep**

No engagement | F2F rep only | Digital only | Mix | Full Multichannel rep (rep + email + teledetailing)

Source: Across Health Navigator EU5 specialists, N=1654

> **Every interaction (...) leaves a digital footprint that can be 'decoded' for richer, deeper insights into emotional and contextual behaviors and preferences.**
>
> **IQVIA 2015**

### Which are the key priorities for your organisation in the next 2 years?

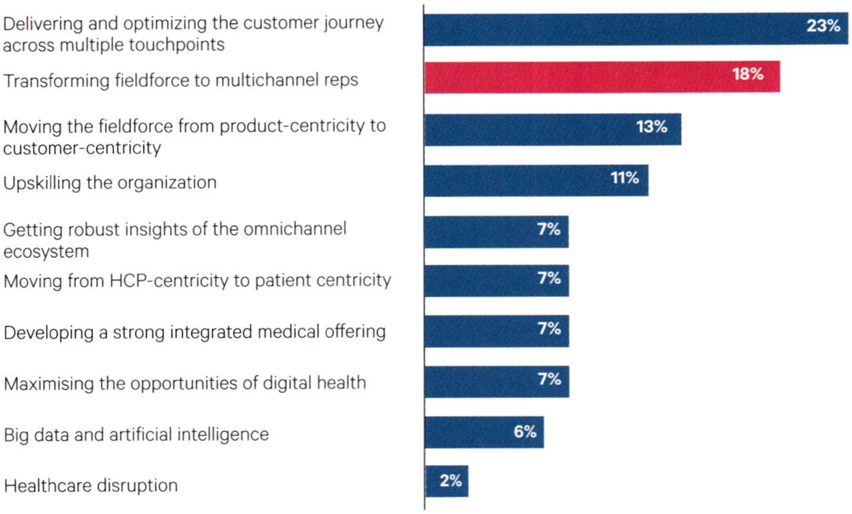


Source: Across Health Multichannel Maturometer 2017 Global, N=256

> ‘By 2017, CEOs will cut selling expenses by one-third as a result of digital marketing activities.’
>
> **Gartner 2015**

## Reach and impact of MC Rep channels in Europe 2017

| | Sales Rep | Tablet detailing | Rep email | Remote detailing |
|---|---|---|---|---|
| **Reach** | 63% | 61% | 43% | 15% |
| **Impact** | 5.8 | 5.8 | 4.6 | 5.9 |
| **MCQ** | 1.00 | 1.02 | 0.39 | 1.03 |

Source: The Across Health Navigator 2017 | N = 3185 | EU5 scope (DE, ES, FR, IT, UK) | Specialists

The Across Health Navigator studies the impact, reach, content preferences and company benchmarks of 57 channels among HCPs. From the impact score, the **multichannel equivalent (MCQ)** is derived: a measurement of relative impact, which makes comparing between channels possible. Find out more on the Navigator data in chapter 1.

# Changing roles, changing world

The changing nature of rep/customer relationships has not happened in a vacuum. There are four fundamental drivers behind it. We are at the beginning of many of these macro-level waves – so early adoption of MC-rep tactics will pay dividends for many years to come.

> **I never fail, I win or learn.**
>
> Nelson Mandela

## 1. Demographic change

Firstly, the physician population is getting younger. Since 2014, over 50% of HCPs are **"digital natives"** (i.e., they received their medical education since the internet was widely available). By 2020, this cohort will represent close to 70%. While all physicians now must to an extent be online some of the time, the amount of time which younger doctors spend online for professional purposes is significantly greater than that of "digital immigrants" (the older generations).

**Average minutes online per day online for professional purposes (EU HPCs)**

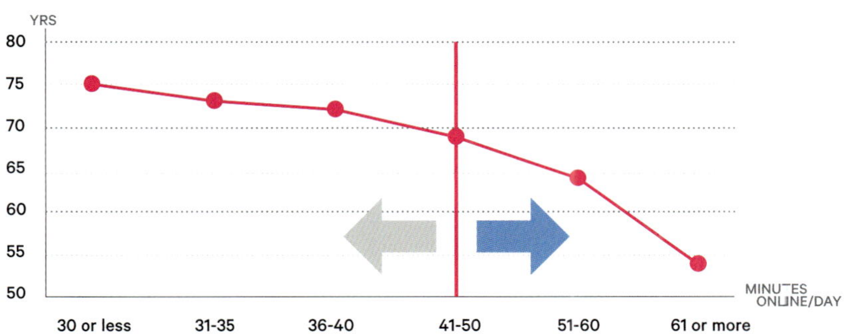


Source: Across Health Navigator EU5 SPEC; 2016-17; n = 1654

It is the same for overall preferences for hybrid (i.e. digital and face-to-face) contact with pharma companies – younger doctors are significantly more open to it, with over 50% of HCPs under 35 preferring this to face to face only. This is even more pronounced when it comes to medical education – with almost 70% of younger physicians preferring a mix for what used to be a purely face-to-face endeavour.

**Communication preferences EU5 Specialists with pharma**

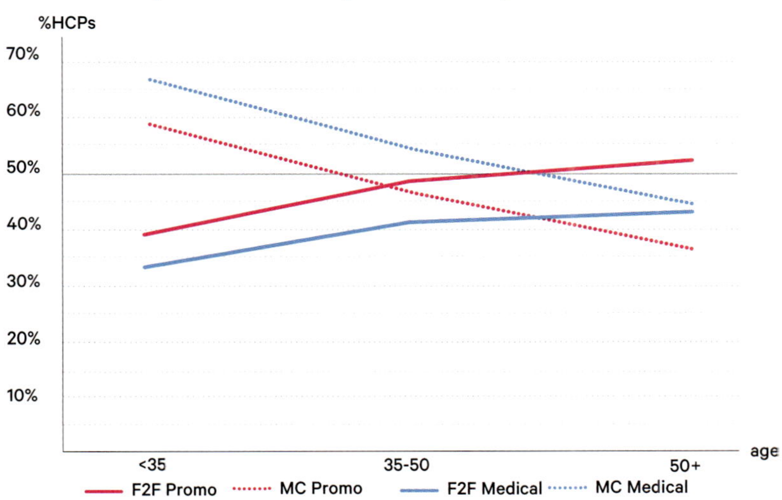


Source: Across Health Navigator, EU Specialists, 2016-2017, N=4305

## 2. Channel affinity changes

Next to demographic changes, there is also clearly a change in the channel affinity preferences of HCPs. Since 2009, physicians across the board have more than doubled the amount of time they spend online for professional purposes. While connected to HCP age, this change is also about the increasing importance of the internet as an information source across the board – hence, even 'older' doctors use it more now than in the past.

Indeed, physicians in general now spend about **40 times more time professionally engaged online than with a rep**. HCPs can now access pharma content at times which were formerly not possible – making continuous communication outside of office hours a reality. Paradoxically, though, the vast majority of pharma budgets are still being spent on personal and face to face channels.

## 3. Contextual changes

Contextual changes are the third major category. The number of different channels, devices, and inputs seeking physicians' attention has exploded. As a result, 'respect for my time', has become the most important criterion when evaluating reps (and hence, granting access). Digital channels (particularly the "pull" type) are much more aligned with this priority, as HCPs can access them "anytime, anywhere".

### Rep quality criteria

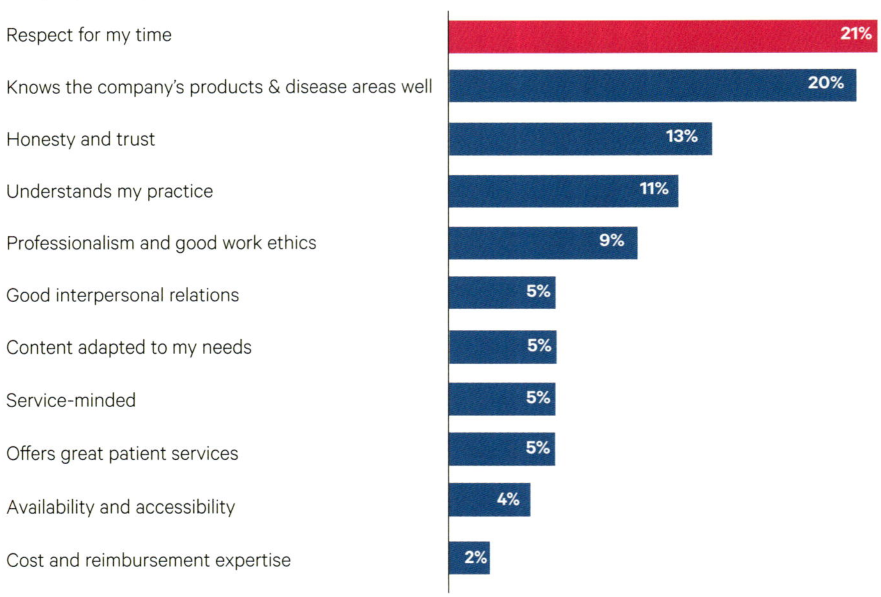


Source: Across Health Navigator, 2017 EU5 Specs, n=3685

## 4. Attitudinal changes

The last type of change is also about the shift in archetypes. One of these models, coined by McKinsey, uses four types: "Independents", "Transactionals", "Knowledge Seekers", and "Relationship Seekers". Importantly, the once dominant HCP archetype of

> Unorchestrated activities can be ineffective at a minimum and potentially detrimental to a brand.
>
> **IQVIA 2015**

> The death of the salesman has been greatly exaggerated
>
> **Economist 2011**

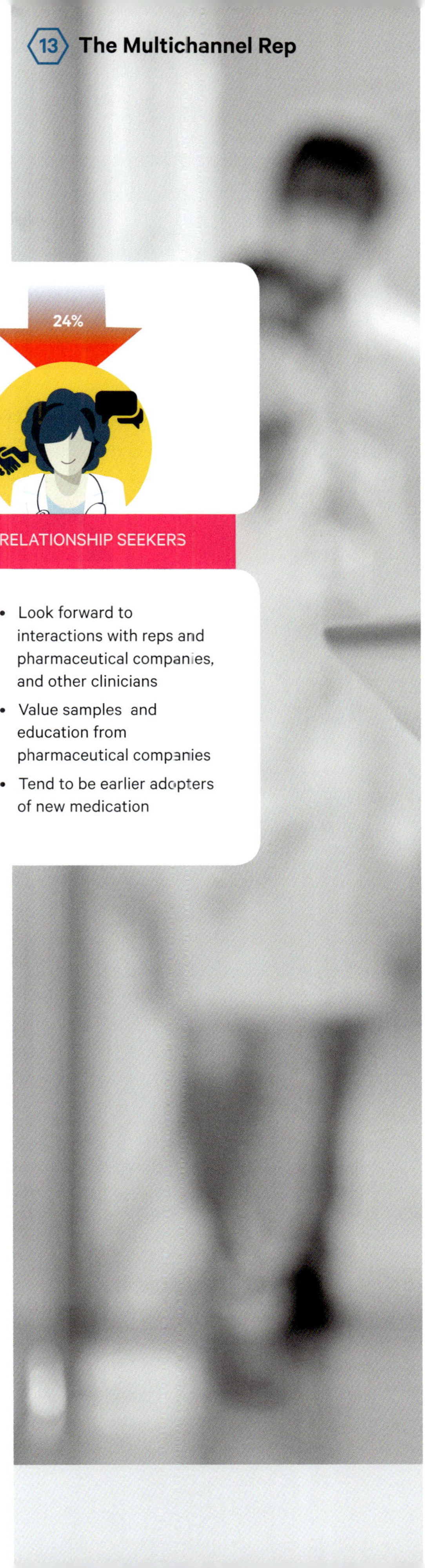

the rep-friendly "relationship seeker" has dropped to rank 3 (24%); "independents" and "knowledge seekers" now constitute two-thirds of specialists in Europe. For more in-depth information, see the eMedical chapter.

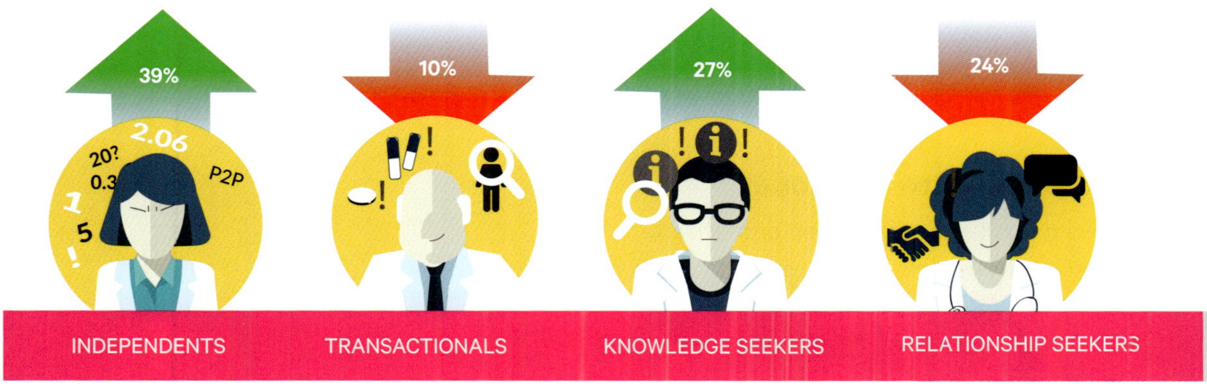


**Independents**

- Do not place much value on interactions with pharmaceutical companies
- Rely on evidence-based materials
- Tend to be slower to try new medication

**Transactionals**

- Only value samples from pharmaceutical companies
- Cost conscious
- Most receptive to patient's preferences
- Tend to be slower to try new medication

**Knowledge seekers**

- Interested in educational programmes offered by pharmaceutical companies
- Do not value informal talks or samples
- Least receptive to patient s preferences
- Tend to be early adopters and pro-pharma

**Relationship seekers**

- Look forward to interactions with reps and pharmaceutical companies, and other clinicians
- Value samples and education from pharmaceutical companies
- Tend to be earlier adopters of new medication

Source: McKinsey's Archetype segmentation model & Across Health Navigator 2016-2017, n = 1654 EU5 Specialists

This too, will have big implications for the go-to-market model for pharma. Physicians increasingly want to engage with other types of content (evidence, science) and a broader variety of (on-demand) channels than the typical "relationship call".

# Becoming an MC rep

*Reps don't become multichannel orchestrators overnight.*

In general, companies that want to transform their field force into Multichannel orchestrators go through 3 distinct stages: reps go from **being Informed**, to **being able to Influence,** and finally, to **Orchestrating** multichannel customer engagement.

## The 3 stages of the Rep Orchestrator model

An evolutionary path - from a detached position to an orchestrator

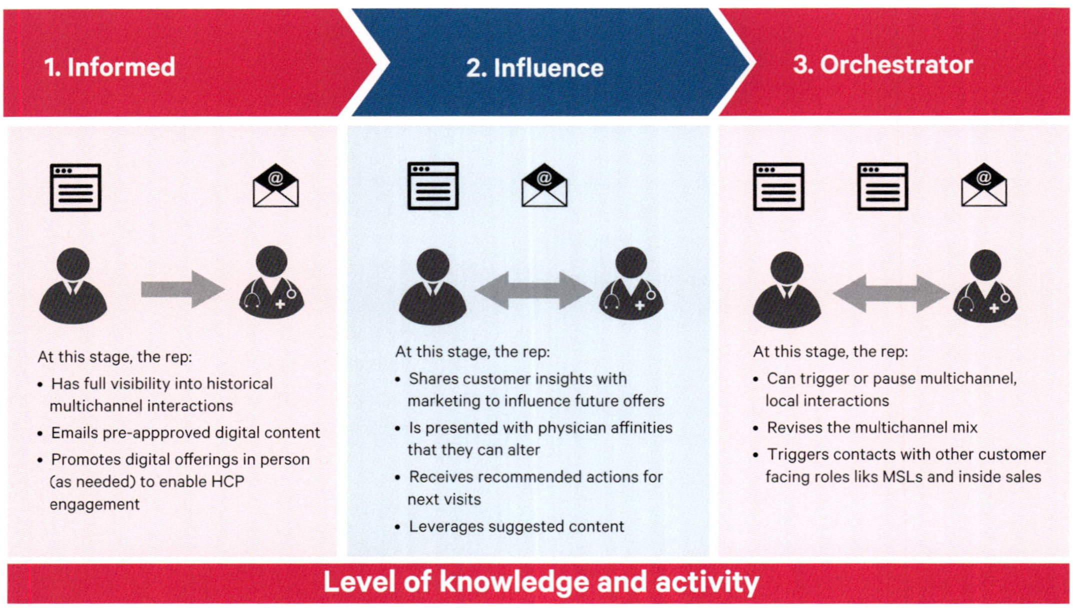


Source: ZS Associates

### 1. Informed

In the first stage of becoming an MC rep, reps are offered full visibility into historical multichannel interactions with their customers. They are also empowered to send e-mails by themselves, containing specific messages that were pre-approved by marketing. In this stage, reps also promote the benefits of using other digital channels (such as an HCP self-service website) to their customers as they understand the value that these channels can add to their personal interactions with customers.

## 2. Influence

The Influence stage begins to leverage the power of collected data to fully translate knowledge about customers' interests into personalized messaging. Based on the profile which the organisation has built up on individual physicians, reps can be advised what may work well, and even have next-best actions suggested to them. Conversely, reps can actively report results and insights back to the organisation.

Some companies may even want to add a decisions support engine on top of their CRM system at this stage, which automatically suggests content that reps should offer through digital channels based on historical interactions.

## 3. Orchestrate

This is the 'ultimate' phase for reps in their path to becoming truly omnichannel. Here, they act as stewards for all engagements with "their" HCPs – meaning that they initiate and follow up on all multichannel communication with their individual customers. This also implies they are in regular contact with other customer-facing roles. In particular Marketing and Medical play an active role in the development and continuous adjustment of the multichannel plan.

As such, they are able to deliver a superior, seamless customer experience, leading to higher customer enagement – and continued access.

## Healthy snack

### The use case for building a decision support engine for multichannel reps

**A pharma company wanted to improve the usage of rep approved email, as after installing the capability they witnessed low levels of uptake by their reps. To do this, the company added a decision support engine to their CRM system, which made suggestions to reps about which emails should be sent, taking into account physician segmentation and content interaction history.**

**After this engine had been introduced, rep uptake of the approved email channel was 23 times higher than previously – when reps had to choose themselves which emails to send to their customers. Additionally, and importantly, HCPs whom received suggestion-driven emails from reps increased their prescription volume by 4%, compared to a control group.**

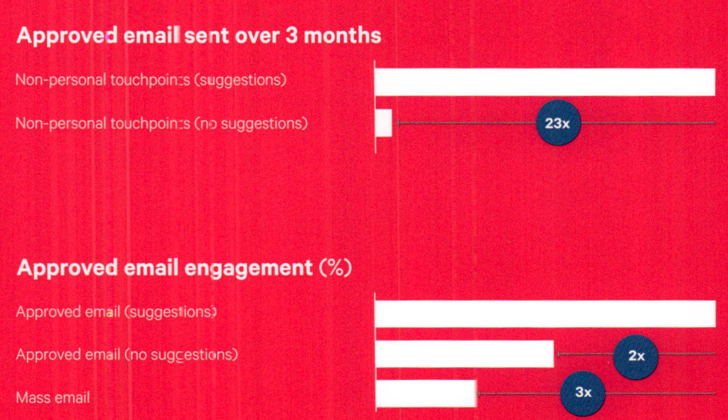

# Value for who?

While conceptually simple, this kind of transformation can prove a challenge. However, within a pharma context the difficulty usually resides not with technology, but with the change management component ("what's in it for me?"). Widespread buy-in to the process leads to widespread value throughout the organisation.

## Value proposition for different stakeholders

**Sales rep** | First-line (district) manager & sales leader | Marketing | HCP

- Increased access through additional channel touchpoints
- Prolonging the conversation through digital channels
- Higher impact through improved insights
- Lead generation and prioritization through historical channel affinity insights
- Improved internal growth opportunities thanks to new skills

Sales rep | **First-line (district) manager & sales leader** | Marketing | HCP

- Improved sales force allocation based on HCP channel affinity and cost-to-serve
- More efficient coverage of remote/vacant territories
- Better achievability of contact ambition level through increased channel spectrum
- Improved ability to reallocate resources to higher margin, higher growth products

Sales rep | First-line (district) manager & sales leader | **Marketing** | HCP

- Move from product to customer centricity based on improved channel affinity and content insights leading to better segmentation & targeting
- Improved engagement through tailored content that meets customer's expectations
- More efficient use of content by repurposing it into additional channels
- Ability to trigger behavioral based communication

Sales rep | First-line (district) manager & sales leader | Marketing | **HCP**

- Seamlessly integrated communication experience
- More tailored information based on true needs
- Ability to engage also through pull channels as opposed to rep push communication only
- Adding pull to rep push communication

> "While it's discouraging that doctors may not meet as often with pharma reps, most physicians still view these reps as valuable sources of information."

**Pratap Khedkar, Principal, ZS Associates**

# Key MC Rep

While theoretically there is no end to the combinations and permutations of channels a digitally empowered rep could use, it generally refers to 4 channels:

| Tactics | | Most common strategy | Interaction type |
|---|---|---|---|
| Tablet detailing | → | Increase impact of F2F | PUSH |
| Rep email | → | Increase frequency on top of F2F | PUSH |
| Remote engagement | → | Increase reach on top of F2F | PUSH |
| HCP self-service website | → | Increase frequency on top of F2F | PULL |

For more in-depth information on these tactics, we refer to the relevant chapters in the book.

# To conclude

**The go-to-market model for pharma has to change. Physicians are – on the whole - very open to digital communication with pharma, particularly digital natives (who will represent 70% of the HCP population by 2020). Next to the age-related channel affinities, there is a broader trend away from the traditional "relationship seeker" customers (only 24% of all specialists in EU5) towards "independents" and "knowledge seekers". In addition, "respect for my time" is the key to continued access and customer engagement.**

**However, seeing the multichannel rep concept as a cost-effective way to merely increase frequency is bound to lead to massive customer disenchantment, increasing the risk of further access restrictions. When done well (ie, "quality over quantity"), the multichannel rep has great potential to improve engagement and create customer delight.**

**Last but not least, the MC rep concept is more than just adding some technology and some change management... indeed, it is a key component of a radical rethink of the commercial organization - one that operates across brands and divisions to plan and execute, with sensitivity, to the needs of individual customers.**

PEAK
DELIGHT
REP

# 14 Agile Mix Planning

> "Marketers must develop an iterative, agile-like approach to test a range of media, read results and make rapid optimization decisions."
>
> **Forrester**

## It's all in the mix

Multichannel, i.e. varying message and channel, yields the highest communication impact (Tannenbaum 1967):

| | Variation of **message**: NO | Variation of **message**: YES |
|---|---|---|
| Variation of **channel**: NO | Lowest effect | Intermediate effect |
| Variation of **channel**: YES | Intermediate effect | Highest effect |

Despite this, pharma has remained in 'monochannel mode'. For decades, the classical rep model has proven incredibly resilient. In recent years, however, new stakeholders have emerged (payers, group practices, patients, referrers, ...), and new channels have proliferated. These changes, along with increasing customer empowerment, are driving the **need to radically rethink the channel mix.**

But most companies in life sciences have only made baby steps in the re-engineering process (see the chapter on the multichannel rep). To achieve impact at scale, organisations should use a robust strategic framework to develop, execute and measure their channel strategy. This will help companies truly capitalise on the channel opportunities, deliver a superior customer experience and also increase profitability (higher sales AND reduced cost to serve).

## The size of the prize

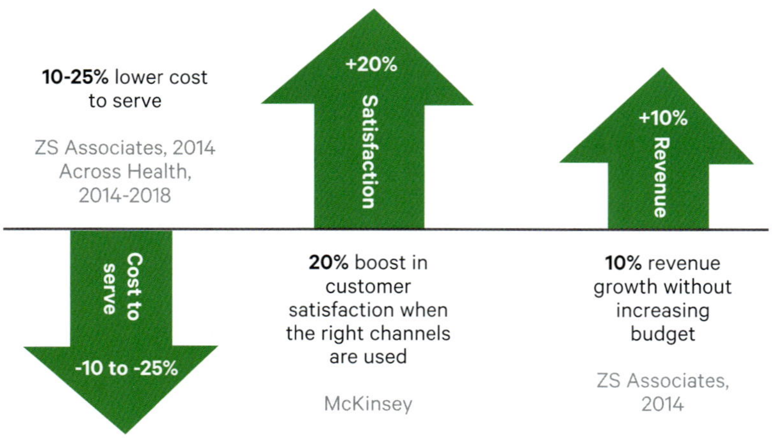


+ more flexibility in terms of resourcing (lower fixed cost)
+ shorter time to critical frequency (and behavioural change)

"The irony is that while there have never been more ways to reach customers, it's never been harder to connect with customers."

**Brad Jakeman, Chief Creative Officer Activision**

## The metrics of Agile Mix Planning

**10%** Optimizing the channel mix can increase revenues by 10%. (Source: ZS Associates)

**8%** ... of pharma staff says they have a robust process for channel mix. (Source: 2017 Across Health Maturometer)

**4%** ... of pharma staff 'completely agree' that they have a high-performing marketing automation platform in place. (Source: 2017 Across Health Maturometer)

**4.6%** ... of pharma's sales & marketing budget is spent on digital, while over 50% of HCPs prefer a mix of traditional and new channels. (Source: IQVIA and the Across Health Navigator)

**<35%** ... of specialists are satisfied or very satisfied with pharma's digital offerings. (Source: Across Health Navigator 2017)

**6%** Only 6% of all EU5 specialists were approached in a truly MCM way in 2017 (rep + email + remote engagement). (Source: Across Health Navigator 2017)

Many companies are hoping that if they throw enough money at problems, and assets at customers, something will eventually hit the (digital) mark. And in that context, digital channels are extremely attractive, as they enable frequency and reach to be increased at very low marginal cost. But from the customer perspective, this "push" barrage may come across as "too much".

Organisations need to create a **channel mix** capable of delivering a valued and differentiated experience at each key interaction, and throughout the customer journey. The classic approach of gaining a deep understanding of the customer's needs must be combined with real-time knowledge of how to engage customers with different channels.

> "We will see the progressive collapse of traditional marketing planning processes into a continuous marketing presence."
>
> **Forrester**

# The maturity level of omnichannel

Integrated multichannel planning and execution still have a lot of room for growth: only 17% of European pharma staff use this as a standard practice today (making this only the 18th most commonly used tactic). A similar picture can be found in the adoption of marketing automation software, one of the key enablers of robust omnichannel engagement (rank 22). On the other hand, the level of pilots in the area of integrated campaigns bodes well, as 56% are currently trialling this key tactic. However, the fact that only 31% are piloting marketing automation software confirms the hesitation of pharma to engage in full digital engagement.

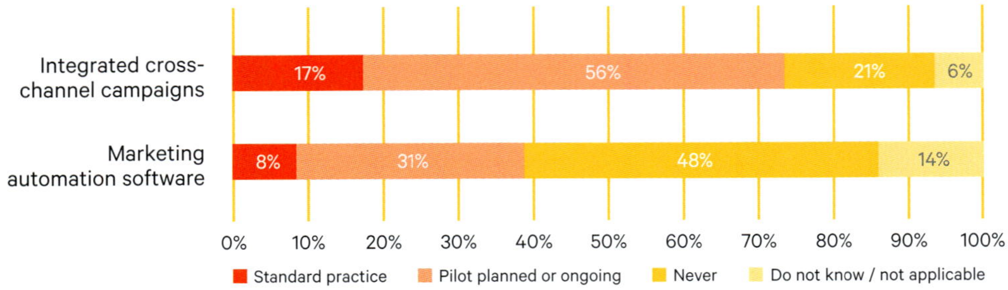


Source: Across Health Maturometer 2017 | N=221 | EU scope

> "In preparing for battle, I have always found that plans are useless but planning is indispensable."
>
> **Dwight Eisenhower**

# Healthy snack

## Marketing mix modelling

**A completely different way of channel prioritization is through marketing mix modelling. This is the process of using statistical analysis to estimate, optimize, and predict the impact of multichannel promotional tactics on future sales. It's a rigorous exercise that incorporates a company's internal marketing and financial information as well as contextual information.**

**Typical inputs** for marketing mix modelling include:

- At least 24 months of historical data (campaign responses, sales/marketing/medical spend, channel-specific ROI,...)
- Contextual information (reimbursement status, pricing changes, weather data (for respiratory products, for instance), ...)
- Competitor information (market share vs competitors, share dynamics after competitor entry, ...)

**Typical steps are:**

1. **COLLECT DATA**
   - Identify data sources
   - Collect historical data to build a database
2. **BUILD THE MODEL**
   - Explore the collected data
   - Build the model using collected data to identify the drivers
3. **OPTIMIZE THE BUDGET**
   - Calculate optimal marketing spend allocation based on different scenarios
4. **IMPLEMENT THE RECOMMENDATION**
   - Make recommendations based on these models and estimates and implement

Next to its many benefits, mix modelling also has several **challenges,** including:

- **Static analysis.** Modelling can prove problematic in the case of rapidly changing customer behaviour and environmental factors. It typically answers questions like: "Did it work?" rather than "Will it work?" or "Will it work again?"
- **Bias toward high-volume marketing activities and channels.** Marketing mix models were originally developed for certain types of traditional high-budget marketing and sales activities. However, the variety of channels has since exploded and the level of data on digital channels is quite "thin" and recent still, particularly in pharma (see "Blinded by science?")

### "Blinded by science"?

**Marketing mix modelling in life sciences**

*Marketing mix modelling can be extraordinarily useful, but may also inspire blind faith in "black box" analytic results. Savvy marketers have long known that the analytical strength of marketing mix modelling is also its Achilles' heel, particularly when it is applied to situations where important market changes are taking place. Here, it may well provide unreliable forecasts. Arguably, this situation is applicable to life sciences too. In addition, pharma typically does NOT yet have the required 24-months of back data on digital channels to kickstart the process.*

# Leveraging a robust campaign planning framework

As a brief reminder, our MCM planning process has 6 steps. In this chapter, we focus on stages 4 and 5. The first 3 components are covered in chapter 1, and measurement in chapter 12. Overall, we recommend the concept of "agile marketing" to **reduce time-to-market** and **maximize the learning opportunities**.

| 1. STRATEGIC IMPERATIVES | 2. STRATEGIC PROXIES | 3. CONVERSION POINTS | 4. TACTICS | 5. PRIORITIZATION AND PLANNING | 6. MEASUREMENT |
|---|---|---|---|---|---|
| Brand strategy<br>• Brand objectives<br>• Positioning<br>• Business opportunities<br>• Key stakeholders | Translate the strategy into something actionable<br>• Leverage points<br>• Behavioural objectives<br>• Messages | What content or services will drive the action/ change that we want? | **What are the ideal channels to achieve this?** | **What is feasible? What is the impact of these tactics?**<br>• Prioritize and plan over time | How can we measure the interactions and engagement? |

## A. Prioritise your channels

Once you have defined your strategic imperatives and defined the proxies and conversion points (steps 1-3), the time has come to **prioritize the relevant channels** (steps 4 and 5). In a world of ever greater channel choice, eliminating some may feel counterintuitive, but strategically this is the right course of action. Deprioritizing channels reduces complexity and cost, freeing up resources to allow the organisation to focus on the core.

Your strategic imperative(s) may already drive you towards specific channels:

| Objective | Most common strategy | Channels |
|---|---|---|
| **1. Add frequency** | Leverage mostly low-touch channels to increase frequency (for instance, rep-triggered email, DM, call centre) | • remote rep<br>• remote MSL<br>• pharma self-service portal<br>• rep triggered email<br>• direct marketing (DM)<br>• call centre |
| **2. Add impact** | Make every encounter count more (for instance, personalized content, dynamic CLM presentation, ...) | • Closed Loop Marketing (CLM)<br>• rich-media content<br>• personalized content |
| **3. Increase reach** | Getting to customers you are not seeing (no-access customers, restricted resources, geographic difficulties, ...); examples include email marketing, 3rd party websites/enewsletters | • pharma email<br>• pharma self-service portal<br>• 3rd party site/newsletter<br>• remote rep<br>• remote MSL<br>• DM<br>• call centre<br>• pharma webcasts<br>• eMeded |
| **4. Facilitate "social selling"** (aka peer-to-peer communications) | Helping customers (mainly HCPs) connect to each other to personally endorse key messages (e.g. via meetings, webinars, HCP communities) | • (KOL) webinars<br>• virtual advisory boards<br>• HCP + patient networks |

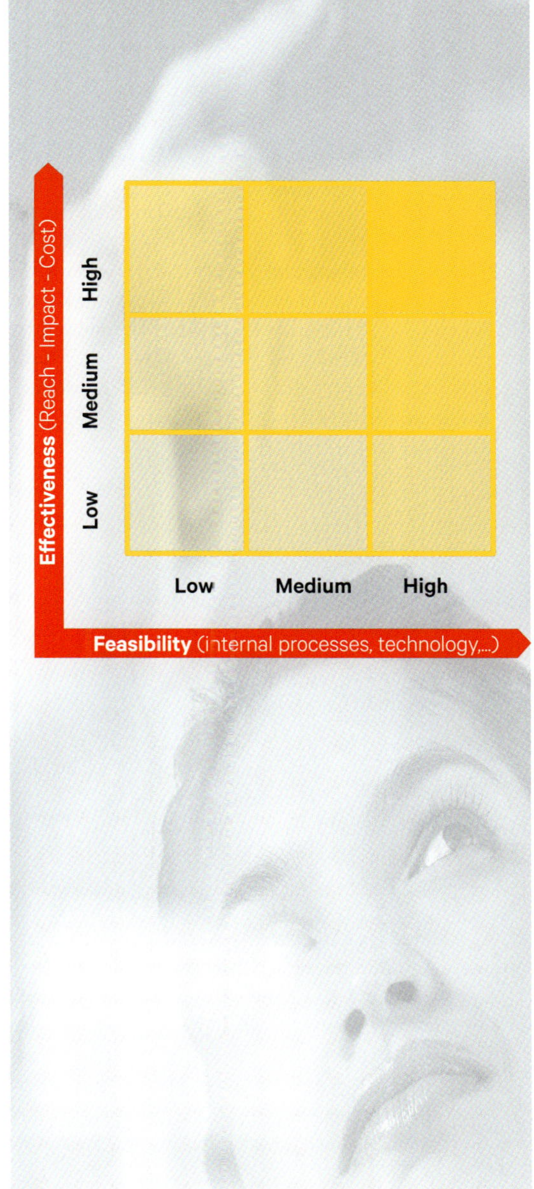


Several other factors may impact your ultimate prioritization exercise. However, when it comes down to it, only two (or three) factors really matter:

- **Effectiveness** (composite of reach, frequency, impact and cost)
- **Feasibility** (a barometer of how ready your organisation is to activate this channel in the short term)

Using an **'effectiveness vs feasibility' graph** is an easy way to demonstrate this visually:

Effectiveness

The **Y axis** looks at the likely effectiveness of channels:

- For best results, use an established framework for reach, frequency, and impact of channels, like the Across Health Navigator
- Use benchmarks (from previous campaigns) to establish the cost per contact or 'MCQ'

Feasibility

The **X axis** looks at the short-term roll-out feasibility of the channel.

This can be more subjective, so it's often a good idea to agree on the parameters upfront, for instance:

- Was the channel used previously in the company?
- Does the channel integrate easily with existing technologies?
- Does the channel add more complexity to the compliance process (compared with an already used channel)?
- Does it involve significant change management (e.g. for the fieldforce or Medical)?

A final check of the level of INNOVATION of the proposed channel set is recommended. Do you leave enough room for **experimentation** and **continuous improvement?** The following distribution has proven to be a good way to ensure constant learning:

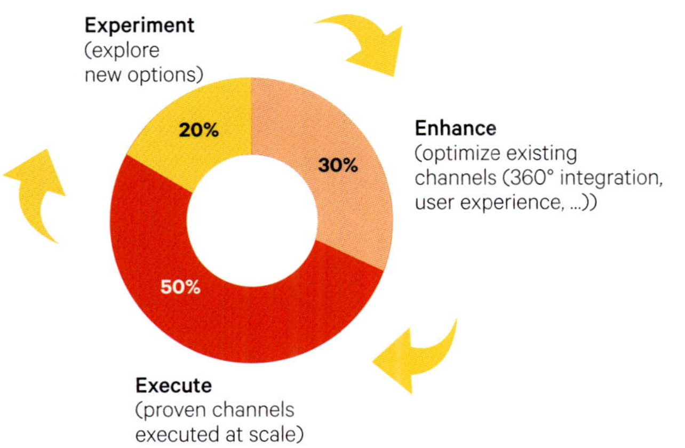


> "20 to 25 percent of spending should finance well-structured experiments."
>
> McKinsey

Over time, the channels you experiment with will need to be enhanced – and then ultimately executed at scale. This virtuous cycle can't happen without the original experimentation and learnings.

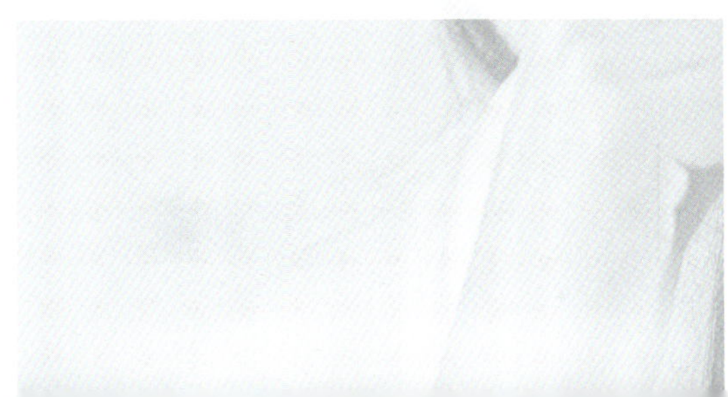

## B. Design your campaign plan

The following dimensions are critical in designing a balanced campaign plan:

**1** **Vary your channels**: "variety is the spice of life". Including a mix of channels, ideally spread between owned, paid and earned, increases customer engagement (the "channel mix flame"). But one should not go overboard on variation: a great-looking plan can easily turn into an execution nightmare if company maturity is (or turns out to be) low; start with 5-7 channels, including a strong "paid media" part. This is relatively easy and fast to implement, with guaranteed & instant reach.

**2** **Content is king:** Using the right channel is vital, but for maximum impact it needs to be integrated with the right content, and offered in the right format and context. How do you identify which content and services should be offered? This should come from identifying the key messages needed to drive the required behavioural change (steps 1-3 in the process above) for each of the selected segments or personas. Things tend to start adding up quickly, though, so it is no surprise that this often leads to the identification of a significant gap between what is needed vs what exists. At any rate, it is vitally important to prepare content well ahead of time to ensure it has been approved before the start of the campaign.

**3** **Design for target frequency**: "Einmal ist keinmal", as they say in Germany ("Once doesn't count"). The principle of "the magnificent 7" is considered the gold standard for frequency, meaning you need to have 5-9 touchpoints to get to behavioural change/conversion.
A few tips:

- Take the **already planned** offline engagements (fieldforce, medical events, ...) into account from the start of the planning process
- Do NOT aim to go over and above the **ideal frequency**, as this may upset customers – and also reduce the efficiency of your campaign.
- Ensure a **balanced mix** of high-frequency channels (email, banner) - which tend to have a lower impact - with low-frequency high-impact ones (rep, webinar,...) to ensure you can reach the required "blended" frequency.

In the end, "ideal frequency" is relative and will vary by situation (high-involvement vs low-involvement products, level of competitor SOV pressure, PLC stage, ...). Hence, each brand should experiment to find its own **proper frequency equation**, using agile marketing principles.

### Tip

**Don't copy-paste**

Be aware of 'best practices', but also **be wary of 'worst practices'**. One of the very worst is copy/pasting last year's marketing plan. Your marketing planning is your opportunity to stand still and re-examine many of your assumptions. Taken-for-granted beliefs inevitably creep into our thinking and leaving this unquestioned holds risks: you may end up with a marketing plan that is suited for yesteryear's market reality, instead of one that is adapting every quarter to a continually changing environment.

> "The greatest danger in times of turbulence is not the turbulence, it is to act with yesterday's logic."
>
> **Peter Drucker**

**4 Give cost-effectiveness (cost per MCQ) a central place**: even digital channels can have a significant fixed and/or variable cost compared to traditional channels. If you then add the impact of the channels (MCQ), you can compare "apples with apples" (see table below). However, customers have different journey needs and should not be channelled into the cheapest option to the detriment of their expected experience. As a rule: the more complex the customer decision, the higher the need for (more expensive) high-touch engagement.

**"Not all apples are created equal"**

| | Fixed cost (setup) | Variable cost Cost/customer | Cost/customer (n = 1000) | Cost/MCQ |
|---|---|---|---|---|
| 3d party remote detailing (MCQ = 1) | 10,000€ | 80€ | 90€ | 90€ |
| Call centre (MCQ = 0.7) | 5,000€ | 8€ | 13€ | 13.5€ |
| Pharma email (MCQ = 0.5) | 2,000€ | 0€ | 2€ | 4€ |

*A ficticious example of values to compare the cost of different channels*

**5 Integrate personal and non-personal channels:** Customers expect organisations to remember their interactions and channel preferences, and adjust their offerings accordingly. Importantly also, MCM programmes show a consistently higher impact when rep efforts are complemented with digital: in a multiyear medtech campaign, Across Health saw a 30% increase in referrals in customer segments who engaged with both reps and MCM, compared to 13% for rep-only and 10% for MCM only. It is critically important therefore to align rep planning with the MCM planning efforts, which may require a significant investment in change management, processes and technology.

**Referral uptake (+%) by type of promotion**

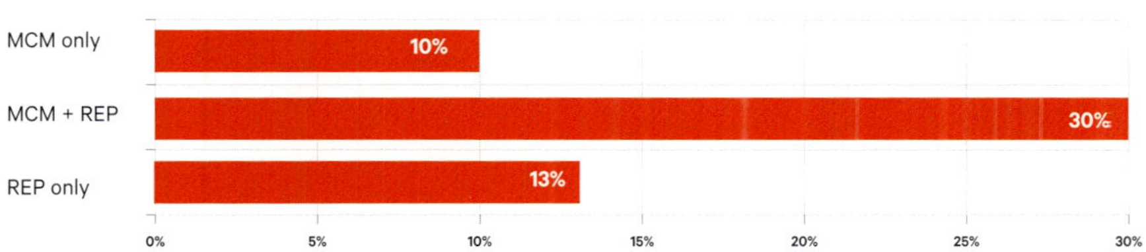


Source: Across Health 2017

## Tip

### "To SOV or QOV, that's the question"

Pharma has traditionally focused on **Share Of Voice (SOV)** marketing, i.e. maximizing the relative share of time customers spend with them, rather than the competition, through setting high visit frequency targets for reps. Indeed, frequency is important, and yes, SOV is a relatively easily measurable activity metric showing that the fieldforce is 'busy' executing the customer action plan.

In recent years, however, customers have been consistently telling the industry that they want something other than one-size-fits-all push marketing. As a result, they have reduced rep access, and started looking online for the content and services they want.

To build a future-proof model for omnichannel customer engagement, QUALITY needs to get a much more prominent place in this quantity-dominated picture. We suggest moving from SOV to **QOV ("quality of voice")**, using the following formula:

QOV
=
RIGHT channels
x RIGHT content
x RIGHT frequency
x RIGHT execution quality
=
optimum customer access
& engagement
& conversion

In the end, QOV assumes a truly customer-centric approach as well as personalized engagement capabilities, as customers typically have different channel, content, and frequency needs.

# Overcoming internal siloes to achieve superior omnichannel

One of the key issues in life sciences (and other industries) is that different customer-facing teams (marketing, sales, medical, digital, ...) are developing and executing customer engagement plans **in (not so) splendid isolation**. Each department may be focused on a different set of goals, metrics and outcomes, resulting in disconnected tactics and a subpar customer experience.

Only 14% of European marketers have an actionable single customer view in place - a *conditio sine qua non* for delivering a consistent and personalised omnichannel customer experience. And while achieving a 360° customer view is already difficult, that 14% would also need technology to act on these new kinds of customer insight, like marketing automation. But in this area too, pharma is just getting started: only 4% of European respondents claim to have such a platform in place (Across Health Maturometer 2017).

> Companies that stick with what worked in the past risk seeing a chasm opening up quickly between them and their digitally-minded competitors
>
> **Nick Taylor**
> **Managing Director Accenture**

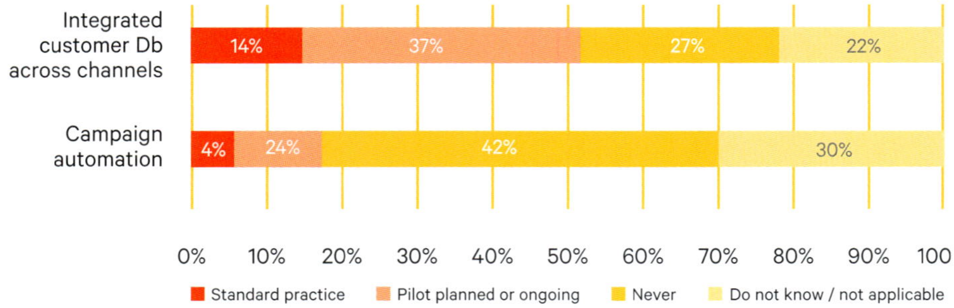


Source: Across Health Maturometer 2017 | N=221 | EU scope

NOTE: In recent years, another type of supportive technology has become available at the rep level, based on the Nobel-prize winning behavioural economics "nudging" concept. The software suggests next best actions and channels to the rep based on an algorithm. Early reports are very positive (see also the "healthy snack" in the MC rep chapter)...

## Healthy snack

### "What's the frequency, Kenneth"?

Despite the popular song by R.E.M., this area has received rather limited attention from the research community, even in other industries. The short answer is: "it depends". In 1982, Ostrow came up with these dimensions for consumer goods (and since then, very little research has been done in this important space):

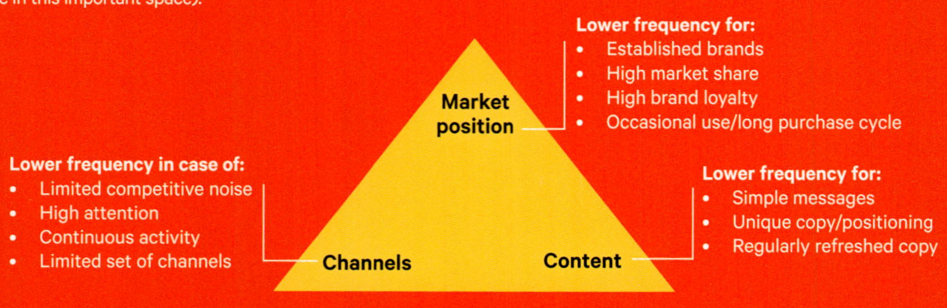


In the FMCG space, media planners recommend 5 to 6 exposures, with the lowest frequency of 3 and the highest frequency of 12 (Makienko 2012). For a more high-involvement, complex industry like life sciences, the "magnificent 7" may therefore indeed be a good baseline for adding or decreasing frequency, based on factors such as the above.

## Checklist: 11 steps to MCM campaign success

1. Run through steps 1-3 of the **strategic MCM framework**
2. Brainstorm on a **relevant set of channels** and prioritize them
3. Define the **time period** for the campaign (rep cycle, before/during/after a congress, 6-12 months, ...)
4. Define the **desired MCQs** per segment/customer
5. Compare with the **already planned "traditional"** MCQs (fieldforce, MSL, meetings, ...)
6. **Add MCM tactics for specific segments/customers** ("surround sound" MC rep tactics, central campaign elements,..)
7. Integrate both parts & develop the **campaign plan**
8. Assess the **campaign blueprint** using a checklist based on:
   - Do you have enough (but not too much) **channel variation** (on- and offline, owned/paid/earned)?
   - Is the **content relevant** enough to achieve the desired behavioural change?
   - Will you achieve the **right frequency** and campaign cadence (with both online & offline customers)?
   - Do you integrate **personal & non-personal** channels in an effective way (+ plan for any change management)?
   - Are all campaign components **cost-effective** (cost per MCQ vs other alternatives)?
9. Define **KPIs**
10. **Execute**
11. **Continuously measure & adjust in an agile fashion**

## Tip

### Agile marketing and multichannel

*The **agile marketing manifesto** (created on the basis of the agile development framework) fits hand-in-glove with the transition to omnichannel customer engagement in life sciences. Agile marketing planning advocates:*

1. **Validated learning**
   *over people's opinions and conventions*
2. **Customer-focused collaboration**
   *over silos and hierarchy*
3. **Adaptive and iterative campaigns**
   *over big-bang campaigns*
4. **The process of customer discovery**
   *over static prediction*
5. **Flexible planning** *vs rigid planning*
6. **Responding flexibly to change**
   *over following a rigid plan*
7. **Many small experiments**
   *over a few large bets*

*You can find out more at* **agilemarketingmanifesto.org**

> "Averages are so old normal."
>
> **Peter Hinssen**

# Healthy snack

## The importance of execution excellence

**Establishing an effective marketing mix requires not only sophisticated strategic planning, but also a great execution plan. Remember "5% inspiration, 95% perspiration"?**

Across Health created the multichannel strategy (campaign plan, content, KPI's) for a GP brand in several markets, with the aim of increasing reach, frequency and, ultimately, sales. We also defined the MCQ targets for the 3 GP segments (high, medium and low).

The execution of the plan was then handed over to a third-party medical portal, and the impact was measured by an independent data provider.

The impact analysis confirmed the value of the strategy, i.e., it drove extra sales (measured vs control groups). On the other hand, execution quality was relatively low – just over 10% of the total universe were reached at the appropriate MCQ level, resulting in a significant "lost sales" opportunity. Additionally, as most campaign items were fixed cost, reach (and sales) could have been increased without any significant cost increase.

| SEGMENT | % of segment universe reached within 6 months | % who achieved threshold MCQ in reached group | % who reached threshold MCQ in total universe |
|---|---|---|---|
| **H** | 62% | 19% | 12% |
| **M** | 60% | 20% | 12% |
| **L** | 31% | 35% | 11% |

This case study underscores the importance of getting a robust and agile execution and measurement process in place following the campaign design strategy work.

# Agile marketing for multichannel success - tips for novices

**Continuous testing**

The agile marketer does not start from certainties but from unknowns. Continuous testing is key:

1. Formulate a hypothesis.
2. Decide quickly how this can be tested and what is needed to measure results.
3. Run the programme to prove (or disprove) the hypothesis

If proven, the next hypothesis can be formulated for further learning. With agile marketing, the learning curve never ends.

**Three reasons for going agile**

With agile marketing, you are able to **respond faster** to market changes (speed); there is **more alignment** between marketing and other departments, not in the least with sales and medical; and there is **more engagement** among the stakeholders, thus increasing the likelihood of better results.

**Don't overdo it**

Agile is a great framework, but it is not necessarily suited for every project. Smaller projects can do with a simpler format. Always consider which mode of operations is best suited for each type of project.

**Don't give up too soon**

Transitioning to agile takes time. The processes and tools to manage projects are new, and you require more collaboration with other teams. So while you're still trying to understand the agile terminology, you must also convince other teams to embark on this adventure with you. Challenging, especially when marketing and budgets are already closely monitored. So, when you decide to go agile, hang in there, as it may be a wild ride at first. But ultimately, increased agility will enable you and your company to respond to changes in the market environment better and faster.

**In with the new, out with the old?**

Agile marketing does not mean you have to do away with all strategic models from the past. In fact, the more models you know, the better equipped you are to question assumptions and look at marketing challenges from different angles. Even better is to mix up different models to create your own new, bespoke model.

**Assign 'bridge builders' and 'agile coaches'**

Many IT departments have dedicated personnel to liaise between IT and the business, but marketing is already expected to be an integral part of it. Assigning 'engagement managers' helps to bring people from different functions together on agile projects. Also worthwhile is bringing in an 'agile coach': someone who helps you to adopt and adapt the agile framework.

## To conclude

Channels and customer interaction models are rapidly proliferating in life sciences. Acting without a plan and an understanding of new channels (and customer adoption of them) will result in suboptimal results – or even disaster. Right channel, right content, right frequency, right context,.. are all key parameters of successful customer engagement in the omnichannel age. Agile multichannel marketing planning offers ways to challenge the "monochannel" status quo and reap the benefits of mix optimization in a robust and future-proof way. Conversely, companies who skimp on experimentation and digitization will be overtaken by changing customer behaviours or forced to assume large risks by rolling the dice on unproven programs when (not "if") markets shift.

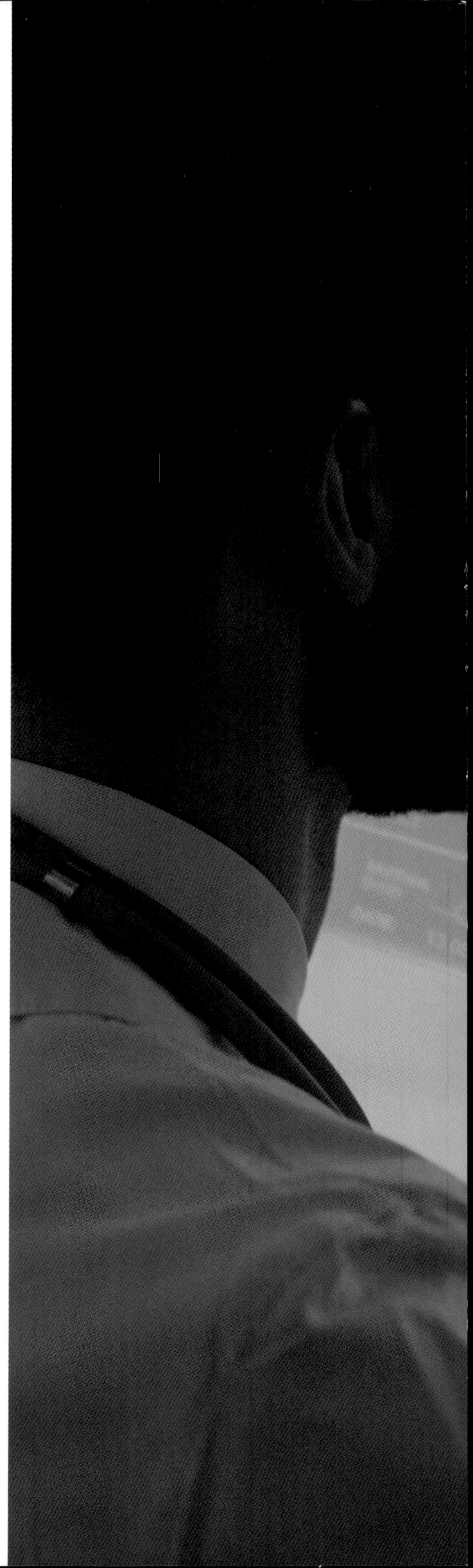

# 15 The Future of Pharma in a Digital World

> "When the human body is the biggest data platform, who will capture value?"
>
> EY

# The perfect storm?

**The operating system of life sciences is fundamentally changing**. If you haven't felt it yet – don't worry, it will catch you soon. Pharma needs to be ready. Broadly, at the moment, it is not.

The traditional model, focused on selling medicines to the 'learned intermediary' (the healthcare professional) is coming under significant pressure, as governments earmark their restricted budgets to products and services that bring value to the healthcare system at large. In a 2012 article, **the Boston Consulting Group** provides a great picture of where pharma has traditionally been "playing" – focused on just a small (although highly profitable) part of the landscape, at the intersection of "intervention and therapy" and "drugs".

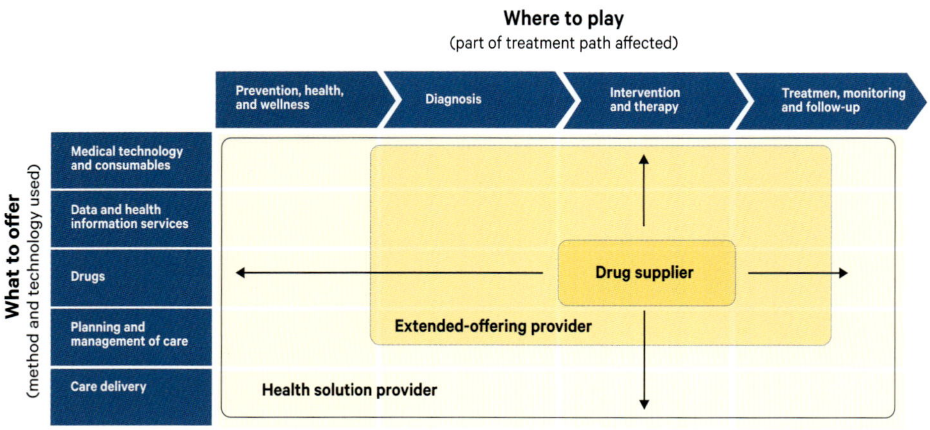


Source: BCG 2012

Forays into other spaces (arrows) remained fairly limited. This has led to large quantities of potential value - and data-fuelled knowledge - leaking away. We need only look at the historic treatment of adherence (the 'forgetful patient') or the limited efforts in prevention programmes, as examples of this.

At the same time, **EY** shows that the importance of these new stakeholders (patients, but also payers and pharmacists) is increasing, while specialists and primary care physicians are losing importance. Interestingly, they also see "other sectors" enter the life sciences market – at speed. The likes of Apple, Google and Amazon have set their eyes on the biggest industry in the world, and are trying to carve out interesting segments. As opposed to pharma, they know digital, big data and the consumer really well, positioning them extremely strongly in the consumer-led prevention & adherence space.

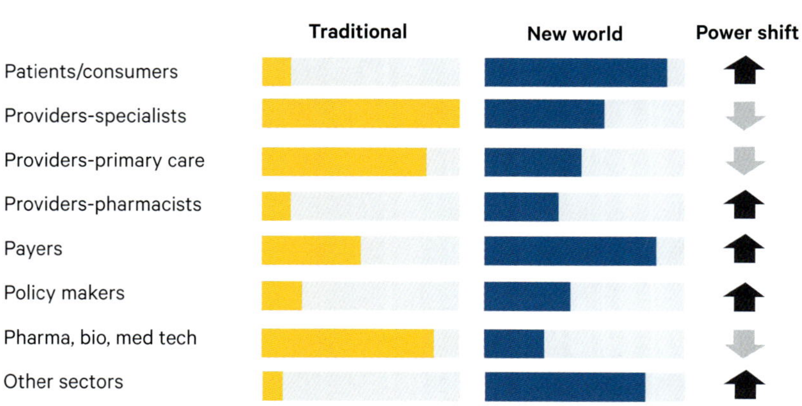


Source: EY, Progressions Life Sciences 4.0

> Pharma will succeed or fail based not on how many drugs they sell, but on whether they improve health outcomes.
>
> **Dave Chase**
> **Entrepreneur**

In addition, pharma as a "drug supplier" is at a significant and ever-widening competitive disadvantage in terms of patient data. Once their products have successfully finished all clinical trials and reached the market, other stakeholders (like payers, health tech startups and Big Tech) have much better access to real-world patient data on pharma's key assets: their products. In telecom, a similar trend is visible, which is referred to as **"the dumb pipe" syndrome**. Is pharma facing the "dumb pill" issue?

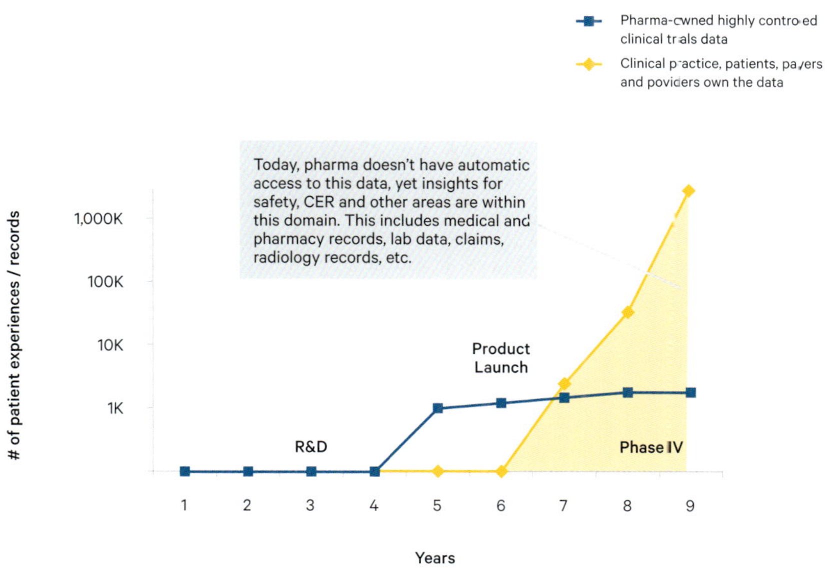


Source: The value of healthcare data for secondary uses in clinical research and development – Gary K. Mallow, Merck, HIMSS 2012

Last but not least, innovative companies are developing increasingly sophisticated, low-cost and robust platforms and technologies, leading to **"super convergence"** (as per Eric Topol, the American cardiologist, geneticist and digital medicine researcher). Super-convergence will lead to an entire reboot of the healthcare industry...with a plethora of opportunities for agile incumbents, Big Tech, and focused startups – and big risks for slow movers.

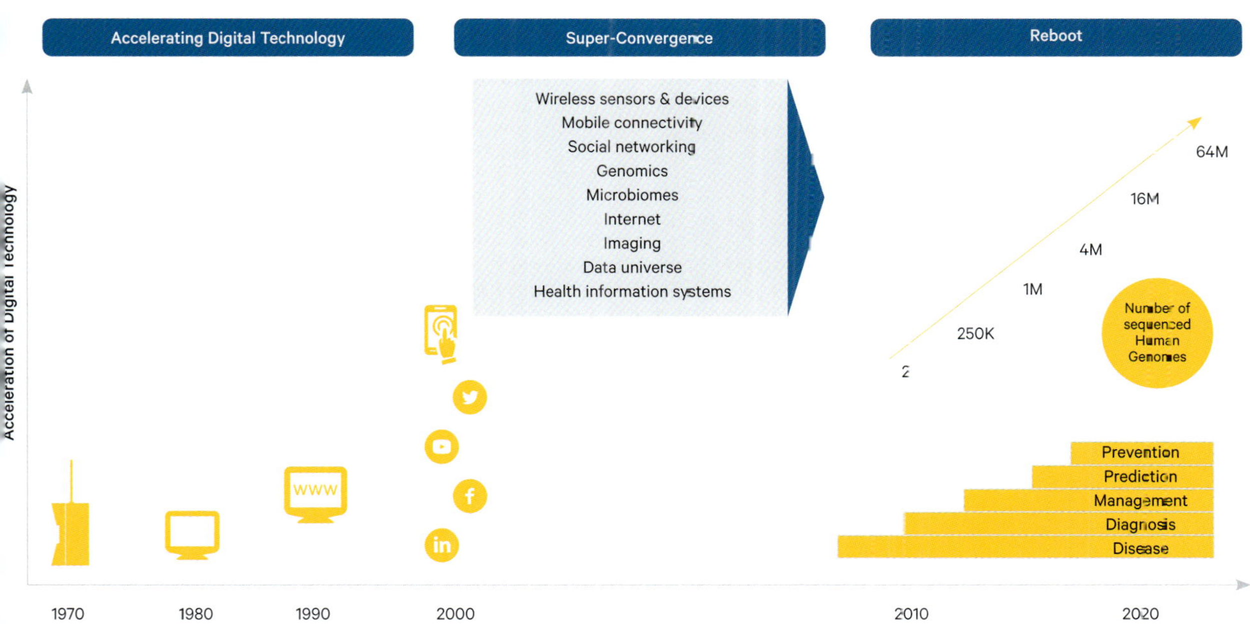


Source: Paul Sonnier, thestoryofdigitalhealth.com

## The metrics of innovative customer engagement in life sciences

**92%** ... of pharma staff believe that digital technologies will disrupt their industry. (Source: Maturometer 2018)

**90%** Healthcare professionals ignore 90% of the data they generate. (Source: McKinsey Global Institute)

**80%** ... of what doctors do now will be eliminated by the mid 2020s. (Source: John Sculley)

**12-17%** ... of total healthcare spend can be saved through big data analytics. (Source: McKinsey)

**12** Healthcare only counts 12 unicorns (health-tech startups with over 1 billion valuation). For reference, there are 27 Fintech unicorns.

**<1%** Fewer than 1% of startups survive

**7x** By 2019, every 1 USD invested by enterprises in innovation will require an additional 7 USD in execution. (Source: Gartner)

> 'One day the utility (of genomic data) will be so high it will surpass the fear.'
>
> **Robin Thurston, CEO Helix**

## The Plantation and the Rainforest

In their book *The Rainforest: The secret to building the next Silicon Valley*, Hwang and Horowitt defined two different modes for companies to be in – rainforests and plantations. The latter is a metaphor for organisations based on the 'efficiency' model of the Industrial revolution – where all tools are focussed on accuracy, precision and quality of one particular crop. Everyone who works in the plantation thinks exclusively about, for instance, bananas.

On the other hand, in the rainforest, there are only weeds. It is dangerous, and uncertain – with outsize risks and rewards. The mentality is that of survival – to try new things, and see if they work. One of these may well be immensely valuable. The venom of a snake that could kill you, may well be the cure to cancer. And to reach scale, you need to trust people (and be trusted).

Large companies usually resemble plantations, with a focus on the value of their current and near future products. However, introducing some 'rainforest' thinking, specifically in bringing new ideas (and types of people) into an organisation may well be vital to sustain long term value.

| Rules of the Plantation ('predictable crops') | Rules of the Rainforest ('unpredictable weeds') |
|---|---|
| **1. Excel at your job** | **1. Break rules and dream** |
| **2. Be loyal to your team** | **2. Open doors and listen** |
| **3. Work with those you can depend on** | **3. Trust and be trusted** |
| **4. Seek a competitive edge** | **4. Seek fairness, not advantage** |
| **5. Do the job right the first time** | **5. Experiment and iterate together** |
| **6. Strive for perfection** | **6. Err, fail and persist** |
| **7. Return favours** | **7. Pay it forward** |

## The maturity level of innovative customer engagement

The 2017 Maturometer data confirm that innovative customer engagement opportunities are still in the early days in pharma, both from a channel and an organization perspective:

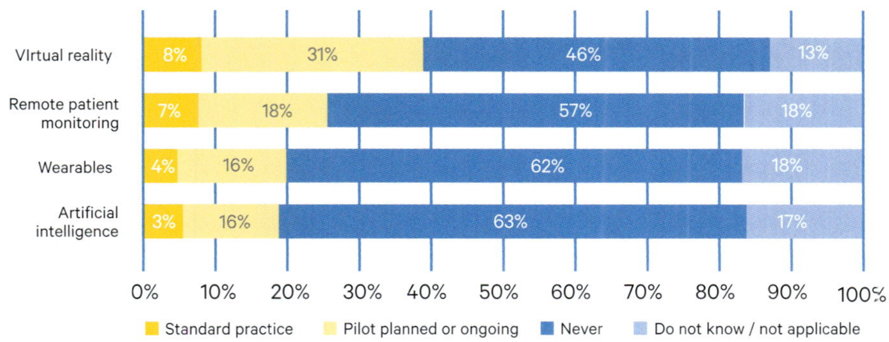


> *It shouldn't take nine months to bring a digital health pilot online. It shouldn't be as painful as having a baby.*

**Dr Ashish Atreja, Mount Sinai**

**15%** Only 15% of pharma staff believes their healthcare innovation team is effective

**37%** Only 37% of pharma staff believe their company is adequately preparing for disruption

**4th** 'Maximizing the opportunities of digital health" is the 4th priority for the next 2 years for pharma staff

Source: The Across Health Multichannel Maturometer 2017 | N = 252 | EU scope

## The fourth industrial revolution is here

In his 2016 book *The Fourth Industrial Revolution*, World Economic Forum founder Klaus Schwab outlined the changes associated with the 4th industrial revolution. While Industry 3.0 focussed on the automation of machines and processes, industry 4.0 is about the end-to-end digitization of all physical assets and the integration of all partners in the value chain into a vast digital ecosystem. Some of the key trends include:

1. Merge of the physical and digital world: digital becomes "pervasive"... think of smartphones, Internet of Things (IoT), voice-based search, robotics, autonomous vehicles, VR and AR, 3d printing,...
2. Digitisation of biology: think of nanotechnology, genome sequencing, crispR,...
3. Everything becomes data-centric: think ubiquitous data, quantum computing, AI, deep learning,...

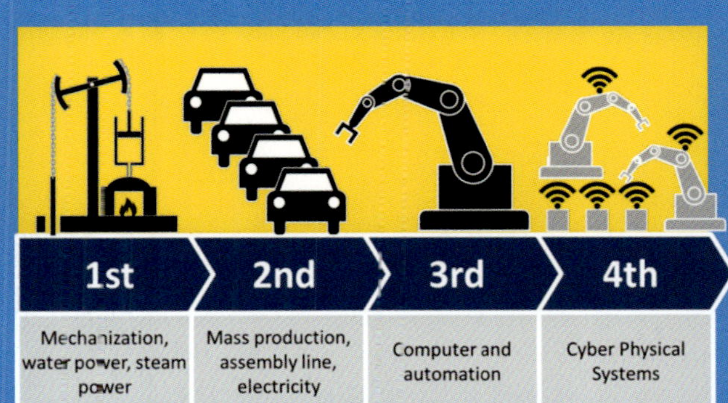


*Graphic of 4IR adapted from: The Fourth Industrial Revolution, Klaus Schwab*

## Where are the biggest shifts likely to happen?

**Basically: throughout the value chain**. Pharma is well positioned at a particular stage in the patient journey – the provision of a medication for a disease (treatment choice and product choice). But what if the game changes and deep-pocketed and/or nimbler companies enter the space? Let's dig a little deeper into the BCG framework from above:

**Prevention, health, and wellness** → **Diagnosis** → **Intervention and therapy** → **Treatment, monitoring and follow-up**

**Prevention, health, and wellness**

- Sensors embedded in our lives (phones, wearables, ...) can give advance warning of changes and recommend specific action in terms of prevention and more rapid diagnosis/referral/treatment, arguably leading to a smaller market for pharmaceuticals.

**Intervention and therapy**

- Data ubiquity and machine learning could eliminate a major job of doctors – making decisions on diagnosis, treatment and product (precision medicine, AI platforms like Babylon, Buoy Health, ...) – and hence strongly reduce the role & impact of the pharma fieldforce
- Amazon/Alibaba/... could eliminate the human interaction for fulfilling prescriptions, reducing the role of the pharmacist even more

**Treatment, monitoring and follow-up**

- Patient adherence and follow-up will see an increasing role for technology:
  - Digital therapeutics (behaviour-modification platforms like Bluestar, Omada, Pear Therapeutics, ...) will complement and sometimes replace pharmaceuticals
  - Internet of things: integrated solutions like Otsuka's Proteus-enabled Abilify or IoT-enabled inhalers (asthma/ COPD) should lead to better adherence and competitive advantage vs. the "have nots"

Organizations that have the right kind of information and use it to deliver new insights about effective care and new value-adding services are likely to capture much of the value. The big question is: **is pharma ready?** And the even bigger question: **is Big Tech, with its B2C leadership, already jockeying for this position?** In extremis, the entire patient journey could be 'owned' by a B2C consumer player, and pharmaceuticals would become a "commodity" in the process. Think Uber vs the "commodity" taxis, as a comparison.

> In the next ten years, genomics will change the world more than the Internet did. It will change how we feed people, how we treat illness, how we develop drugs.
>
> **Dr. Sanjay Patil**

# Healthy snack: Disruption, anyone?

**Clayton Christensen** introduced the theory of 'disruptive innovation' in his 1997 book *"The Innovator's Dilemma"*, defining it as "an innovation that creates a new market and value networks that will eventually disrupt an existing market and replace an existing product." Here, the incumbent targets the profitable customers at the high-end of the market, while the challenger goes for the low end. Disruption happens when the incumbent's mainstream customers start taking up the innovator's products or services in volume.

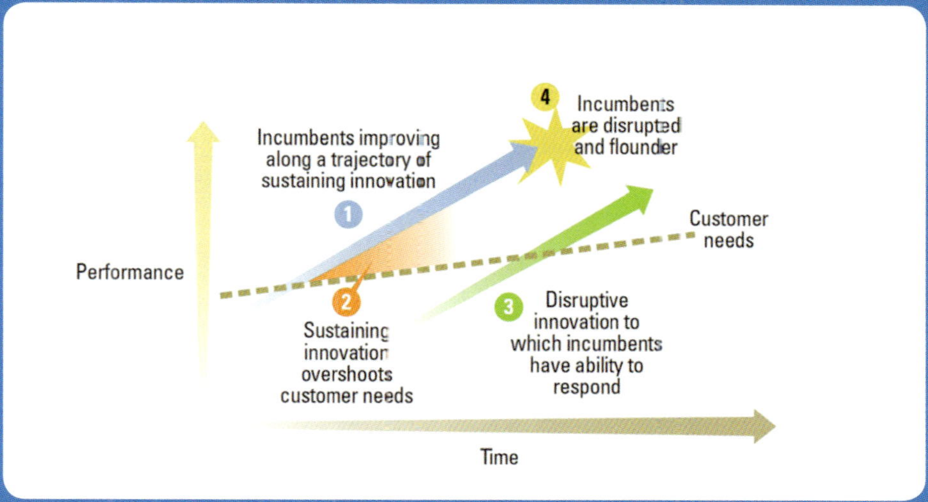


*Source: King et al, MIT Sloan Management Review, 2015*

**McKinsey** also has a powerful visualization of the disruption process - from the incumbent perspective:

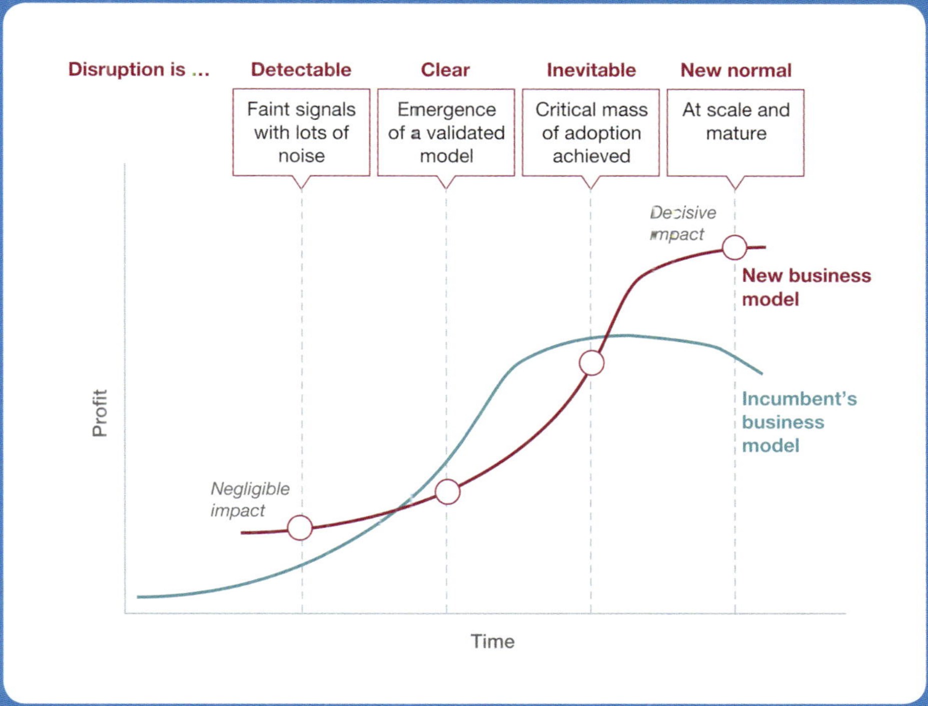


*Source: McKinsey, 2016*

Unfortunately, disruption theory is in danger of becoming a victim of its own success... Christensen now believes that the theory's core concepts have been widely misunderstood and its basic tenets misapplied (Christensen, HBR 2015).

# How to stay ahead of the game?

Pharma excels at its "sweetspot" – developing and marketing innovative pharmaceuticals. Should they expand horizontally - upstream (diagnosis and prevention) or downstream (treatment monitoring) - or even vertically? Should they consider capturing and offering data and health-information services in addition to medicines? These are big questions... but pharma's past successes and traditional functional siloes make the industry ill-suited to succeed in new environments. Fortunately, high regulatory hurdles and the specialized nature of the R&D process have given the industry some breathing space (unlike, say, the book industry being eaten by Amazon). So, how can pharma not only limit this threat, but turn it into an opportunity? These are some of the key questions to address to ensure **a future-proof strategy** (as per EY 2017):

- **For a given therapy area or patient group, will you provide services or stick to selling products?**
- **Are you aiming to prevent, treat or manage disease?**
- **Where, and how, will you fit into disease-focused, integrated-care platforms?**
- **Do you consider patients/consumers your true customers?**
- **Are you focused exclusively on creating shareholder value or on building stakeholder value?**

> Success breeds complacency. Complacency breeds failure. Only the paranoid survive.
>
> **Andy Grove**

In terms of strategic options, there is a lot that companies can do to get started:

### 1. Get serious about scenario planning

Unpredictability cannot be 'solved' by planning. Strict planning and colourful forward-looking line charts and models are irrelevant when faced with **truly** unpredictable markets. Of course, planning and strategies will remain relevant for many "stable" parts of the organization, but these processes too will need to become highly agile and adaptive.

**Scenario planning** offers a good way to create different views of possible longer-term futures. This is not a prediction exercise, but the scenarios do describe a series of extreme futures, against which current and alternative strategies can be tested. The origin of this methodology lies in military strategy, and is composed of a series of steps:

1. Once a specific topic or area of research is defined, past and current events are described, using a **PESTEL** or similar framework.
2. Through a series of external and internal **interviews**, a longlist of possible drivers for change for the next 10 to 15 years are identified
3. From these drivers for change, the most uncertain and impactful drivers are used to construct a series of **possible scenarios for the future.**
4. These are then used to **test the robustness** of the current strategy and alternative strategies. The key question being: "how would your company respond to these extreme situations today to ensure an optimal outcome for the future"?

The idea behind scenario planning is that companies are better prepared for unforeseen events, while suppressing a climate of complacency.

## Tip

PESTEL **PESTEL planning**

A PESTEL framework is one which evaluates the:

- **P**olitical
- **E**conomic
- **S**ocial
- **T**echnological
- **E**nvironmental
- **L**egal

factors which have a macro-environmental impact on an organisation

## 2. Think ecosystem rather than Not-Invented-Here

Assess where the healthcare landscape is going, what your core competitive advantage is today & tomorrow, and where you are better off partnering. Plenty of partnering options exist:

- **Big Tech**:
  - They have a strong legacy in digital and B2C marketing
  - Technologies in which they are strong (cloud/big data/pervasive/ logistics) are becoming more than just the infrastructure layer
- **Startups:**
  - Think of AI companies like Babylon Health or digital therapeutics like Omada/Woebot, or blockchain startups focusing on the personal health record...and this is only the beginning

> The battle between every startup and incumbent comes down to whether the incumbent innovates before the startup gets distribution.
>
> **Alex Rampell, Andreessen Horowitz**

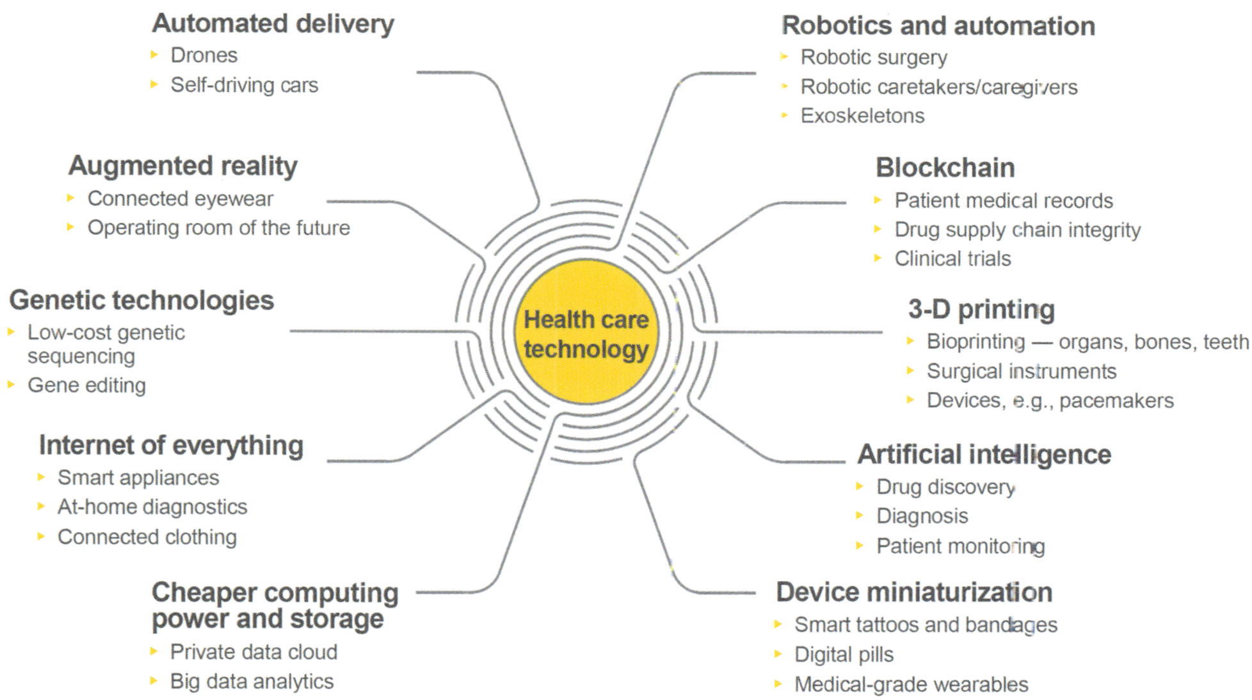


Source: EY – Life sciences 4.0, Securing value through data-driven platforms, 2018

## From multichannel to multistakeholder

Doctors are becoming much less the 'sole purveyor of knowledge', and life science companies will need to move to a multistakeholder engagement, with the new key focus on patients and payers. A fundamental problem with today's system is that patients lack knowledge and control. This is changing rapidly. Patients are becoming more empowered thanks to better information and health data. As a case in point, Sweden aims to give all its citizens electronic access to their medical records by 2020; over a third have already set up accounts. Estonia has almost universal access to electronic health records, and even Belgium is beginning the roll-out. Studies confirm that patients with such access get better treatment results..."Welcome to Doctor You" (The Economist).

"The **Doctor** will see you now"
(Ancient Egypt - 2015)

↓

"The **Patient** will see you now"
(E. Topol 2016)

↓

"The Doctor will be **you**"
(Economist 2018)

## Tip

### DAT How to prepare for your Day After Tomorrow

*Peter Hinssen* summarizes the key issues for incumbents in 4 great questions. What is your take on them?

- **Big question 1:** "Why is it almost impossible for large organizations to spot new and radical technologies quickly, and develop their potential? What explains this organizational blindness to new opportunities?"
- **Big question 2:** "Why are large corporations so eager to acquire new startups, and why are they capable of messing them up so profoundly in record time?"
- **Big question 3**: "How is it possible that large corporations – even when they understand their own challenges and the direction they need to take – are incapable of moving on their own, without external help and guidance?"
- **Big question 4:** "How can companies become agile in their 'Day After Tomorrow' thinking and be successful in developing an approach that works?

## The Day After Tomorrow concept (DAT)

Peter Hinssen's "Day after Tomorrow" model is in fact very simple. It's about dividing your attention, budget, resources, talent etc. into three simple buckets: Today, Tomorrow and the Day After Tomorrow (DAT). Most people think they spend about 70% of their time on Today, 20% on Tomorrow and 10% on the Day After Tomorrow. However, when they measure their real activities, it is more like 93%, 7% and 0%. Of course, Today is important – hugely so, even. Because it generates the current value of your activities. And Tomorrow is huge as well, because that takes care of your future value. But the Day After Tomorrow can generate huge amounts of long-term value for your company. If you do not make sure that DAT becomes embedded into the DNA of your organization, then the odds are that you won't even make it to the Day After Tomorrow.

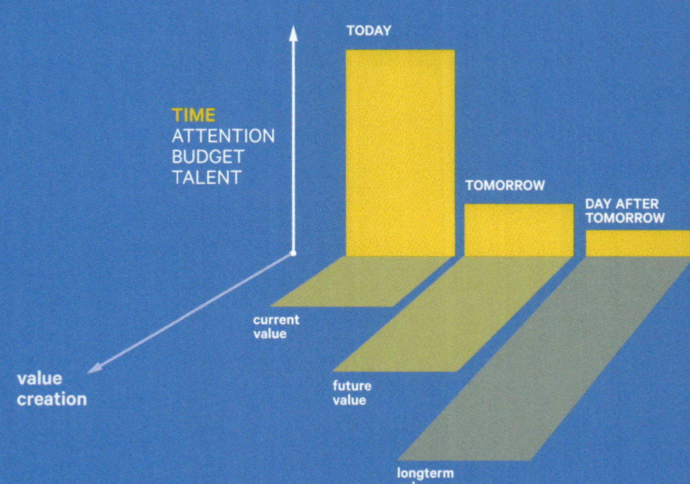

## Averages are so "old normal"

**There is no such thing as an "average" patient** – every patient is unique. Nevertheless, medicine has been focusing on the average patient for hundreds of years. Billions of dollars are wasted annually in the US alone because of unnecessary or inappropriate care. Treatment decisions continue to be made via trial and error. Thanks to powerful new technology platforms like genomics (and other flavours of –omics) and AI we are moving away from the 'average' patient who receives a 'blockbuster' product, towards personalized treatment based around 'nichebusters' ("precision medicine"). In addition, life sciences companies must also begin to define personalization more broadly than clinical data. Precision should incorporate an understanding of individual behaviour. 'Beyond the pill' services, wearables and data platforms powered by multichannel communications will have a stronger role in the post-prescription phase to optimize adherence and the value of treatment to the patient, the provider, the payer and pharma itself.

## From product-centricity to customer-centricity

Being customer-centric is the holy grail of any organization, from the smallest biotech right up to the largest incumbent. It is on websites, in mission statements and weaved through strategies. We really do believe that our 'Customer IS King'. And yet, if we are honest, we are not really obsessed with making our customers happy. We are still controlled by the one question: 'how can we sell more products and maximize our profits?'

We still put our products, processes and departments well before the customer experience. In fact, we are probably even putting the customer last. But with the arrival of empowered customers and the seamless omnichannel experience they get from digital leaders like Amazon, Uber and Netflix, service expectations are shifting fast. These expectations are increasingly being imported to the world of healthcare, too. The ones who thrive will be those who reverse their organizations and put the customer **FIRST**.

In such a customer-driven market, it is suicide to remain a product-led organization focussed on educating and selling to physicians through one dominant channel, the rep. So, how can you redesign your company, and yourself, to remain relevant in the coming years? By **pulling all different customer groups into the heart of your company**. Being truly customer-centric needs to be engrained into the very DNA of your company. It is not just about culture, but about completely inverting processes, structures and KPIs. Organizations need to become networks - more fluid, flat, experimental, creative, simple, low-cost and radical.

> ‘Stop lying about customer-centricity – it is poisoning you.’
>
> **Steven Van Belleghem**
> **Thought leader and inspirator**

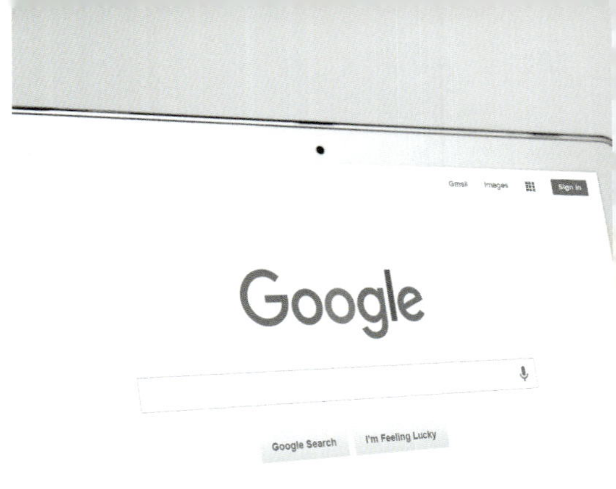


## Data, data, data

**Data is the new oil.** Whoever sits on the largest reservoir can generate the most insights. Beyond customer intelligence and personalized customer engagement, big data is also key to digital health. The Internet-of-Things (IoT), wearables and ingestibles (aka 'the quantified self'), genomics, cloud-based electronic / personal health records, companion diagnostics... are creating a never-seen mass of structured and (mostly) unstructured data.

With the advent of superior big data technologies and new-generation data scientists in healthcare, the 'race to value' has begun.

As Big Data becomes more mature within organizations...

- Data becomes an asset, not a cost
- Analytics is considered intellectual property
- Decision-making is increasingly based on data and analytics

## Agility as the facto position

In a **VUCA (Volatile-Uncertain-Complex-Ambiguous)** world, agility is key to survival. 'Agile' aims at overcoming strict planning methods and replacing them with more flexible approaches, rapid feedback loops and short cycles. This allows business leaders to respond to change better and faster. Eric Ries' 'The Lean Startup' centres around the 'build-measure-learn' feedback loop. With his background in technology start-ups, Ries found that success is best achieved when an idea is built into a minimal viable product (MVP). This product is trialled with real customers to gain learnings. The company can use this data to decide whether to persevere ("we're on the right track") or to pivot ("this is going nowhere") to a new idea. This feedback loop is repeated over and over again, until the right match between product and market is found.

## Tip

### MVP The minimal viable product

In 'The Lean Startup', author Eric Ries introduces the **minimal viable product (MVP).** Instead of developing a product in full, the MVP "is that version of a new product which allows a team to collect the maximum amount of validated learning with the least effort". It enables start-ups to test their assumptions about which product and features best meet a market need. That way, sunk costs are avoided and the start-up can still iterate before a point of no return is reached. This approach is increasingly used at large corporates too: typical examples are the **'beta'** versions of new products. Google, amongst others, often probes the market with new beta products before betting big on it.

> Without order nothing can exist. Without chaos nothing can evolve.
>
> **Oscar Wilde**

## To conclude

There is no denying it: pharma companies have been very successful with product-focused innovation so far. However, the future looks foggier and more uncertain than ever before.

The rise of the super consumer and robust technologies that deliver real-time insights to other health stakeholders may well disrupt their business model. Innovation will have to be redefined in terms of outcomes and personalization, which means products will no longer be the only driver of value.

To remain successful, flexible approaches are needed that allow these companies to go beyond their products. Short-term plans need to be more agile, while for the Day After Tomorrow, scenarios need to be tested, re-validated and translated into implications for Today and Tomorrow.

There is no silver bullet when it comes to radical innovation. The truth is that there are as many methods as there are companies. In his book, Peter Hinssen highlights 10 different approaches...and then goes on to say that there are many more ways companies can accelerate and boost their innovation ventures!

The future is clearly not about digitizing the current operating model ("the better mousetrap fallacy"). To lead in a VUCAnized world, incumbents will need to embrace the DAT thinking, apply agile approaches and minimal viable product (MVP) concepts, as well as leveraging selected strategic partnerships, building a data-fueled multistakeholder engagement framework and organizing internally in novel ways. Whoever can best pull this delicate balance off will reap truly magnificent rewards, and lead in this Brave New World.

> We think there's an extraordinary opportunity for pharma to have a seat at the table that it hasn't had before.
>
> **Aman Bhandari, M2I2 (MSD's venture capital group)**

# Keywords

**A/B testing** = different designs, wording or flows are trialled to see which generates the best results. Often used for campaigns and websites.

**Agile marketing** = an iterative and adaptive process where small, highly-collaborative teams work in a series of short cycles, incorporating rapid feedback, to deliver emergent solutions, emphasizing transparency among all stakeholders.

**Analytics 3.0** = an umbrella term for an agile, real-time big data type of analytics used to provide rapid insights that generate business impact.

**Attribution problem** = the difficulty or impossibility to tell which touchpoint attributed to the eventual behavioural change.

**Big Data** = a blanket term for datasets so large and complex that it becomes difficult to process them. Big data technologies and architectures are needed to process the data. A rule of thumb is that when normal (personal) computers stop being able to process data, it becomes 'big'.

**Bounce rate** = percentage of total emails sent that could not be delivered to recipients' inboxes.

- 'hard bounce' = an email is rejected as the email address is no longer functional
- 'soft bounce' = the recipient is temporarily unavailable (on vacation, mailbox is full...).

**Brand ambassador** = a person who favours and promotes a brand.

**Build-measure-learn feedback loop** = a concept that states that success is achieved when an idea is built into a minimal viable product, which is trialled by real customers to gain learning, from which a start-up can decide whether to persevere ("We're on the right route!") or to pivot ("This is going nowhere!").

**Buyer persona** = a descriptive profile of a typical customer.

**Buying cycle or process** = a visualization of the steps a (future) customer can potentially follow, divided over a pre-purchase, a purchase and a post-purchase phase (also called "customer journey")

**Channel conflicts** = conflicts that occur between competing sales channels. For example: telesales versus field sales versus e-commerce.

**Chatbot** = a software programme, often based on AI, which simulates a character with whom a user can interact through a text-box or messaging app.

**CLV** = Customer Lifetime Value. A prediction of the total net profit from a customer for the entire duration of the customer relationship.

**CME** = continuing medical education.

**Content marketing** = the art of communicating without selling. A marketing technique of creating and distributing relevant and valuable content to attract, acquire and engage a clearly defined target audience – with the objective of driving profitable customer interactions.

**Contextual content** = content that is adjusted to the context of a person's media consumption, behaviour, desires and needs.

**CPC** = cost per click. A system where advertisements are shown but the advertiser only pays for actual clicks, not for the number of views. Sometimes referred to as pay per click (PPC).

**CPL** = cost per lead. An advertiser pays per actual lead generated through advertising (e.g.: only for completed online lead forms). CPL is often combined with CPC or CPM.

**CPM** = cost per mille. An advertiser pays per thousand views of an advertisement.

**Crowdsourcing** = the process of outsourcing a task which, previously, was done by employees or a supplier to a group of people or a community (= a crowd). Often announced through an 'open call', in which a broad group of people are invited to voluntarily table ideas and offer their skills to 1) solve a problem, 2) provide innovative ideas, 3) come up with a creative slogan or design and more. The term is a portmanteau of `crowd' and `outsourcing'. Various online crowdsourcing platforms are available to facilitate the process of co-creating value.

**CTA** = call to action. A clear invitation towards web page visitors for a next action, like completing a form, taking a test, ordering online, ...

**CTR** = click-through rate. The number of times a message (ad, email, ..) is clicked as a percentage of the total number of times it is viewed (CTR = # of clicks / # of views). For example: 50 clicks out of a total of 1,000 views = 5% CTR.

**Customer centricity** = a series of strategies and tactics a company uses for the development and delivery of its products and services centred around the current and future needs of customers (vs "product centricity").

**Customer journey** – see buying cycle

**Demand side platform (DSP)** = a technology platform that enables marketing agencies and advertisers to buy media across different inventory sources.

**Descriptive data** = data which describes a situation or a problem.

**Detail aid** = a printed or digital sales aid that contains product information.

**Digirati** = a terminology to identify that a company or industry scores highly on both digital and transformation intensity.

**Digital footprint** = the trail, traces or `footprints' that people leave online. Also known as 'digital shadow'. A company's digital footprint examines how well represented a company is online. It is a measurement of online 'Share of Voice'.

**Digital immigrant** = someone who received their higher education before the Internet came to the scene.

**Digital marketing** = building customer relationships through a myriad of digital activities.

**Digital native** = someone for whom the Internet has always been around (vs. the digital immigrant).

**Earned media** = customers become the channel; you have to "earn" them, thanks to your reputation etc., rather than "pay" them.

**eMedical** = online medical education.

**eMSL** = online medical science liaison.

**F-rule** = eye-tracking studies showed that people read web pages in an F-pattern. Web copywriters should consider this pattern when writing for the web.

**Generation C** = generation 'connected'.

**Geo-targeting** = the physical location of a website visitor is used to deliver specific content tied to their location.

**GIGO** = 'garbage in, garbage out'. The need for stored data to be correct and complete. Sometimes also changed to 'garbage in, gospel out', when data analytics are no longer scrutinized.

**GP** = general practitioner.

**HCP** = healthcare professional – usually a doctor, but also nurses, pharmacists etc.

**Inbound Marketing** = marketing tactics and strategies that enable prospects and customers to connect with a company.

**Infographic** = a visual representation of information, data or knowledge.

**KOL** = key opinion leader.

**KPI** = key performance indicator, a metric that tells you how you are doing compared to your objectives.

**Ladder of adoption** = an overview of the possible stages of brand adoption by an HCP (or other stakeholder).

**Landing pages** = optimized (and often stripped down) web pages tailored to the context of the visitor.

**Lead nurturing** = a gradual relationship building process to keep prospects engaged until they are ready to become leads and, ultimately, customers.

**Lead scoring** = a methodology for ranking leads.

**Live chat** = a web-based tool, enabling visitors to chat directly to a sales or customer service person.

**Marketing automation** = automation of a sequence of activities (email, call centre, banner, ...) for prospects and customers; most often scenario-based.

**Marketing dashboard** = the visualization of marketing performance.

**Maturometer** = a study on the digital maturity level of life sciences companies. Also known as the Across Health Multichannel Maturometer.

**Minimal viable product (MVP)** = the version of a new product that allows a team to collect the maximum amount of validated learning with the least effort.

**Mobile commerce** = e-commerce through mobile devices.

**Mobile-first strategy (or mindset)** = a strategy in which campaigns and initiatives are devised from a mobile perspective. Mobile is no longer an add-on but a cornerstone for planning.

**Mobirati** = a concept to identify how well adopted mobile is within a company's overall activities. The framework separates mobile from other digital activities and compares 1) the level of mobile marketing intensity to overall digital intensity and 2) the degree of integration between both.

**MSL** = medical science liaison.

**Multichannel equivalent (MCQ)** = a methodology to recalibrate the impact of channels vs that of a standard channel, enabling a comparison between channels. Based on the Across Health Navigator data.

**Multichannel (or omnichannel/orchestrator) rep** = The idea that reps, when given electronic communication tools, can lead and guide more components of digital interactions with HCPs

**Navigator** = an analysis of several key dimensions of omnichannel customer engagement: reach/impact of channels, content & context type by channel, channel-level benchmarking and the Media Optimizer for "paid" media. Also known as the Across Health Navigator.

**Native advertising** = an online advertising method that provides contextual content.

**NPS** = Net Promoter Score. A metric to gauge the overall sense of active engagement of customers.

**Omnichannel** = bringing a unified message to the market, regardless of channel.

**Owned media** = media channels that are fully controlled by the brand/company.

**Paid media** = presence on these channels is bought by the brand/company.

**Predictive data** = past data is used to predict future outcomes.

**Prescriptive data** = 'cause and effect' data analysis provides multiple options on 'what to do'.

**Product centricity** = a product-centric company focuses primarily on the products it brings to market (see also 'customer centricity').

**Pull marketing** = a series of tactics and strategies in which the customer is being 'pulled in' through relevant content. Nowadays more often referred to as inbound marketing.

**Push marketing** = an earlier term for outbound marketing. Products and services are 'pushed' towards the customer through promotion and advertising. Often referred to as traditional marketing.

**QR code** = (Quick Response) codes enable a person to visit a web page by scanning a 2D image with a smartphone camera. Recognizable by a square pattern of black dots.

**Responsive design** = websites and web pages are optimized so that they scale properly to whatever mobile device is being used.

**Retargeting** = your ads are shown to people who have visited your website before. A widely used practice in many industries, but not allowed in pharma product marketing.

**Scenario planning** = a strategic exercise that describes a series of extreme futures against which current and alternative strategies can be tested.

**SEA** = search engine advertising. An advertising technique where companies pay per click for their text ads to be shown in search engine results pages and on relevant 3rd-party websites.

**SEM** = search engine marketing. A combination of search engine optimization and search engine advertising.

**SEO** = search engine optimization. A series of techniques to optimize online content so that search engines can better find and index this content.

**Social selling** = the practice of leveraging social networks and social tools in the sales process.

**Spam** = unsolicited bulk email.

**Stakeholder analysis** = a process to identify the individuals or groups that are affected by a change or project. Stakeholders are sorted according to the interest and impact they (could) have on a project.

**TA** = therapeutic area.

**Tablet detailing** = interactive presentations on a tablet device aimed at adding impact to a rep's face-to-face conversations with an HCP.

**Teledetailing** = conducting an interactive, online, real-time meeting with an HCP. Also referred to as 'remote detailing' or 'web calls'.

**Telemarketing** = a marketing tactic centered around outbound call center activities.

**Thought leader** = an individual or a firm recognized as an authority in a specialized field and whose expertise is sought and often rewarded.

**T-shaped profile** = a concept that stresses the need for people to be well equipped in a breadth of fields (the horizontal bar of the T) while also possessing a level of expertise in a specific field (the vertical bar). A T-shaped person is both generalist and specialist. In marketing, the concept of the "Fat T marketer", ie staff with key strengths in strategy and martech, is emerging.

**Viral marketing** = when marketing communications are being shared and distributed at high speed and with an enormous reach, similar to a virus, for example, through word of mouth or network effects. Viral marketing is hard or impossible to control or generate.

**VUCA** = a concept that states that the world today is typified by Volatility, Uncertainty, Complexity and Ambiguity.

**Wearable** = a device that is worn on the body and which continually collects data, such as biofeedback and physiological data.